*New England Earthquakes*

# *New England Earthquakes*

## *The Surprising History of Seismic Activity in the Northeast*

John E. Ebel

## Globe Pequot

*Guilford, Connecticut*

## Globe
## Pequot

An imprint of The Rowman & Littlefield Publishing Group, Inc.
4501 Forbes Blvd., Ste. 200
Lanham, MD 20706
www.rowman.com

Distributed by NATIONAL BOOK NETWORK

British Library Cataloguing in Publication Information available

**Library of Congress Cataloging-in-Publication Data available**

ISBN 978-1-4930-3577-9 (paperback)
ISBN 978-1-4930-3187-0 (e-book)

∞™ The paper used in this publication meets the minimum requirements of American National Standard for Information Sciences—Permanence of Paper for Printed Library Materials, ANSI/ NISO Z39.48-1992

Printed in the United States of America

*To my wife, Martha*
*For her constant and generous love and support*

# Contents

# Acknowledgments

My interest in and research into the historical earthquakes of the northeastern U.S. and adjacent Canada has extended back almost 40 years, and numerous people have helped me with various aspects of this work. My first encounter with the topic of the historical earthquakes of New England took place shortly after I completed my PhD in 1980 at Caltech when one of my professors, Clarence Allen, gave me a pamphlet that had been discarded from the library of Caltech's Seismolab. That pamphlet was a copy of William Brigham's 1871 publication on the earthquake history of New England. Clarence thought that I might be interested in it because I was soon to head off to my new faculty job at Boston College and to take over running the New England Seismic Network, which was operated at the Weston Observatory of Boston College. Even today I still often refer to that skinny volume that Clarence gave me so many years ago, a volume that launched my research interest into historical earthquakes.

Over my time at Weston Observatory and Boston College, I have enlisted the assistance of many students, faculty, colleagues, and members of the public to help me with various aspects of my research into the history of the earthquake activity of the northeast region. Although there are too many to mention all by name, I do want to single out with gratitude the contributions of several persons who have helped me over the years. Boston College undergraduates Jennifer Quinlan, Megan Dupuy, and Serafina Zeringo spent some busy summers researching and compiling accounts of historical earthquakes for me. Outside of Boston College, information on historical earthquakes has come my way from Gabriel Leblanc, Kathleen Langone, Alan Ruffman, Ken Burke, Ed Myskowski, and France St. Laurent, among others. Field investigations of the probable locations and sizes of past strong earthquakes by Martitia Tuttle, Justin Starr, Katrin Monecke, Brad Hubeny, and the late David Roy, along with many Boston College students, have added geological constraints on the occurrences of historical and even prehistorical earthquakes. Finally, I am indebted to the work of many earlier generations of researchers into the earthquake history of the northeastern U.S., including the Jesuits who worked at Weston Observatory beginning with its founding in 1928. Among the many researchers from earlier times, those at the Weston Geophysical Corporation in the 1960s and 1970s produced a rich set of reports in which they documented and reproduced hundreds of accounts of past earthquakes from the northeastern U.S., reports that are as valuable today as they were on the day that they were published. For earthquakes in Quebec province, the late Fr. Pierre Gouin, S.J., produced a monumental volume with transcriptions of a large number of primary accounts of some of the most important historical earthquakes of eastern Canada. I salute him posthumously for his comprehensive book and thank him for translating the French accounts into English.

Finally, I wish to express my gratitude to the administration and staff of Boston College for the many different ways that they have supported my work over the years. Boston College research grants to a number of my students have paid their summer research internships and expenses for fieldwork, money that earned a very rich academic reward for both myself and for the students. Support from the Department of Earth and Environmental Sciences (formerly the Department of Geology and Geophysics) for class projects involving geological studies of historical earthquakes is most appreciated. Over the years members of the staff of the Boston College library system and of the academic support group of the Boston College Information Technology department have greatly facilitated the work of my research group to collect, compile, and make available to others data on historical earthquakes. I believe that there is still much to be learned about the historical earthquakes in the northeastern U.S. and southeastern Canada, and I hope that future support from university, government, foundation, and private sources will be made available to continue this important line of research.

# Introduction

New England and nearby areas in the U.S. and Canada have a long and storied history of earthquakes that goes back to the times of the earliest exploration and settlement of the region by Europeans. This may come as a surprise to the many living in the region today who have never felt a local earthquake. Nevertheless, not only is it true, but there is every reason to believe that earthquakes, including some earthquakes large enough to cause damage, will strike New England and the surrounding states and provinces in the future. In fact, in the 1960s Boston, Massachusetts, was given the same seismic hazard rating as Los Angeles, California, because both had experienced strong earthquakes in their historic pasts. Since then, seismologists have learned much about the rates at which earthquakes occur throughout the country and about the effects of the earthquakes when they occur. Today, we know that the probability of damaging earthquake shaking in Boston is about 25 times less than in Los Angeles. Even so, the threat of earthquakes in Boston, throughout New England, and in adjacent regions is one that cannot be ignored.

In order to properly assess the probabilities of future damaging earthquakes in Boston, in the New England region, and in other parts of the northeastern U.S. and southeastern Canada, seismologists must have a complete record of the past earthquake history of the region. Starting in the 20th century, the earthquake history is known from earthquake recordings made by seismic instruments. However, prior to the last century, the only available information about past earthquakes comes from historical reports or from geologic studies. The historical reports compose the most complete record of the past earthquakes that occurred, typically giving information on the dates and times of the events as well as reports from different localities of felt effects and damage if an event was strong. The Native Americans also preserved some memories of past earthquakes in their oral traditions. Unfortunately, the dates, locations, and effects of these events in their lore are remembered in only general terms, and so

Native American lore is less useful for assembling a precise earthquake chronology for the Northeast. Even so, the Native American legends do confirm that earthquakes were taking place in the northeastern U.S. and southeastern Canada even before the first Europeans came to this part of the world.

The need to compile a precise earthquake history of New England and adjacent regions and tell others about that history led me to write this book. For almost four decades, I have studied the current and past earthquakes of the region, hoping to learn more about where the past earthquakes have taken place and where future earthquakes might occur. I am also interested in better estimating how strong future earthquakes might be and how often damaging earthquakes might occur. The ultimate goal of this research is earthquake prediction, but earthquake prediction is not feasible at all at the present time, nor do I expect that it will be feasible in the foreseeable future. A more immediate goal of my work is to provide data for the computation of the seismic hazard for the northeastern U.S. and southeastern Canada, a heavily populated area with many old buildings that are vulnerable to damage in strong earthquake shaking. Every several years the U.S. Geological Survey produces updated versions of its U.S. national seismic hazard maps. These maps show the estimated levels of earthquake ground shaking with different probabilities of occurrence for the entire country. The maps are used in building codes as the basis of the seismic-resistant design of structures. In the codes the parts of the country that have higher estimated levels of earthquake ground shaking have more stringent building design specifications to withstand earthquake shaking. For New England and the Middle Atlantic states, the seismic hazard ground motions are much lower than for the major cities of California, which means that the design codes for buildings are somewhat less stringent for the former than for California. Even so, all of the states in the northeastern part of our country incorporate some level of earthquake-resistant design in their building codes.

Everything said here about the seismic hazard for the northeastern U.S. also applies to southeastern Canada. Like the U.S., our Canadian neighbors also update their national seismic hazard maps every several years, with corresponding updates in the seismic provisions in their building codes. Because earthquakes and earthquake shaking ignore international boundaries, a strong earthquake in Canada can cause damage in the U.S., and vice versa. For this reason, not only does this book discuss earthquakes that were centered in the northeastern U.S., but the book also describes some important past earthquakes that were centered in southeastern Canada but affected the northeastern U.S.

The chapters of this book describe the largest, most important, and most interesting earthquakes that have been centered in New England and adjacent areas from the time of the first European settlements along the U.S. east coast until today. However, the earthquakes described in this book are far from an exhaustive list of the earthquakes that have taken place in the region. Each year New England experiences about half a dozen earthquakes that are felt in one part or another of the area, and a comparable number of felt earthquakes take place in the Middle Atlantic U.S. states and even more are felt each year somewhere in southeastern Canada. Many more earthquakes that are not felt are detected by modern seismic network monitoring throughout the region, including some offshore events. Almost all of these earthquakes are relatively small in magnitude (magnitude 4.0 or less) and cause no damage, but they contribute bits and pieces of information to help seismologists better understand the seismic hazard in the region. The real seismic hazard comes from the strong earthquakes that have magnitudes above about 5.0, because these are the ones that are strong enough to damage structures. It is these strong earthquakes that are the primary subjects of this book.

# Chapter 1

# The Basics of Earthquake Seismology

Throughout my professional career at Weston Observatory of Boston College, I have fielded many questions about earthquakes, particularly earthquakes in the northeastern part of the country. The most common question, one that I seem to deal with almost on a weekly basis, is, "Did we just have an earthquake?" Perhaps the inquirer's house shook, or maybe the person heard a boom and felt a vibration. In any case I dutifully check the seismic records. If this is a single report with no other calls, the answer is almost always that no earthquake took place. Whatever shook their house was not an earthquake. Sometimes an earthquake did indeed occur, and in those cases calls from other residents soon follow. The existence of the earthquake is easily verified from the seismic records at Weston Observatory.

Sometimes the questions are more involved. One question that I have received a number of times is, "Was there an earthquake or a tremor that just happened?" The person asking the question mistakenly thinks that the phenomenon of an earthquake is somehow different from that of a tremor. In fact, what some people perceive as a tremor is nothing more than the shaking of an earthquake felt far from its epicenter. To a seismologist like myself, a tremor is merely one manifestation of the set of phenomena that together we refer to as an earthquake. In any case a quick check of the seismic records at the time reported by the caller can verify whether or not the shaking experienced was from an earthquake.

Another set of questions elicits a more detailed and complex answer from me. One common form of the question is, "Where is the fault in our region?" and another common form is, "Where is the closest fault to my house?" In both cases the callers think that by asking a question about faults that they will learn something about the possibilities of facing the effects of a future earthquake. To these callers I give a detailed explanation of what a fault is, what an active fault is, and the fact that at the present time no one has identified any active faults in New England. Indeed, it is not from the study of the local faults but rather from the study of the earthquakes themselves in the region that seismologists are learning the most about the possibilities of future earthquakes in places like New England. I don't blame people for asking any of these questions, primarily because these questions are based on images that propagate through our popular media. Unfortunately, the questions and the ideas on which they are based arise from an incomplete understanding of the causes and effects of earthquakes by the public at large.

So, if people have misunderstandings about the causes and effects of earthquakes, what is the scientific understanding of earthquakes? What causes earthquakes? How are earthquakes related to faults? What happens during earthquakes and what are the effects of earthquakes? What phenomena are observed before an earthquake, and can those observations be used to predict earthquakes? Answering these questions is what this chapter is all about. The information presented in this chapter is important to understand what happens when earthquakes occur, and it is also important because it provides the basis for understanding many of the historical earthquake reports that are presented in subsequent chapters.

## EARTHQUAKES AND FAULTS

Laboratory experiments have shown that earthquakes occur due to differential pressures in the rock of the earth. Differential pressure refers to a situation where the strength of the pressure in the rock in one direction is different from the pressure in another direction. For example, the horizontal pressure might be much greater than the vertical pressure in the rock. One-half of the difference in pressure between the maximum direction and the minimum direction is a quantity that scientists call shear stress. Earthquakes occur when the shear stress in rock exceeds a critical shear stress that represents the breaking strength of the rock. If the shear stress equals or exceeds the rock breaking strength, the rock cracks and an earthquake initiates. A simple thought experiment illustrates this phenomenon. Imagine a standard bench vise in which a clay brick has been placed along its long axis. The vise squeezes the brick at the two sides of its long axis, whereas there is no excess pressure against the other four sides of the brick. Now imagine very slowly turning the screw on the vise, which slowly increases the squeezing of the brick. As long as the vise handle is being turned, the pressure in the one direction of the brick increases. This increases the shear stress inside the brick. At some point, as the pressure on the brick increases, the brick will no longer be able to withstand the shear stress. At this point the brick will suddenly break into two (or more) pieces as a crack forms and breaks the brick apart. The crack typically forms diagonally across the brick. The different pieces of the brick will slide past each other as the excess horizontal pressure is suddenly relieved. In fact, the brick will likely fall out of the vise because it will no longer be intact.

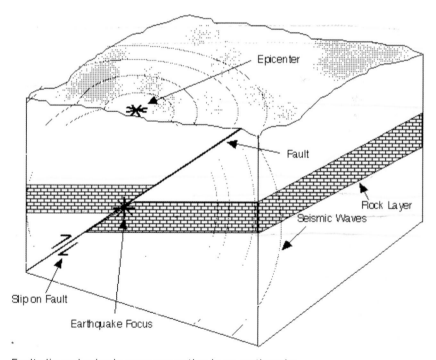

Fault slip and seismic wave generation in an earthquake

Offset rock layers due to past movement on small faults

The sudden breaking of the brick is exactly the same thing that happens inside the earth when an earthquake initiates. In an earthquake a crack forms with the rock on one side of the crack sliding past the rock on the other side of the crack, and in doing so the sliding releases some of the excess pressure or shear stress that had previously built up. In the laboratory as well as in the earth, the rock always slides away from the direction of maximum pressure and toward the direction of minimum pressure. In the earth the crack along which the sliding takes place is called the fault. One popular misconception is that there must be a fault present before there can be an earthquake. This is not true. There must be differential pressures in the rock with shear stress large enough for the rock strength to be exceeded. Rock can break in an earthquake even if there is no fault present. In fact, every fault that exists in the earth today was initially formed in an earthquake that occurred in unfaulted rock. Once a fault forms, the rock is usually weaker along the direction of the fault and a new buildup of pressures in the rock in the same direction as before can cause a later earthquake slip on the same fault, and this can repeat many times on the same fault over long geologic time intervals. On the other hand, if the directions of rock pressure change over geologic time as the configuration of the tectonic plates that move over the surface of the earth evolves, then the later pressures in the earth may no longer be capable of causing rock slip along an old, existing fault. Changes in the rock pressure directions change the orientations of the faults that can be active. In summary, earthquakes are caused by pressures in the rock and not simply by the existence of local faults.

Laboratory experiments show that the directions of the rock pressures in the earth control the orientations of the faults that have earthquakes and the directions that the rocks slip in earthquakes. In some places on the earth like California, the directions of the greatest and least pressures in the earth are horizontal. In these areas the faults tend to be vertical and the rocks slip horizontally on either side of what is called a strike-slip fault. The famous San Andreas Fault in California is one example of a strike-slip fault. Strike-slip faults are always oriented at an angle to both the maximum and minimum pressure directions. In some parts of the earth well outside of California, the maximum pressure direction is horizontal and the minimum pressure direction is vertical. In these cases the fault where an earthquake takes place dips into the earth at an angle, and the rock on the upper side of the fault is pushed up over the rock on the underside of the fault. This is called a thrust fault, and such faults typically are found in the many different places on the earth where one tectonic plate is pushing into another tectonic plate. The largest earthquakes globally have all taken place on thrust faults. A third situation is found at those places on the earth where two tectonic plates are pulling away from one another, such as is happening at the mid-Atlantic spreading ridge. In these places the maximum pressure direction is vertical (due to the weight of the rock), and the minimum pressure direction is horizontal because the plate movements are trying to pull the rocks apart at the plate boundary (the horizontal pressure is away from rather than toward the fault). Earthquakes that take place with these pressure directions dip into the earth at an angle, and the rock on the top side of the fault slips downward relative to the rock below the fault. These faults are called normal faults, and they are found where valleys are opening. The valleys of the East Africa rift system are forming today with normal-fault earthquakes. The directions of the maximum and minimum pressures in rocks in a region

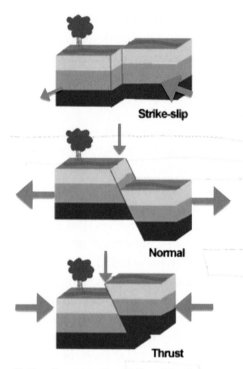

Strike-slip, normal, and thrust fault movements and the pressure directions associated with each fault MODIFIED FIGURE FROM THE USGS

control both the orientation of the faults that have earthquakes and the directions that the rocks can slip on those faults.

One common misconception about faults that has become increasingly prevalent in recent years is the idea that there is such a thing as a "fault line." As described above, a fault is a crack surface in the earth along which rock has slid during an earthquake. It is not a line, but a planar feature, just as the wall or floor of a house is a planar feature. Where, then, did the mistaken concept of a "fault line" arise? The answer comes from the fact that geologists create maps of the geology of the earth's surface, and on those maps faults are depicted as lines. In actuality a line that represents a fault on a map shows where that fault surface intersects the surface of the earth. Indeed, the geologist who drew a fault "line" on a geologic map knew that he or she was simply representing the position of the fault on the earth's surface and that the fault is a surface that plunges deep into the earth. Indeed, most geologic maps are accompanied by geologic cross-sections, which are drawings that show how the geology, including the faults found in that geology, project downward into the earth. People who are not geoscientists tend to ignore the cross-sectional drawings and focus only on the maps themselves, and thus they likely get the mistaken impression that faults are lines on the surface of the earthquake. The fact is, faults can extend many miles into the earth, and if those faults are not vertical faults but rather dip at some angle into the earth, then the position of a fault at some depth below the earth's surface will not coincide at all with the surface position of that fault as drawn on the geologic map. This is an important consideration when one tries to correlate earthquake epicenters with local geology.

Another common misunderstanding about faults that often shows up in movies is that during an earthquake a fault is a place where a large chasm opens up in the earth. The fact is that faults are not open chasms in the earth. Rather, they are places where there are thin cracks in the rock and where the rock has slid on either side of the crack. The pressures inside the earthquake act to close these cracks as much as possible, and in small faults the crack is often completely closed. Early in my days as a graduate student at the California Institute of Technology (Caltech) in Pasadena, I participated in a student field trip led by one of our faculty members, Prof. Clarence Allen. Among other things, Professor Allen was an expert on the San Andreas Fault, which he had studied throughout his professional career. One of the first stops on our field trip was at the San Andreas Fault north of Los Angeles. He led the students to a rock hill and pointed to a place within the hill where there was a boundary with noticeable change in the rock on either side of the boundary. On one side of the boundary, the rock was filled with boulders and was a light tan color, whereas on the other side of the boundary, the rock was made of fine crystals and was medium brown in color. He pointed triumphantly to the boundary zone between these two very different rock types and announced proudly, "There is the San Andreas Fault!" The fault itself was nothing more than a thin zone, about one or two inches thick, that was filled with a crumbly, rusty-colored rock that fell apart in one's hand if it was pulled out of the hillside. I would easily have walked right by the fault without noticing it if it had not been pointed out to me. Since then, I have visited many faults in many different places, including California, New England, Germany, and Turkey. Faults, including major plate-boundary faults, are unimpressive features up close, and they are easy to miss unless one has a trained eye. Faults are nothing more than thin cracks in what was once intact rock.

Ground fault gouge eroding out of a fault zone PHOTO COURTESY OF JIM TALBOT

The geology at the location where Professor Allen showed me the San Andreas Fault on our field trip gave me an important lesson on how geologists recognize faults in rock. A contrast in rock types on either side of a sharp boundary is often (but not always) indicative of a fault. The friable rock within the thin fault zone is another important clue about the existence of a fault. This material is called fault gouge by geologists, and it is one of the important indicators of past earthquake fault movements. Fault gouge forms from the rock along the fault being ground to powder due to repeated fault movements over long periods of geologic time (many thousands to millions of years). The existence of fault gouge tells a geologist that a fault has experienced a long history of earthquake slips. Some fault zones have not had enough slips for fault gouge to form, but if the fault surface is exposed, one may find parallel scratches on the rock surfaces on either side of the crack. These scratches are caused by the fault slip, where the rock on one side of the fault leaves scratches on the surface of the rock on the other side of the fault. These scratches are called slickensides, and they are a sure indicator of past earthquake slip on the fault surface. Unfortunately, although slickensides demonstrate the existence of a past

8

earthquake, they do not indicate when that earthquake occurred.

An important characteristic about earthquake faults that many people do not appreciate is that once rock is cracked in an earthquake, that crack stays in the rock as long as that rock exists intact. Unlike human skin, cracks in rocks never heal, and so even very old faults can be found in the rocks of the earth today. The existence of a fault in rock is an indicator only that an earthquake slip took place at some point in the history of that rock. The earthquake slip might have taken place yesterday, or a million years ago, or even a billion years ago (if the rock is that old). Over the millions and billions of years of

Slickenside scratches running from lower left to upper right on an exposed fault surface FROM DOCUMENT SUBMITTED TO THE U.S. NATIONAL SCIENCE FOUNDATION

geologic time, all rocks experience various episodes when the rock pressures build up to the point where earthquakes can occur. Thus, all rocks found today at the surface of the earth tend to have faults in them, and usually those are old faults that have not had recent earthquake activity. It is for this reason that the relationship between earthquakes and local faults is uncertain in many parts of the world, even in places in seismically active areas where we know about many faults that have experienced earthquakes in historical times. Thus, an important goal of earthquake research is to identify those faults that are seismically active today. To an earth scientist, a seismically active fault is one that has the potential for having an earthquake in the near future. The term "near future" in geoscience refers to a time period sometime between the present and the next several thousand years. To some people the next several thousand years might seem like a long time, but compared to the total history of the earth, it is a tiny tick of time.

The search for active faults is an important line of research that occupies many earth scientists. In fact, motivation for the research into the historic earthquakes that are described in this book ultimately involves the search for active faults in northeastern North America. Even in seismically active parts of the world, there likely are many active faults that are still to be discovered. For example, over the past century there have been several strong earthquakes in California where the active faults had not been recognized prior to the occurrences of the earthquakes. In these cases the earth scientists who had mapped the faults had not found good geologic evidence of recent slips on those faults. Earth scientists still have much work to do before they can pinpoint all of the active faults in different parts of the world. It is hoped that studies of the faults that experienced strong earthquakes in historically recent times can help identify previously unrecognized active faults.

Confirming that a crack in rock is indeed a fault can be difficult. Rocks in the earth crack not just in earthquakes but also due to natural weathering processes. As the rock at the surface erodes due to the action of water, ice, and wind, the rock below becomes exposed. The erosion of surface rocks relieves the pressures on the rock below the surface, and this can lead to the formation of short cracks in the surface rocks that are called joints. Unlike faults where the rock pressure causes slip on faults, joints are small cracks that show no rock slip. Thus, not all cracks in rocks are faults, even if all faults are cracks in rocks.

Even if a crack in rock can be confirmed as a fault that had one or more past earthquakes, determining when the past earthquake(s) occurred can be fraught with uncertainty. Obviously, the age of the rock gives the oldest possible time when the fault might have formed. But this does not date the earthquake itself. The only way to estimate the date when the earthquake occurred is to find different geologic layers of different ages in which the fault is found and then to find other, younger geologic layers where the fault is not found. The age of the earthquake, then, is sometime after the date of the youngest layer with the fault and before the date of the oldest layer without the fault. With luck and knowing where to look, this possible age range might be small, but often the possible time range when the fault was active might be quite large. For example, in New

England the age range of many faults cannot be constrained to less than 100 million years. This is hardly useful to an earth scientist who wants to show that a fault is active today.

Even if the time period when a fault was active cannot be determined with any certainty, some other information about its past earthquakes can be inferred from measurements taken from the fault. From scientific observations of earthquakes taken globally over the past century, seismologists have now established some scaling laws about earthquake sizes. It is now firmly established that the magnitude is related to the size of the fault surface that had rock slip during an earthquake; a larger magnitude earthquake has a longer and wider area where the fault slipped. Furthermore, a larger magnitude earthquake has a greater amount of slip of the rock on either side of the fault than does a smaller magnitude earthquake. The first scaling law is useful because it means that the maximum magnitude that could take place on an active fault can be estimated from measurements of the size of that fault. Long active faults can potentially have large magnitude earthquakes, whereas short active faults can only have small magnitude earthquakes. The second scaling law is most useful if the rock slip on a fault from a past earthquake is observed. A small amount of slip means that the past earthquake had a small magnitude, whereas a large amount of slip means that the past earthquake had a large magnitude. Thus, much can be learned about the potential magnitudes of future earthquakes if active faults can be identified.

## SEISMIC WAVES AND EARTHQUAKE SHAKING

Although the focus of the discussion so far in this chapter has been about what happens on faults during earthquakes, this is only half the story when an earthquake occurs. When rock slips in an earthquake, the slip releases vibrational waves that spread out in all directions away from the fault. These vibrational waves are called seismic waves, and they come in two forms. In one form the rock is stretched and compressed as the wave passes. This is called a P wave, and it is the fastest seismic wave that is radiated from a fault. The second form of seismic waves causes the rock to bend sideways as the wave passes, much as a flag flutters on a flagpole when blown by the wind. This is called an S wave, and it travels at a slower

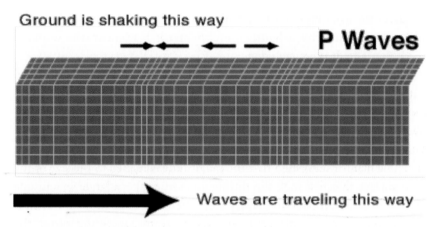

P waves squeeze and stretch the ground as they travel FIGURE FROM THE USGS

speed than a P wave, although it usually has a higher amplitude than the P wave. Some P and S waves get trapped along the surface of the earth, and these are called surface waves. These usually are the highest amplitude waves generated by earthquakes, and they move slower than S waves. Thus, when an observer feels an earthquake, the person usually initially experiences a vertical shaking associated with the P wave, then a stronger horizontal shaking associated with the S wave, and finally very strong horizontal and vertical shaking associated with the surface waves.

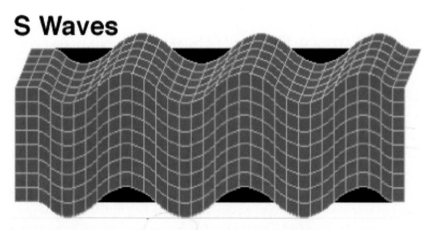

S waves bend the ground as they travel FIGURE FROM THE USGS

Because all of these seismic waves can reverberate within the shallow rock layers in the earth, the earthquake shaking does not stop when the surface waves pass; rather, it gradually abates as the reverberations die away. These later waves that die away with time are called coda waves by seismologists. As felt by humans, earthquake ground shaking from the first P wave to the last of the coda waves lasts only a couple seconds in a magnitude 2.0 earthquake to about 15–20 seconds in a magnitude 4.5 earthquake to more than four minutes in a magnitude 8.0 earthquake. Thus, the length of time during which earthquake ground shaking is felt can be used to estimate the magnitude of the earthquake. The development of earthquake shaking differs depending on how far an observer is from the earthquake epicenter. For observers close to an epicenter, the shaking of a strong earthquake starts with great force, with the strongest shaking experienced within a few seconds of the beginning of the earthquake. On the other hand, for observers far from the epicenter, the earthquake shaking seems to gradually build up in strength over many seconds,

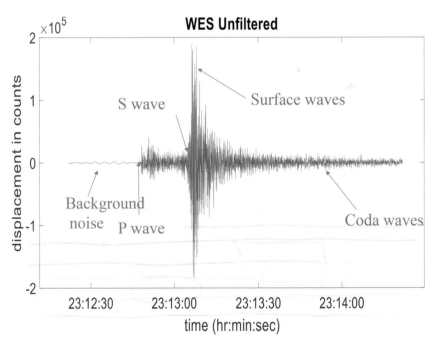

Example of an earthquake seismogram

with the strongest shaking perhaps 10–20 seconds or more after the first shaking is experienced. This means that the description of the development of earthquake shaking as experienced by an observer can give clues about how far the observer was from the earthquake epicenter.

P waves in the earth are the same as sound waves in the atmosphere, and for this reason earthquakes generate sounds that can be heard as the seismic waves pass. The strength and type of the sounds associated with seismic waves depends on the distance of the observer from the place in the earth where the seismic waves originate. As seismic waves pass through the earth, the higher frequency energy in the waves is preferentially absorbed. At close distances to a fault where an earthquake takes place where the travel path from the fault to the observer is short, all frequencies are transmitted with approximately equal strength, and observers report that the earthquake sounds are quite loud and can be high-pitched as well as low-pitched. However, at greater distances from the fault the high-pitched seismic energy is absorbed by the earth and only low-frequency energy makes it to the observer. In this case the observer hears only a low-pitched rumble like distant thunder. At even greater distances, the earth absorbs all of the acoustic frequencies, and so only those vibrations that are at frequencies below those of human hearing are experienced. At these distances the earthquake is experienced as a vibration with little or no sound at all, other than perhaps the rattling of windows and objects on shelves. Thus, a description of the sounds (or lack of earthquake sounds) when an earthquake is experienced can be an indicator of how far from the earthquake source the observer is located. In historic reports about earthquakes, information on the sounds (or lack of sounds) can be an important indicator of how far a person may have been from the earthquake epicenter.

One characteristic of all seismic waves (P, S, and surface) is that the amplitudes of the waves decrease as those waves spread away from the earthquake fault. This decrease happens for two reasons. The first is that the earth absorbs some of the energy as the seismic waves pass through it. This absorption is greater for waves with higher frequencies as described above, and it explains why earthquake sounds are strongest near an earthquake fault and become weaker as those waves propagate away from the fault. The absorption of seismic waves is different in different parts of the world. In places where the rock temperatures are relatively high at depth in the earth, the rock tends to absorb larger amounts of seismic energy than in those places where the rock temperatures are lower at depth. For example, in California the rock at 6–20 miles (10–30 kilometers) deep in the earthquake is much hotter than the rock in the eastern U.S. at the same depths. There is good geologic evidence for this because in California there are a number of places where there have been volcanic eruptions during the past few thousand years. On the other hand, in the eastern U.S. the youngest volcanic rocks are over 100 million years old. It is for this reason that earthquake wave amplitudes decrease much faster with distance in California than they do in the eastern U.S. This means that an earthquake in the eastern U.S. can be felt over a much greater area than the same magnitude earthquake in California. It also means that an earthquake in the eastern U.S. has the potential to cause damage at a greater distance from the fault than the same size earthquake in California.

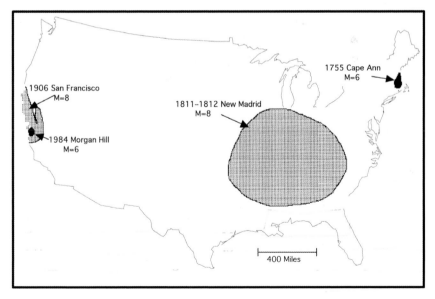

Comparisons of the damage areas of earthquakes in the eastern and western U.S.

The second reason that earthquake wave amplitudes decay with distance from the fault is due to the spreading of the wave energy over greater volumes as the waves spread away from the fault. This phenomenon is familiar to anyone who has thrown a rock into a still body of water like a lake or river. Where the rock hits the water, the wave is noticeably large, with perhaps a splash of water. The water wave then spreads away from the place where the rock hit, becoming lower in amplitude as the wave spreads over ever greater circles. If the body of water is large and quite still, the wave can be seen to very large distances, although the amplitude of the wave might be barely discernible. This spreading of the seismic energy takes place in the same way in all parts of the world. Everywhere on and within the earth, seismic-wave amplitudes are affected by both rock absorption and by circular spreading. It is the combination of these two effects that controls how strongly earthquake shaking is felt at different distances from an earthquake.

## Earthquake Magnitude

The decrease in the amplitudes of seismic waves as they spread away from a fault has been known from the very early days of seismology. The early seismologists used seismic-wave observations to measure the decrease in wave amplitudes at different distances from earthquake sources. They observed that stronger seismic sources generated higher amplitude seismic waves, but they also found that the seismic-wave amplitudes decreased at the same rate away from the earthquake fault no matter how strong the earthquake was. Prof. Charles Richter at the Seismological Laboratory of Caltech was one of the seismologists making such measurements in Southern California. In carrying out his research, Richter realized that the size of the earthquake source could be computed from earthquake amplitude observations if the rate of decay of the seismic waves was known. In 1935 he developed a mathematical formula, which came to be known as the Richter scale, in which the strength of the earthquake was determined by measuring the amplitudes of the seismic waves at different seismic stations and then inputting those amplitudes into Richter's magnitude formula. At its most fundamental level, the Richter magnitude formula extrapolates the size of the seismic waves back to the seismic source, thus providing an estimate of the strength of those waves at the source. Because the range of the amplitudes of seismic waves is extremely large for earthquakes of different sizes, Richter proposed to use a simple mathematical function called a logarithm to compress the range of earthquake sizes into a simple range of numbers. He set that range of numbers to fall between roughly 0 for the smallest earthquakes to just less than about 10 for the largest known earthquakes. Because the Richter magnitude scale is logarithmic, a change in magnitude of one unit corresponds to a change in wave amplitude of a factor of 10. Thus, the seismic waves from a magnitude 5.0 earthquake are 10 times stronger than the seismic waves from a magnitude 4.0 earthquake.

Although Richter's original magnitude scale was a major step forward in earthquake science, it had some major shortcomings that seismologists needed to accommodate. One shortcoming was that Richter's magnitude formula only worked in California because implicit in that formula is the rate of seismic wave absorption for Southern California. In order to apply Richter's idea to other parts of the world, seismologists needed to account for the different seismic-wave absorption characteristics in different parts of the world. For global earthquakes Richter teamed with Caltech colleague Prof. Beno Gutenberg in the 1930s and 1940s to develop two different magnitude scales, one based on P-wave amplitudes and one based on surface-wave amplitudes. For decades these magnitude scales have been applied to measure the sizes of earthquakes that are recorded widely across the globe. For the smaller local earthquakes in different parts of the world, seismologists were required to adapt Richter's original formula based on local earthquake observations. For example, in 1973 Prof. Otto Nuttli of St. Louis University developed a modified version of Richter's original magnitude scheme for use in central and eastern North America.

Another shortcoming of Richter's original magnitude formula as well as the P-wave and surface-wave magnitude scales of Richter and Gutenberg is that for technical reasons these methods underestimated the size of the largest earthquakes that take place on the earth. This shortcoming was resolved in the 1970s with the development of the moment magnitude scale by Prof. Hiroo Kanamori of Caltech and Dr. Tom Hanks (not the actor) of the U.S. Geological Survey (USGS). Their magnitude scale made use of new seismic data analysis methods not yet developed at the time that Richter and Gutenberg were active. Kanamori and Hanks designed their magnitude scale so that it gives moment magnitudes that are the same as the P-wave and surface-wave magnitudes of Richter and Gutenberg at lower magnitudes, but it also gives the correct magnitudes to the largest recorded earthquakes. It is for this reason that the moment magnitude scale has become the preferred earthquake magnitude scale in use by seismologists today.

The magnitude scales just discussed are used by seismologists to rate the strengths of the seismic waves that are radiated by earthquake sources. Larger magnitude earthquakes radiate larger amplitude seismic waves from the faults where they occur. Furthermore, as discussed earlier, larger magnitude earthquakes occur on faults that are longer and wider than smaller magnitude earthquakes, and larger earthquakes also have a greater amount of rock slip on their faults than do smaller magnitude earthquakes. In addition, larger magnitude earthquakes are felt over larger areas and for longer time periods than are smaller magnitude earthquakes. On the other hand, the magnitude of an earthquake in itself cannot be used to tell how strong the earthquake ground shaking is at any individual site that experiences that earthquake. The strength of the ground shaking depends on both the magnitude of the earthquake and the distance from the earthquake fault to the location where the earthquake is experienced. Sites at different distances from the same earthquake experience different levels of ground shaking, with stronger ground shaking generally occurring closer to the fault and weaker ground shaking occurring farther from the fault.

## EARTHQUAKE SHAKING: DAMAGE TO STRUCTURES, SHAKEMAPS, AND EARTHQUAKE INTENSITY

The strength of ground shaking is the most important indicator of the felt and damage effects due to earthquakes. At very low amplitudes of ground shaking, only a few people might even sense the ground shaking. As ground shaking amplitudes increase, more people sense the ground motions, and they become more aware of the vibrational nature of the seismic waves that are causing the ground shaking. At still higher amplitudes of ground shaking, people notice buildings, trees, and other man-made and natural structures noticeably swaying, and they may become fearful that buildings are going to be damaged. At even higher amplitudes the ground shaking can feel so violent that people in buildings report that it feels like the building is being hit by a giant sledgehammer, and they fear that collapse of the building is imminent. From decades of compiling both reports of felt effects and building damage due to earthquake shaking and instrumental recordings of the strong ground shaking at sites where felt and damage reports were collected, seismologists and earthquake engineers now can pinpoint the different amplitudes of ground shaking where felt effects occur with no building damage, where buildings start to crack, and where buildings start to collapse. This has not been a simple task because different kinds of buildings are damaged at different levels of ground shaking. Even so, the relationships between amplitude levels of earthquake shaking and potential for damage for many different kinds of buildings are now understood well enough that they are used as a basis for specifying earthquake resistance in modern building codes.

In central and eastern North America, studies of earthquake shaking amplitudes and amounts and severity of damage in earthquake shaking have been carried out every time a damaging earthquake has taken place. Furthermore, many of the kinds of building types in central and eastern North America are also common in the western U.S., and particularly in California, where the database of earthquake ground motions and corresponding earthquake damage is very large. This database is very useful because it allows seismologists and earthquake engineers to take historic reports of earthquake damage and estimate the probable amplitude of the earthquake ground shaking that caused that damage. The database, along with the ability to estimate the amplitude of earthquake ground shaking at a site by knowing the earthquake magnitude and the distance of the site from the fault where the earthquake was centered, can also be used to estimate how damage could have occurred at a site due to an earthquake of a specified magnitude on a specified fault.

Today, immediately following the occurrence of an earthquake, the USGS publishes what it calls a ShakeMap, which is a map of an area where the earthquake occurred that shows the epicenter of the earthquake along with colors or contours of the levels of ground shaking that

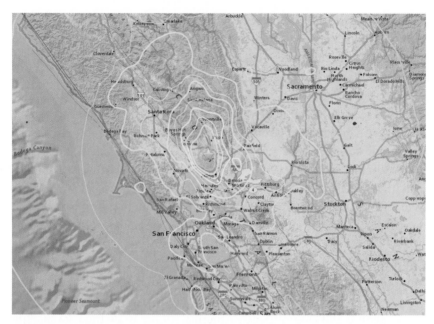

ShakeMap showing the contours of different levels of shaking from an M6.0 earthquake at Napa, California, in 2014 FIGURE FROM THE USGS

are calculated to have taken place at locations surrounding the epicenter. The highest amplitudes of ground shaking are those closest to the epicenter, and the amplitudes of estimated ground shaking decrease with increasing distance away from the epicenter. The USGS also provides charts that estimate the potential for damage to buildings for the different amplitudes of ground shaking shown on their maps. Thus, the potential severity of an earthquake can now be assessed even before the first damage reports are received from the affected area.

Although ShakeMaps are a twenty-first-century invention, a much less sophisticated system of maps of ground shaking due to earthquakes has been around since the early 1800s. At that time seismologists started going out to places where earthquakes had recently taken place, and they compiled accounts of the locations affected by the earthquake and the kinds of effects reported at each of the locations. At some locations damage to buildings was reported, and that was so noted. At other locations people felt the earthquake but reported little or no damage. At still other locations the earthquake was barely noticed or not noticed at all. These seismologists then compiled this information on a map of the region affected by the earthquake, and from the map they were able to draw contours showing the areas where the earthquake caused significant damage, where it caused minor damage, and where it was felt but caused no damage at all. They used the term "earthquake intensity" to describe the effect that they were contouring, and the maps that they drew came to be called

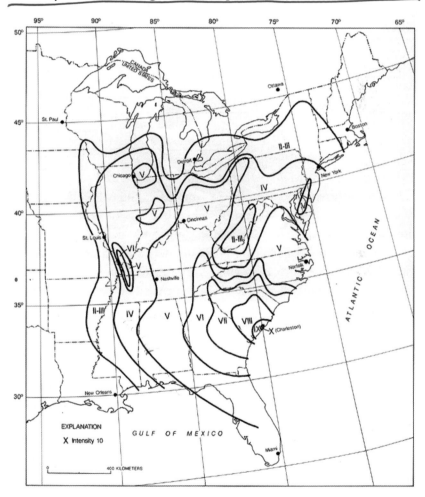

Isoseismal map of Modified Mercalli intensities of the Charleston, South Carolina, 1886 earthquake

intensity maps. In hindsight these maps were very crude ShakeMaps. The localities with the highest intensities probably encompassed the area where the fault that slipped in the earthquake must have been located.

To standardize intensity maps seismologists developed intensity scales, which are lists of the felt and damage effects of earthquakes that are divided into a number of different levels. Weak shaking noticed by only a few people was assigned one intensity level, strong shaking but with no damage was assigned another intensity level, and strong shaking with considerable damage was assigned another intensity level. Intensity-level assignments were made using Roman numerals to indicate that these are not instrumental measurements but rather subjective assignments based on subjective reports. Seismologists in different countries developed their own earthquake intensity scales. In the U.S. seismologists settled on the Modified Mercalli scale as the preferred seismic intensity scale. The Modified Mercalli intensity scale is spelled out in the appendix. Modified Mercalli values are indicated by MMI and range from MMI I (not felt) to MMI XII (total destruction). MMI values from II to V describe increasing strengths of ground shaking where no damage has occurred, whereas MMI values from VI to XII describe increasing strengths of ground shaking based on the amount of damage to buildings and other structures. Seismologists have developed relationships between MMI values and measures of ground shaking, such as peak ground acceleration. Thus, it is possible to relate seismic intensity maps to ShakeMaps and vice versa.

One might guess that ground-shaking amplitudes and seismic-intensity values should decrease in a regular way away from an earthquake fault. On average this is true, but there can be some notable variations to this trend. One important variation arises in local areas where there are thick layers of soft soils at the surface of the earth. In general seismic-wave amplitudes tend to be lower when measured on hard rock at the earth's surface than when measured at nearby sites that are underlain by soft soils. Because of their low seismic velocities, local soft soils tend to amplify earthquake ground shaking compared to nearby rock sites. This effect is predicted by seismic theory and is routinely observed on seismic-intensity maps where places with locally higher seismic-intensity values reflect areas where thick soil layers are found. Many instrumental measurements on soft soil sites and nearby rock sites have confirmed this effect. Thus, earthquake-shaking effects and even earthquake damage is affected by the local soils (or lack of soils) where the earthquake is experienced.

Another reason that earthquake intensities may not always decrease in a regular way from an earthquake fault is that different kinds of buildings suffer damage at different amplitudes of ground shaking. Well-built, seismically resistant buildings require much higher amplitudes of ground shaking before they are damaged, whereas brittle buildings with little or no seismic resistance are damaged at much lower amplitudes of ground shaking. Thus, MMI VI and MMI VII intensity assignments depend on the types of local buildings as well as the strength of the seismic waves that shook those buildings. For example, building collapses are common at relatively low amplitudes of ground shaking when the buildings are made of mud-brick, which has very low seismic resistance. In the U.S. masonry buildings made of bricks and mortar with no other support are easily damaged in earthquake shaking. The problem here is that the brick walls tend to break and fall apart when subjected to horizontal shaking, with the tops of the brick walls breaking first. On the other hand, well-built wood-frame buildings tend to flex in horizontal earthquake shaking without breaking, and so it takes a higher ground-shaking amplitude to damage a wood-frame building than to damage a brick building. For the typical home in eastern North America, earthquake shaking will damage a brick chimney and brick walls before it damages the wood-frame house to which the chimney and walls are attached.

## LANDSLIDES AND LIQUEFACTION

Strong earthquake shaking not only can damage man-made structures, but also can affect the natural landscape. In mountainous and hilly areas, landslides are common in strong earthquake shaking. Loose rocks can be shaken from unstable perches, standing rocks can be tipped over, and steep hillsides can give way in landslides. Landslides can be triggered under two different conditions. The first condition is controlled by the angle of repose of the slope of a hillside. Every earth material (soil and rock) has an angle of repose, which is simply the maximum slope angle at which that material can sit indefinitely without the danger of a landslide. A loose material like sand has a low angle of repose, whereas a hard material like granite has a very high angle of repose. If the slope of a hillside made of an earth material is less than the angle-of-repose slope, then the hillside will be stable and not slide even if affected by an earthquake. On the other hand, if the slope at some part of a hillside exceeds, even by just a small amount, the angle of repose of the earth material that makes up that hillside, then a landslide can be triggered by a stimulus such as heavy rainfall, strong winds, or earthquake shaking. A hill can sit stably for many years at a slope beyond its angle of repose, only to become unstable and slide when a sudden stimulus like an earthquake affects the hillside. Landslides are very common in mountainous areas during strong earthquakes and often can pose a greater hazard to human settlements than the earthquake shaking itself. For example, most of the 944 deaths in a moment magnitude Mw 7.7 earthquake in El Salvador in January 2001 were due to landslides from the mountains into populated areas. The earthquake epicenter was offshore, and the landslides were triggered by the strong shaking of the seismic waves as they spread onshore away from the fault.

The second condition under which a landslide can be triggered is on hillsides where the earth materials that make up the hillside surface are sitting at a slope than is smaller than the maximum stable slope based on the angle of repose. In this case the expectation is that the slope should always be stable, even in strong earthquake shaking. However, if there is a weak layer beneath the surface that has a smaller angle of repose than for the surficial materials, then a stimulus like strong earthquake shaking can cause a landslide to initiate in the subsurface material, which then slides downhill and carries the surface materials with it. This is a hidden danger because an investigation of the surface earth materials may not reveal the weak underlying layer. It is for this reason that the danger for landslides following earthquakes is difficult to assess with high accuracy.

Both kinds of landslides are triggered when earthquake ground shaking exceeds some minimum critical level. The critical level is somewhat different for slopes composed of different kinds of rock or soils, but below the critical level of ground shaking, no landslides are observed. Thus, the observation of the occurrences of landslides in historic earthquakes gives an indication that the ground shaking due to the earthquake exceeded the minimum critical level, and this in turn can be used to infer the minimum magnitude of that earthquake.

In addition to landslides, another type of physical change in the local landscape that can be caused by strong ground shaking due to an earthquake fault slip is called soil liquefaction. In places where liquefaction takes place, there is a subsurface soil layer with a high sand content. Liquefaction can take place in the sandy soil layer if the layer is below the groundwater table and hence is saturated with water. Under normal conditions natural settling of the ground during the formation of the soil layers causes the layer to act as a solid that can support a surface load, much as a person standing on the wet sand of a beach does not immediately sink into the sand. However, when a water-saturated sandy soil layer is agitated by strong earthquake shaking, the pressures in the water and in gases dissolved in the water in the layer build up rapidly, much like shaking a bottle that contains a carbonated soft drink. As the pressure builds up in the shaking, the soil layer starts behaving like a liquid instead of a solid. If the sandy soil layer is at the surface of the earth, objects on the surface start sinking into the layer, much like a person who is standing on the wet sand of a beach can start sinking into the sand by wiggling his or her toes and feet. If the sandy soil layer is below the surface and covered by a layer with a high clay content that traps the pressurized water and gas below, then a different kind of liquefaction phenomenon can take place. In this case the pressure in the liquefied soil layer may build up to the point where it can break through the impermeable covering layer. In this case the pressurized water and gas may burst out in places through the covering layer and onto the surface, bringing a wet layer of sand and mud with it. These eruptions leave deposits on the surface that look like little sand or mud volcanoes, and they are often described that way by amateur observers. Geologists and seismologists call them sandblows. Sandblows can be as small as a couple feet across or they can approach the size of a football field in extent. Sandblows are not observed in all earthquakes because they can only occur in the places where the geologic conditions

Sandblow that formed in the Charleston, South Carolina, 1886 earthquake

of the local soils are those described above. As for landslides, soil liquefaction can only take place when the local ground shaking exceeds a critical level. Thus, as for landslides, soil liquefaction effects are only observed within some distance of an earthquake epicenter, and their existence can be used to infer the minimum magnitude of the earthquake that caused the liquefaction.

As mentioned earlier, some landslides take place when weak subsurface soil layers are shaken at levels above their critical shaking level. Sometimes situations arise where the subsurface layer has a high sand content and is water saturated. In this case the water-saturated sandy layer can liquefy and cause the land to slump, even for terrain with very gentle surface slopes. Slopes as small as 1 degree can slide under these very special conditions. In the cases where a soil with a very low slope moves downhill due to a subsurface liquefied soil layer, geologists and seismologists call the surface deformation a lateral spread. The surface may look almost flat to the naked eye, but in fact a lateral spread is nothing more than a combination of liquefaction and landsliding. For example, in the moment magnitude 6.9 Kobe, Japan, earthquake of 1995, the dock areas of the city of Kobe were heavily damaged due to lateral spreading. Although the land surface of the dock areas appeared to have no topographic slope, major lateral spreading heavily damaged the areas as the very strong earthquake shaking liquefied sandy layers beneath the docks. Subsequent geological and geotechnical investigations discovered the liquefied layers beneath the area.

## EARTHQUAKE STATISTICS

Because earthquakes are natural phenomena ultimately caused by the steady movements of the tectonic plates over the surface of the earth, earthquakes follow a generally repeatable pattern over time, magnitude, and location. For example, areas that were very seismically active a century ago are the same places where most of the world's earthquakes take place today. The rates of earthquakes in active places like California and Japan seem to be quite comparable today to those that were reported a century ago. It has long been known that in all parts of the world smaller magnitude earthquakes take place much more frequently than do larger magnitude earthquakes. Even though seismologists cannot predict exactly when and where future strong earthquakes will strike, they have become adept at estimating the probabilities of future earthquakes of different magnitudes in different parts of the world. Earthquake statistics are now widely used to help seismologists understand the past earthquake history of different parts of our planet and estimate the probabilities of future earthquakes in different areas.

An important statistical tool for estimating the potential of future earthquakes was developed by Beno Gutenberg and Charles Richter at Caltech in the 1930s and 1940s. It is called the Gutenberg-Richter relation (or GR relation), and it comes from analyzing the numbers of earthquakes of different magnitudes that are observed over a period of time in a region. Although earthquakes in different parts of the world tend to take place at different levels of activity, in general the GR relation indicates that the average rate of earthquake activity decreases by about a factor of 10 for each unit increase in magnitude. Thus, if an area has about 1,000 magnitude 2.0 or greater earthquakes in a year, it averages about 100 magnitude 3.0 or greater earthquakes per year, about 10 magnitude 4.0 or greater earthquakes per year, and about 1 magnitude 5.0 or greater earthquake per year. Although it does not make intuitive sense to talk about 0.1 magnitude 6.0 or greater earthquakes per year, this number can be inverted to indicate that a magnitude 6.0 earthquake takes place once every 10 years, on average. The universality of the GR relation means that the expected number of large earthquakes in a given time period can be estimated if the rates of small earthquakes are known.

In addition to the GR relation, there is an important statistical law in seismology that describes how the rate of aftershocks following a large earthquake changes with time. Aftershocks are smaller earthquakes that tend to occur at an increased rate on a fault immediately after a larger earthquake takes place. Aftershocks tend to decrease in number with time following the occurrence of an earthquake, with the greatest rate of aftershock activity immediately following the largest earthquake, called by seismologists the mainshock. In 1894 Fusakichi Omori published a study in which he showed that the number of aftershocks per day changes inversely with time. Quantitatively, Omori's Law for aftershocks states

## Average Number of Earthquakes per Year in Southern California (Gutenberg-Richter Distribution)

| Magnitude | Number per Year | Average Time between Earthquakes |
|---|---|---|
| 2 | 1,500 | 5.8 hours |
| 3 | 162.5 | 53.9 hours |
| 4 | 17.5 | 20.9 days |
| 5 | 1.88 | 194.8 days |
| 6 | 0.20 | 5.0 years |
| 7 | 0.021 | 47.1 years |

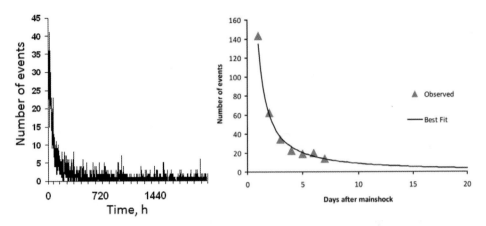

Examples of Omori's Law decay

that if there are about 100 aftershocks on the first day after a mainshock, there are about 100/2, or about 50, aftershocks on the second day after the mainshock. Furthermore, there are about 100/3, or about 33, aftershocks on the third day after a mainshock; about 100/4, or about 25, aftershocks on the fourth day after a mainshock; and so on. There can be considerable deviations from Omori's Law from day to day, but on average Omori's Law is very good at estimating how the average rates of aftershocks change with time following a mainshock.

Omori's Law does not take into account the magnitudes of the earthquakes; rather, it counts equally earthquakes of all magnitudes in the rates of aftershocks per day. On the other hand, even for aftershocks the GR relation holds, so smaller magnitude aftershocks take place more frequently than larger magnitude aftershocks. Seismologists can use Omori's Law and the GR relation together to estimate the rates of aftershocks of different magnitudes on a fault following the occurrence of a mainshock.

One of the reasons that there are variations in the number of aftershocks per day when compared to predictions from Omori's Law is that earthquakes have a strong random component in their occurrences with time. Because of this randomness there is no regularity to the times when earthquakes occur. During some time periods there are large numbers of earthquakes that occur, whereas during other times there are relatively few earthquakes. The time periods from more to less activity change with no discernible pattern. Because of their randomness, earthquakes display no obvious predictability with time, whether seismologists are talking about foreshocks, mainshocks, aftershocks, or any kinds of earthquakes. In random processes like earthquakes, the only consistency is the average number of earthquakes per time. If one takes a time duration that is long compared to the time between individual earthquakes, the average number of earthquakes in that time duration is approximately the same no matter when that average is computed.

## INTERPRETING HISTORICAL EARTHQUAKE RECORDS

An important scientific goal in the study of an historical earthquake is to learn as much as possible about what happened on the fault during the earthquake and what happened at human settlements due to the earthquake shaking. The work is conducted much in the same way that a forensics expert investigates a crime scene. The historical seismologist carefully analyzes the available historical records about a past earthquake, looking for clues that are consistent with the modern understanding of the effects that are observed when earthquakes take place. Of course, the historical seismologist must view all records with careful skepticism, since they can contain exaggerations, misinformation, and the prejudices of the person giving the report. Furthermore, many historical earthquake reports are secondhand reports, where the reporter records the earthquake as recounted by another person. Secondhand reports frequently suffer from distortions of the original report due to information that was excluded, exaggerated, or misinterpreted by the person who wrote the report. Even so, earthquake descriptions may contain important clues that can help constrain the magnitude of the earthquake, the possible location of the epicenter, and the strength of the ground shaking where the earthquake was experienced. Historical earthquake descriptions can be combined from different locations to look for consistencies and patterns between the reports that can help aid in the interpretation of the source location and size of the earthquake.

Traditionally, one of the most important results from a study of an historical earthquake has been the intensity map, which shows the assigned intensities across the region where the earthquake was felt. In theory the isoseismal contours dividing different intensity regions should have circular or oval shapes that are centered on the epicentral region of the earthquake. Many seismic intensity maps show such shapes, but these are the interpretations of the map compilers rather than the actual contour shapes that are required by the data. In fact, maps of intensities at different locations with no isoseismal contours superimposed show a complex pattern of intensities with the greatest intensities near the epicenter and progressively smaller intensities (but with much local variation) at farther distances from the greatest intensity region. These variations are due to local site amplification effects, to differences in the construction and conditions of the local buildings from place to place, and to the inherently subjective nature of intensity assignments. Today seismologists have developed several methods that use mathematical analyses of the sites and values of the intensity assignments from an intensity map to estimate the epicentral location and magnitude of an historical earthquake. Such methods have been calibrated where both intensity reports have been accumulated and the magnitude and location of recent earthquakes have been determined using modern seismographic data and methods.

With our modern understanding of earthquakes and the various phenomena associated with earthquake shaking, even a single terse felt report about an earthquake can contain important clues about the earthquake source information. For example, it is now well known that the shaking in a larger magnitude earthquake lasts longer than that for a smaller magnitude earthquake. This means that a report that gives an indication of the duration that earthquake shaking was felt can be used to give a rough estimate of the magnitude of the earthquake. Sometimes a felt report contains information about the time between the beginning of the earthquake waves and the arrival of the strongest ground shaking. The beginning of the earthquake occurs at the arrival time of the P wave, whereas the strongest shaking is during the arrival of the surface waves. The time difference between the arrivals of these two wave types is proportional to the distance of the observer from the earthquake fault. If this time difference is short (no more than a few seconds), the earthquake fault was near the observer, but if the time difference is large, then the observer was at a great distance from the fault on which the earthquake took place. If the time difference between these two arrivals can be estimated based on an historical earthquake report, then the distance of that observer from the fault location where the earthquake slip took place can be inferred. Some historical accounts give surprisingly reliable accounts that can be used to determine the approximate distance of the observer from the earthquake fault.

There is another piece of information that is sometimes found in an individual earthquake report that can be used to infer how far the observer may have been from the earthquake fault. That piece of information is a description of the sound of the earthquake or the lack of sound during the earthquake shaking. Observers near the epicenter of an earthquake magnitude 2.0 to about 3.5 typically describe the earthquake sound as a loud boom, like a nearby explosion or clap of thunder. If the earthquake is above about magnitude 5.0, observers near the epicenter often report a roaring sound that accompanies the earthquake shaking. My wife, Martha, grew up in California, and she lived only a few miles from the fault that had the magnitude 6.7 San Fernando earthquake in February 1971. That earthquake took place about 6:00 a.m. She was in bed asleep at the time of the earthquake, and she remembers being awakened by the earthquake. What she found most scary about the earthquake was the loud roaring sound that accompanied the violent earthquake shaking. She said it sounded like a jet plane was landing on the roof of her house, and she worried that a nuclear bomb had exploded nearby. The earthquake sound that she heard was nothing more than the seismic waves from the earth converting into sound waves in the atmosphere. As discussed earlier in this chapter, at close distances to the earthquake fault, the seismic waves have ample energy at acoustic frequencies that can be heard by human beings. As earthquake magnitude increases, the strength of the sound as well as the time duration of the sound increase for observers near the fault where the earthquake slip took place. The roaring sound that my wife heard in 1971 lasted about a minute, a terrifying amount of time to her.

For observers at progressively greater distances from an earthquake epicenter, the nature of the earthquake sounds progressively changes. The intensity of the sound decreases, and the nature of the sound evolves from a roaring or crashing nature near the fault to a low rumble sound,

THE BASICS OF EARTHQUAKE SEISMOLOGY

like distant thunder, at farther distances from the fault. At the greatest distances where an earthquake is felt, observers often do not report any sounds from the earth at all, but perhaps only sounds from the buildings due to the shaking (such as bouncing of glassware on shelves, creaking of the building, rattling of building windows, etc.). The same earthquake can be experienced very differently by observers depending on their distance to the fault where the earthquake took place, and these differing experiences can often be inferred in the written reports of historical earthquakes.

As described above, aftershocks inevitably follow earthquakes. For small mainshocks, say magnitude 2.0 to 3.0, the aftershocks are so small that they are not felt or heard by humans. However, as the magnitude of an earthquake that is a mainshock increases, so does the number of aftershocks that follow that mainshock. Also, larger magnitude mainshocks can have larger magnitude aftershocks. The GR relation described previously holds for aftershocks, and so the smallest magnitude aftershocks are the most common after a mainshock, and larger magnitude aftershocks are less common. Typically, the magnitude of the largest aftershock is about 1.0 to 1.3 magnitude units smaller than the magnitude of the mainshock. Thus, the largest aftershock of a magnitude 6.0 mainshock is often about magnitude 4.7 to 5.0. Reports of aftershocks in historical records can give important information about the distances of the observers from the mainshock fault. In some cases aftershock reports may also help constrain the location and magnitude of the mainshock.

Historical earthquake reports created by observers who were located very near the fault that slipped in the earthquake often describe the aftershocks that were experienced. Being very close to the fault where the earthquake took place, these observers were able to feel and hear the small aftershocks as well as the large aftershocks that occurred. Observers at greater distance from the fault will be outside the area where the smallest aftershocks can be experienced, but they may still feel the larger magnitude aftershocks. Observers still farther away may only report the very largest aftershocks that take place. Thus, the number of aftershocks reported in an historical earthquake account can be used in some cases to infer how far that observer was from the fault where the earthquake slip took place. Knowing the number of aftershocks and the distance of the observer from the earthquake fault may also help constrain the magnitude of the mainshock that caused the aftershocks. If the number of felt aftershocks can be gleaned from the accounts from different localities for an historical earthquake, then the relative distances of those different localities to the earthquake fault can be estimated, which in turn can be used to constrain the location of the earthquake fault itself.

The strength of the local ground shaking associated with a report of an earthquake can sometimes be estimated from details given in the report, and this in turn can help assess how far the person giving the report was from the earthquake fault. Obviously, localities with reports of damage to structures experienced stronger ground shaking than places where the earthquake was felt but no damage was reported. The type of damage that is reported also gives an indication of the strength of the local ground shaking. Minor damage such as cracks in walls indicates ground shaking that was weaker than shaking that causes major damage to parts of walls or that causes chimneys to fall down. In general, brick and stone walls of masonry structures are less able to withstand ground shaking than are wood-frame or well-built steel-frame buildings. Because of this, damage to wood-frame and steel-frame structures is indicative of very strong ground shaking, whereas the ground shaking was not as strong if the damage is confined to masonry structures. The number of damaged structures is also indicative of the strength of the ground shaking, with stronger ground shaking damaging more structures than weaker ground shaking.

The strength of local ground shaking can also be inferred by reports of landslides and liquefaction effects. Landslides are triggered by ground shaking above some minimum level, and landslides become more numerous as the ground shaking level increases above this minimum level. Thus, localities where many landslides were reported experienced much stronger ground-shaking than a place where only a single landslide was experienced. The same is true of sandblows. More numerous and larger sandblows occur at localities where stronger ground shaking is experienced, whereas the number of sandblows and their sizes decrease as the level of ground shaking decreases. As for landslides, there is some minimum level of ground shaking that must be exceeded before any sandblows can take place. The same statement is true for other types of ground liquefaction due to earthquake shaking. Thus, reports that quantify in some way the number and severity of landslides or of liquefaction features provide important information about the amplitude of the local ground shaking at the locality where the observation that was recorded in the report was taken.

# CHAPTER 2

# 1638: The Pilgrim's Earthquake

THE YEAR 1620 IS FAMOUS IN NEW ENGLAND HISTORY BECAUSE IT WAS the year when the first permanent settlement of European pilgrims was established in the region at Plymouth, Massachusetts. The conditions were very difficult for the first Europeans as there was so much about their new home that was unfamiliar to them. The plants, the animals, the weather, and the Native Americans all posed challenges because they were different from what the pilgrims had experienced in Europe, and yet there were some similarities as well. For the pilgrims their first years after their initial landing in 1620 were consumed with the vital tasks of building homes, planting crops, and developing the resources they needed to survive in their new home.

It was in the year 1638 that the pilgrim settlers experienced their first earthquake in their new, strange land. The date was probably June 1 on the Julian calendar, which was the calendar that was in use in England and its colonies at that time; June 1 on the Julian calendar corresponds to June 11 on the modern Gregorian calendar. Today the custom is to follow a date on the Julian calendar with the initials O.S. (which stand for Old Style) and to follow a date on the Gregorian calendar with the initials N.S. (which stand for New Style). That custom is followed in this book.

## THE NEW ENGLAND COLONIES EXPERIENCE AN EARTHQUAKE

The earthquake on June 1, 1638 (O.S.), was a strong shake that greatly startled the residents of New England. William Bradford, the governor of the settlement at Plymouth, Massachusetts, at the time, wrote the following description of the earthquake:

*This year, about the first or second of June, was a great and fearful earthquake. It was in this place heard before it was felt. It came with a rumbling noise or low murmur, like unto remote thunder. It came from the northward and passed southward; as the noise approached nearer, the earth began to shake and came at length with that violence as caused platters, dishes and suchlike things as stood upon shelves, to clatter and fall down. Yea, persons were afraid of the houses them-selves. It so fell out that at the same time divers of the chief of this town were met together at one house, conferring with some of their friends that were upon their removal from the place, as if the Lord would hereby show the signs of His displeasure, in their shaking a-pieces and removals one from the other. However, it was very terrible for the time, and as the men were talking in the house, some women and oth-ers were without the doors, and the earth shook with that violence as they could not stand without catching hold of the posts and pales that stood next to them. And about half an hour or less came another noise and shaking, but neither so loud or strong as the former, but quickly passed over so it ceased. It was not only on the seacoast, but the Indi-ans felt it within land, and some ships that were upon the coast were shaken by it.*

There are several interesting details in this report that help with the modern interpretation of the location and magnitude of this earthquake and of the amplitude of the ground shaking at Plymouth. The report states that the earthquake started with a low rumbling noise like distant thunder. As explained in chapter 1, this descriptions indicates that Plym-outh was far enough from the earthquake fault that the loudest noises associated with the faulting had been damped out by the rock through which the waves traveled but also that Plymouth was not so far away that the sounds from the seismic waves had been completely lost. Thus, Plymouth was probably somewhere between 62 and 370 miles (100 to 600 kilometers) from the earthquake fault. This is also supported by the following statement that the shaking took some time to build up to its maximum strength. Thus, there was some noticeable although unstated time period between the arrival of the fastest wave (the P wave) and the highest amplitude waves (the surface waves). This also confirms that Plymouth was at some distance from the fault upon which the earthquake took place.

Another important detail in this report is the strength of the earthquake ground shaking at Plymouth. The shaking was strong enough to cause items on shelves to fall down, but apparently it did not cause damage to any of the buildings themselves, although the residents were clearly afraid that the buildings might collapse. One statement in the report indicates that those who were standing outdoors were so affected by the ground shaking that they had trouble standing without holding on to something like a post in the ground. Taken together, these reports suggest that the ground shaking was about MMI V or VI at Plymouth. No chimney damage is reported by Bradford, a point that is discussed more fully at the end of this chapter.

The Bradford report states that ships in the harbor felt the earthquake. This is not at all surprising because seismic waves in rock will transmit into water bodies on the rock and thus be felt in the water and on the water surface. Whereas the ocean gives a ship a rolling or rocking motion, earthquake shaking is felt as a sharp vibration, similar to that felt by those who experience earthquake ground shaking on the land surface. Given the strong shaking felt onshore at Plymouth, it would be expected that the earthquake shaking would also be felt on the nearby ocean, and that is indeed confirmed by Bradford.

Not only does Bradford provide many details about the mainshock, but he also reports that an aftershock was felt at Plymouth. This aftershock was felt about half an hour after the mainshock, and the ground shaking due to the aftershock was apparently much weaker at Plymouth than was the mainshock. There are no other indications of aftershocks in the Bradford report.

Another important description of the 1638 earthquake was written by Governor John Winthrop of the Massachusetts Bay colony. The city of Boston was founded in 1630 and Harvard College was founded in 1636, and so Winthrop's report provides information about how the earthquake was experienced in what is today the Boston area. Winthrop's description is as follows: "June 1. Between three and four in the afternoon, being clear, warm weather, the wind westerly, there was a great earthquake. It came with a noise like a continued thunder or the rattling of coaches in London, but was presently gone. It was at Connecticut, at Narragansett, at Pascataquack, and all the parts round about. It shook the ships, which rode in the harbor, and all the islands, etc. The noise and the shakings continued about four minutes. The earth was unquiet twenty days after, by times."

Like Bradford, Winthrop reports the earthquake on June 1, but he puts the earthquake somewhat later in the afternoon than does Bradford. Timekeeping was very crude in those days with no established time zones, and so discrepancies in the reported time of the earthquake among the original reports are not meaningful. Like Bradford's report from Plymouth, Winthrop indicates that the ground shaking in the Boston area was accompanied by noise like thunder or the rattling of coaches on the cobblestone streets of that time, which suggests that Boston was not close to the fault but also was not too far away. Thus, Boston probably also was between 62 and 370 miles (100 to 600 kilometers) from the earthquake fault.

Winthrop does not describe how strongly the ground shaking was perceived by the Boston residents other than to indicate that the earthquake was felt on ships and islands offshore at Boston. However, Winthrop does provide one important detail that was not specified in the Bradford report. Winthrop states that the ground shaking lasted about four minutes. This is a very long time period for the shaking due to a single earthquake, and if taken literally would suggest that this earthquake was probably well above magnitude 7.0. However, given the few clocks that were available at the time and the simple construction of those clocks, the time duration of four minutes reported by Winthrop must be viewed with a large dose of skepticism. A time duration of two minutes for the mainshock is more in keeping with the probable magnitude of this earthquake that is estimated later in this chapter. Another possibility is that a strong aftershock took place within two to three minutes following the occurrence of the mainshock, and that this was felt at Boston at the end of the shaking of the mainshock. If two consecutive earthquakes took place only a couple of minutes apart, then the four minutes of ground shaking in Winthrop's report would have represented the total duration of shaking due to the two different earthquakes and not the duration of ground shaking from a single mainshock.

John Hull from Dorchester, Massachusetts, also recorded the earthquake in his diary. He wrote, "The 1st of the 4th month, about noon, was a great and general earthquake. The vessels upon the river, and the goods that were in the said ships, moved much. Many upon the land could scarcely stand upright."

Similar to that at Plymouth, Hull describes the shaking at Boston, where he was at the time of the earthquake, as being so strong that people had trouble standing. He indicates not only that it was felt by persons on ships on the Charles River but also that the goods stored in those ships were moved by the shaking.

Another surviving report about the earthquake was provided by Roger Williams from the Rhode Island colony in Providence. In a letter to John Winthrop dated June 1638, Williams wrote,

> SIR,—I sometimes fear that my lines are as thick and over busy as the musketoes, &c., but your wisdom will connive, and your love will cover, &c. Two things at present for information. First in the affairs of the Most High; his late dreadful voice and hand: that audible and sensible voice, the Earthquake. All these parts felt it, (whether beyond the Narragansett I yet learn not), for myself I scarce perceived ought but a kind of thunder and a gentle moving, &c., and yet it was no more this way to many of our own and the natives' apprehensions, and but one sudden short motion. The younger natives are ignorant of the like: but the elder inform me that this is the fifth within these four score years in the land: the first about three score and ten years since [1568]: the second some three score and four years since [1574], the third some fifty-four years since [1584], the fourth some forty-six since [1592]: and they always observed either plague or pox or some other epidemical disease followed; three, four or five years after the Earthquake, (or Naunaumemoauke, as they speak). He be mercifully pleased himself to interpret and open his own riddles, (and grant if it be pleasing in his eyes) it may not be for destruction, and but (as the Earthquake before

*the Jailor's conversion) a means of shaking and turning of all hearts, (which are his,) English or Indian, to him. To further this (if the Lord please) the Earthquake sensibly took about a thousand of the natives in a most solemn meeting for play, &c.*

Unlike the strong shaking reported at Plymouth, Williams's report suggests a weaker level of ground shaking, indicating that he was farther from the epicenter than was Plymouth. Even so, Williams states that the earthquake was widely felt by the colonists in Rhode Island as well as by the Native Americans. Williams learned from the Native Americans that earthquakes like the one that they experienced were not an uncommon occurrence in the region, with four being remembered by older natives from between 1568 and 1592. Earthquakes were common enough in the region that the Narragansett tribe had a word for it (*Naunaumemoauke*) in their vocabulary.

## THE EARTHQUAKE IN QUEBEC

One other report about the effects of this earthquake came from Fr. Paul Le Jeune, a Roman Catholic missionary who was a member of the Society of Jesus (S.J.), commonly called the Jesuits, and who was working with the Native Americans in Canada. Father Le Jeune was based in Quebec City, but he had traveled to Trois-Rivières in Quebec, from whence he provided the following account of the earthquake as recorded in the *Jesuit Relations*: "On St. Barnabas's day, we had an earthquake in some places; and it was so perceptible that the Savages were greatly surprised to see their bark plates collide with each other, and the water spill out of their kettles. This drew from them a loud cry of astonishment."

In 1638 St. Barnabas's day was Friday, June 11, 1638 (N.S.), which corresponds to June 1, 1638 (O.S.), and the earthquake is reported at a time when the Native Americans were cooking, likely in the middle of the day. Thus, it is safe to assume that the report from Father Le Jeune is about the same earthquake that was reported from the British colonies of Massachusetts, Rhode Island, and Connecticut. It is not certain where the Native Americans were when they experienced the earthquake, since the account is not specific and was written at a later time as part of Father Le

Jeune's annual report to Rome. Fr. Pierre Gouin, a French-Canadian Jesuit who in 2001 published *Historical Earthquakes Felt in Quebec (1534–1925)*, speculated in his book that Father Le Jeune's report may be describing the earthquake experience at Trois-Rivières.

These are the only localities in eastern North America from which reports of the 1638 earthquake are known. The area of New Brunswick and Nova Scotia that was called Acadia at the time had its first permanent settlement established in 1636, and no indication of the earthquake at that settlement is reported. It is likely that the earthquake was felt

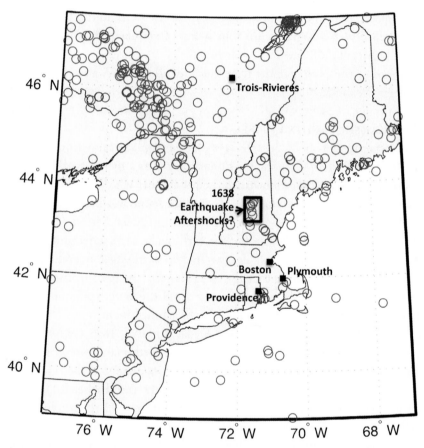

M≥3 earthquakes from 1975 to 2017 and the suspected location of the 1638 earthquake

in this area but that its effects were minor enough that they were not included in the local historical tradition. Likewise, there is no indication of the earthquake in the surviving accounts of the Dutch settlement of New Amsterdam in what is today Manhattan Island in New York City. The earthquake should have been felt by these settlers, but here also the effects of the earthquake may have been minor enough that they were not remembered later.

With the reports from only a few places about the earthquake and its effects, it is difficult to determine the location and magnitude of the event. My guess for the location of this earthquake is that it took place in south-central New Hampshire, with the active fault rupture having taken place between Concord and Sanbornton. Today this is the most seismically active area in New England. My estimate of the moment magnitude of the 1638 earthquake is 6.5 to explain the strength of the shaking at Boston and Plymouth, where people had trouble standing during the shaking, and at Trois-Rivières, where water splashed out of cooking pots. From this postulated fault area, aftershocks of about moment magnitude 4.0 and above would have been felt in Boston. A magnitude 6.5 mainshock would probably have generated a number of aftershocks above magnitude 4.0 during the weeks after the mainshock. I believe that the paleoseismicity model points to the Concord-to-Sanbornton area in New Hampshire as a possible location for the 1638 earthquake fault rupture, and the aftershock evidence from the Winthrop report adds support to this speculation.

## DAMAGE TO CHIMNEYS?

None of the primary reports about the 1638 earthquake that were written immediately following the earthquake mention any damage to buildings. However, in 1764 Thomas Hutchinson published a history of the Massachusetts Bay colony, and in that history he recounts the following about the 1638 earthquake: "The year 1638 was memorable for a very great earth-quake through New-England. The shake, by the printed accounts of it, and from manuscript letters, appears to have been equal to that of 1727, the pewter in many places being thrown off the shelves, and the tops of chimneys in some places shook down, but the noise, though great, not so surprising as that of the last mentioned. The course of it was from west to east."

This account by Hutchinson is the first one known that mentions damage to chimneys in the 1638 earthquake. At first I was always puzzled by this reference to chimney damage when I read it. Sometime later I visited Plymouth Plantation, which is a reconstruction of the Plymouth colony from about the year 1627. It was on this visit that I believe I learned part of the answer to my puzzlement. None of the reconstructed homes from the original Pilgrims' colony at Plymouth Plantation have chimneys, but rather smoke was vented from each home through a hole in the roof. I subsequently learned the reason for this. During the early colonial days, the European settlers did not have ready access to lime, which is a necessary ingredient for making cement. Without cement they could not mortar stones or bricks into a standing chimney. John Abbot Goodwin, in his history of the Plymouth colony that was published in Boston in 1888, wrote that the chimneys from this period were constructed of small straight sticks placed vertically upward and lined on their interior with clay. Such chimneys were prone to fire if they were not well clayed. Years later some deposits of lime were found in the area that could be used to make cement. Also, as their settlements grew in number and the wealth of the settlers increased, some colonists had cement shipped over to the colonies from England. This access to cement probably all happened after the 1638 earthquake. Thus, one likely reason that no chimney damage was reported in 1638 is that there were no stone or brick chimneys to damage at the time of the earthquake.

If my speculation about chimneys in the previous paragraph is true, why then does the history by Hutchinson mention chimney damage for the 1638 earthquake? I believe that this is an example of a common problem that must be accounted for in historical research, namely that later historical writers sometimes embellish their historical descriptions with details that the writers assume were true but in fact did not happen. This can explain the Hutchinson description of chimney damage in 1638. From his 18th-century perspective, and especially from his personal experiences of the 1727 and 1755 earthquakes (described in later chapters), Hutchinson was well aware of later earthquakes in New England where chimney damage was the most common form of damage. He probably assumed from the original descriptions that the 1638 earthquake was strong enough to damage chimneys and therefore included that idea as part of his description of the 1638 earthquake. He may have been unaware that chimneys were not being constructed in New England before the 1638 earthquake. This is an example of the kind of improper statements that are sometimes inserted by an author into the description of an earthquake and its effects.

# CHAPTER 3

# 1658: The Earthquake That May Have Never Happened

FOR THOSE OF US WHO WANT TO DETERMINE THE LOCATIONS, MAGNI-tudes, and effects of historical earthquakes, a starting point for our research is invariably to consult existing earthquake catalogs to determine when past earthquakes took place. An earthquake catalog is nothing more than a compilation of the dates, times, locations, and estimated sizes of some or all of the earthquakes that are known for a region. Some earthquake catalog compilers published catalogs of global earthquakes, whereas many other compilers have focused on including some or all of the earthquakes of a particular region in their publication.

Catalogs of historical earthquakes typically contain anywhere from tens to hundreds (or more) of events. Assembling the data for an earth-quake catalog is a major task because multiple sources must be consulted and pertinent information from those sources must be extracted and recorded. It is easy to make mistakes during this process, and those of us who work with earthquake catalogs always seem to find some mistakes in them. One kind of mistake, that of inserting into the description of an earthquake an observation that did not happen, was described in the previous chapter of this book. Here I talk about another kind of mistake, namely that of inserting into an earthquake catalog an earthquake that may have never taken place.

An entry in an earthquake catalog of a purported earthquake that in fact never took place represents what historical seismologists call a false earthquake. How can false earthquakes happen? Actually, there are many ways that such mistaken events can be created in an earthquake catalog. Sometimes catalog compilers made a mistake on the date and/or time of an earthquake. This is especially a problem for earthquakes that took place before the changeover to the Gregorian calendar in the British colonies, because sometimes earthquake catalog compilers mistook an Old Style (Julian) date for a New Style (Gregorian) date. Sometimes catalog compilers included as separate earthquakes the same event with the same date and time but with different locations. This mistake usually arises when more than one earlier investigator had each assigned a different epicenter to an earthquake, and a later catalog compiler assumed that these represented different earthquakes at different locations rather than different estimated locations of the same earthquake.

The case of the 1658 earthquake seems to be an example of another way that a false event may come to be included in an earthquake catalog. In 1871 William T. Brigham published a catalog of earthquakes from New England and vicinity in the *Memoirs of the Boston Society of Natural History* (volume II, pages 1–28). As the source of this earthquake, Brigham cites *New England's Memorial*, a history of New England written by Nathaniel Morton and published in 1669. Brigham wrote, "A very slight shock was noticed in 1653 (October 29), but did not attract general notice, and is not mentioned by Mallet in his catalogue. Five years later occurred what is usually styled in the old histories, 'a great earthquake.' Morton says, 'This year there was a very great earthquake in New England', but no account of the day, hour or direction is given; perhaps it was April 4. Von Hoff enumerates this in his list, but gives no further particulars, referring simply to the Philosophical Transactions as his authority; Mallet does the same."

The possible date of April 4 that Brigham mentions is attributed in a footnote by Brigham to the publication *Canadian Naturalist and Geologist*, volume V, page 369. The article by J. W. Dawson of McGill University in the *Canadian Naturalist and Geologist* references the earthquake catalog of Robert Mallet of Ireland, published in 1858, as the source of his information on this earthquake. Mallet's entry on the earthquake in New England in 1658 notes only that it was "violent." In the printed version of the earthquake catalog of Mallet, there is listed an earthquake on

April 4, 1658, at Messina, Italy, and the New England earthquake is given two entries later. Dawson seems to have interpreted the three consecutive earthquake entries in the Mallet catalog, starting with the Messina earthquake in 1658, as having occurred on the same date of April 4. By his wording in the above quotation, Brigham appears skeptical that the New England earthquake took place on April 4. I believe that Dawson misinterpreted the Mallet catalog entry and that Mallet did not give a date for the New England earthquake other than that it took place in 1658.

Brigham notes that a listing of the 1658 earthquake was included in the worldwide earthquake catalog of Karl von Hoff of Germany that was published posthumously in 1840. Brigham indicates that von Hoff and Mallet found their information about this earthquake in the *Philosophical Transactions*. For the Mallet catalog Brigham notes that the information came from volume L, page 9, of the *Philosophical Transactions* of 1757, which is an article by Professor Winthrop of Harvard University about the 1755 earthquake. In that article Professor Winthrop mentions a great earthquake in 1755 but gives no other information about the event. In addition to this reference, in volume XXXIX of the *Philosophical Transactions*, number 437, starting on page 63, published in 1735, there is an article by Paul Dudley in which he discusses a number of early earthquakes in New England. He includes in his article the following sentence: "In 1658, there was another very great earthquake, but no particulars are related." He gives no date for the earthquake, nor does he give any details about it. In summary, of the early earthquake catalogs of Brigham, Mallet, and von Hoff, the only reference to a primary source that comes from the time shortly after 1658 is Brigham's citation of Morton's *New England's Memorial* of 1669.

With all of the early catalogs listing a great earthquake in New England in 1658 and a primary source from 1669 also mentioning a great earthquake that year, why do I consider this to be a false earthquake? The major problem is that there are no primary sources from the time, other than Morton's *New England's Memorial*, that mention an earthquake in 1658. The *Jesuit Relations*, which describe in detail the day, time, and shaking effects of the earthquakes of 1638 (chapter 2) and 1663 (chapter 4), mention no earthquake at all in 1658. The Reverend Samuel Danforth of

Roxbury, Massachusetts, mentions earthquakes in 1660, 1661, and 1663 in his diary, but he has no mention of an earthquake in 1658. John Hull in nearby Dorchester, Massachusetts, and Increase Mather across the Charles River from Boston in Cambridge, Massachusetts, also are silent about a great earthquake in 1658. The same is true for all other sources in New England from that time except for that of Nathanial Morton.

Morton lived through the year 1658 as an adult, and so he would have had a memory of a strong earthquake if one had taken place in 1658. Even so, I think he added a false earthquake into his *New England's Memorial*, and I think there is a simple explanation of how this might have happened. In the 1600s a compiler of historical events like Morton would have been consulting many different written sources to gather his data, including the data on past earthquakes. His compilations would have been made using handwritten notes, and later he would have relied on those notes taken during his research when he was writing by hand his manuscript for publication. Somewhere in this process, it would have been very easy to misread the year 1638 as 1658 and to include a reference to a strong earthquake in 1658 in the published version of his *New England's Memorial*. The mistake might have happened when he read the sources that he consulted, since most of these sources would have been handwritten and the handwriting may have been hard to read. The mistake might have happened later, such as when consulting a handwritten research note on the earthquake in New England he mistook his handwritten 1638 for 1658.

Morton likely would have felt the earthquakes of 1660 and 1661 that are mentioned in the diary of Reverend Danforth, and perhaps he misremembered the year of one of those earthquakes. The lack of an earthquake in 1658 would explain why there are no details of the earthquake, such as the date, time, or strength of ground shaking, that are provided by any source from the time, including Morton. Even if false, Morton's indication of a great earthquake in 1658 would have become enshrined in the later earthquake catalogs of von Hoff and Mallet and then copied into subsequent earthquake catalogs by even later compilers like Brigham. Everyone can cite someone else as the authority on the earthquake, but the one primary source from the time period is almost certainly a mistake.

The story of this likely false earthquake provides an important example that one cannot accept something as true simply because it was recorded in a recognized historical or scientific document. Mistakes can occur, and if they are not recognized as such by later users of the document, then those users may spread the misinformation far and wide. Of course, there is a chance that New England did indeed experience a strong earthquake in 1658 and that Morton, and perhaps later von Hoff and Mallet, had access to primary reports of this earthquake that are now lost. In my opinion this is a very unlikely possibility, and I believe that the listing of a strong New England earthquake in 1658 is simply a false earthquake report that has been propagated into almost all modern earthquake catalogs.

CHAPTER 4

# 1663: A Major Earthquake Strikes Quebec

WHEREAS THERE ARE NO EXISTING RECORDS THAT DOCUMENT A STRONG earthquake in New England 1658, there is no doubt from the documentary record that a major earthquake rocked what is today the northeastern U.S. and southeastern Canada in 1663. Numerous contemporaneous reports survive today that give rich accounts of the effects of the 1663 earthquake. Compared to the time of the 1638 earthquake, by 1663 there were many colonial settlements in northeastern North America, and records describing this earthquake and its aftershocks have been preserved from many of these settlements.

## AN EARTHQUAKE ON FEBRUARY 5, 1663, IN QUEBEC

In 1663 a number of Jesuit missionaries were spread throughout Quebec, providing church services and religious education to the Native American and colonial French populations. In 1663 Fr. Jerome Lalemant, S.J., was the head of the Jesuit missionaries in Quebec, and it was his job to provide regular written reports to Rome concerning the activities of the Jesuit missions. His report about the 1663 earthquake in the *Jesuit Relations* was written in French in Quebec City in the summer of 1663, and a translation of a part of that report is provided here:

> On the fifth of February 1663, toward half past five in the evening,
> a loud roaring was heard at the same time throughout the length and
> breadth of the Canadas. This noise, which gave one the impression that
> the house was on fire, made all rush outdoors to escape so unexpected
> a conflagration; but instead of smoke and flames, people were much

*surprised to behold the Walls tottering, and all the stones in motion, as if they had been detached. Roofs seemed to bend down in one direction, and then back again in the other; Bells rang of their own accord; beams, joists and boards creaked; and the earth leaped up, and made the palisade stakes dance in a way that would have seemed incredible, had we not witnessed it in different places.*

*Then all left their houses, animals took flight, children cried in the streets, and men and women, seized with terror, knew not where to take refuge, — expecting every moment to be either overwhelmed under the ruins of the houses, or swallowed up in some abyss that was to open beneath their feet. Some knelt in the snow and cried for mercy, while others passed the rest of the night in prayer; for the Earthquake continued without ceasing, maintaining a certain swaying motion much like that of Ships at sea, so that some experienced from this tossing the same heaving of the stomach that one suffers on the water.*

Father Lalemant's description makes clear that this was a great earthquake. The shaking was strong enough that people left their buildings in fright, bells were rung, the houses and palisades of the fort were visibly deformed, and people on the solid earth suffered motion sickness as though they were on a ship at sea. These are all common reports that take place in strong earthquake shaking, both historically and in modern times. Father Lalemant indicates that the earthquake was felt throughout all of Canada. He further indicates that the earthquake took place at 5:30 p.m. on February 5, 1663 (N.S.). In another part of his report, he gives additional details about the earthquake:

*Item, during Shrovetide. This time was remarkable, among other things, for a frightful and sudden Earthquake. It began half an hour after the close of benediction on Monday, the 5th of February, the feast of our holy martyrs of Japan, namely at about 5½ o'clock, and lasted about the length of 2 misereres. It took place again at night, and was repeated many times on the following Days and nights, sometimes more and sometimes less violently. It injured some chimneys and caused other slight losses and damages, but did a great deal of good to souls; for on shrove Tuesday and Ash Wednesday one would have said that it was Easter Sunday, so many Confessions and Communions were there, and all devotions were frequented. This lasted until the 15th of March, or thereabout, quite perceptibly.*

A miserere is a Roman Catholic prayer. A Jesuit colleague of mine, Fr. James McCaffrey, S.J., once gave me the estimate that it takes about one and a half minutes to recite a miserere. Thus, Father Lalemant's report suggests that the earthquake shaking lasted about three minutes, consistent with an earthquake of very large magnitude. There is a discussion later in this chapter about the magnitude of this earthquake.

· The time of the earthquake is confirmed by reports from other observers. For example, Sr. Marie Morin from the fort at Montreal wrote that the earthquake took place on Maundy Tuesday (the day before Ash Wednesday), February 5, while they were serving food to the poor who were sick. In 1663 February 5 was a Monday (as correctly stated by Father Lalemant), and so ascribing February 5 to Tuesday is a mistake in Sister Morin's report. Sister Morin states that the shaking lasted about a miserere and then came with even more force. She further states that people had to lie down on the ground because the shaking was too strong to permit people to remain standing.

## DAMAGE IN QUEBEC DUE TO THE EARTHQUAKE

The existing reports indicate that the towns along the St. Lawrence River in Quebec experienced very strong ground shaking due to the earthquake. For example, in the *Jesuit Relations* Father Lalemant relays a report from Fr. Charles Simon, S.J., from Trois-Rivières, that states, "Those who returned from the fort . . . relate that the earth was shaken with so great a force that it leaped up to the height of a foot, and rolled in the manner of a skiff tossed by the waves."

Father Lalemant's report includes something similar from Montreal: "Word comes from Montreal that, during the Earthquake, fences-stakes were plainly seen to jump up and down as if in a dance; of two doors in the same room, one closed itself and the other opened, of its own accord; chimneys and housetops bent like tree-branches shaken by the wind; on raising the foot in walking, one felt the ground coming up after him and rising in proportion to the height to which he lifted his foot, sometimes giving the sole a quite sharp rap; and other similar occurrences, of a highly surprising nature, are reported from that place."

As Father Lalemant was accumulating and summarizing reports from many diverse places in Canada, it is possible that he mixed up the ground-motion report from Trois-Rivières with that from Montreal. On the other hand, it is also quite possible that a similar strength of ground shaking was experienced at both Trois-Rivières and Montreal, and hence similar descriptions of the ground shaking came from both places.

Although the mainshock ground shaking was quite strong, lasted for at least several minutes, and was followed by some strong aftershocks, the historical records do not describe much damage to settlements in the region due to the earthquake. As can be seen in one of Father Lalemant's reports that is reproduced above, aside from some chimneys being damaged, apparently there was relatively little destruction in the region due to the earthquake shaking. At Beauprè, a town on the St. Lawrence River close to the fault that moved in the earthquake, there is no record of damage due to the earthquake, although Sr. Marie de l'Incarnation, superior of a convent of Ursuline nuns in Quebec City, provides some details about a church candle that was knocked over several times, probably by the mainshock and/or strong aftershocks: "At the Church of Beauprè, which is that of Château-Richer, the earth trembled so roughly on Ash Wednesday that the walls trembled as if they had been of cards. The Blessed Sacrament, which was exposed, trembled at the same time: it did not fall, however, having been restrained by a small crown of infringing flowers. The lamp, which was extinguished, fell three times, but the Ecclesiastic who took care of this church, kindled it and remounted it in its place, it did not fall."

The Blessed Sacrament, a religious object probably no more than one to two feet high, was restrained from falling from its altar by some flowers that had been placed around it, although a nearby candle apparently fell and was remounted three times before it stayed in its place and fell no more. No mention is made of any damage to the building in which the objects were placed, from which it may be inferred that the church itself sustained no damage. This report states that the events described took place on Ash Wednesday, which was two days after the mainshock took place. It is possible that the ground motions described in the report do not pertain to the mainshock but rather to one or more of the stronger aftershocks that were experienced a couple days after the mainshock.

At Quebec City, about 25 miles (40 kilometers) farther from the earthquake fault than Beauprè, the reports that survive today also do not contain any mention of damage to man-made structures, although the ground shaking at Quebec City was clearly very strong, as can be seen in the report from Father Lalemant that is reproduced at the beginning of this chapter. On the other hand, damage to buildings was indeed described at the towns of Trois-Rivières and Montreal, even farther from the earthquake fault than Quebec City. Regarding the houses at Trois-Rivières, Sister l'Incarnation wrote, "As the houses are all of wood because there is no stone at Trois-Rivières, the exterior effect [of the earthquake] ended at the fall of some chimneys."

The same kind of damage was reported from Montreal by Sister Morin: "Our house was preserved on the Island of Montreal without any injury being done; also the evil was not as great on our island as in Quebec. There were only chimneys, barns, and stables that fell in fairly good numbers."

It appears that at Montreal, aside from the chimneys, the houses stayed intact without damage, although some larger structures such as barns and stables were collapsed by the earthquake shaking. This report also suggests that there was substantially more damage at Quebec City than at Montreal. Unfortunately, no record exists today that tells what that damage at Quebec City might have been.

The reports from Trois-Rivières and Montreal are quite consistent with the damage expected in a strong earthquake given the building construction practices of the time when the earthquake took place. Because wood was cheap and plentiful, whereas brick and mortar had to be manufactured from specific raw materials, buildings were constructed of wood with only some chimneys being made of stone or brick. The structures of the wooden buildings were supported by timber frames that were held together by wooden pegs. The heavy timber frames typical of that time period resulted in strong, flexible structures that could be shaken very greatly without breaking apart and collapsing. At Montreal damage was reported to some barns and stables, larger structures that may not have been built with as much care as the houses in which the people lived. It is also possible that it was older wooden structures that suffered damage, structures that may have had other problems such as rotting in the wood support posts and beams. Masonry structures such as chimneys, especially those built with the relatively weak mortar that was the only product available at the time, are not flexible and easily break apart in strong earthquake shaking. Thus, it is quite possible that the wood-frame structures at Quebec City, Beauprè, and other towns near the fault where the earthquake took place suffered less damage than one today might expect simply because of the earthquake-resistant construction practices of the time.

## PROFOUND EFFECTS ON THE RIVERS OF QUEBEC DUE TO THE EARTHQUAKE

Whereas the effects of the 1663 earthquake and its aftershocks may have been far from catastrophic in the settlements of Quebec and beyond, the natural landscape of the region around the fault that slipped in the

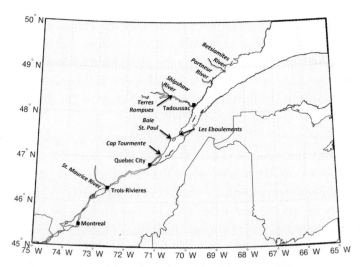

Locations with major effects due to the 1663 earthquake

56

earthquake was altered greatly by the strong ground shaking. In particular, landslides were numerous on the bluffs along a number of the rivers of the region. Many of the landslides slid into the rivers of the region and deposited soil, rocks, and foliage into the waters. As the earthquake took place in midwinter, it is likely that all the rivers flowing into the St. Lawrence were frozen at the time and even the St. Lawrence itself was choked with ice, and so the observations of landslides and changes in the color of the rivers were probably made many months after the earthquake took place. In his report Father Lalemant included the following description from Trois-Rivières of some of these changes:

> According to the report of many of our Frenchmen and Savages, who were eye-witnesses, far up on our river, the Three Rivers, five or six leagues from here, the banks bordering the Stream on each side, and formerly of a prodigious height, were leveled — being removed from their foundations, and uprooted to the water's level. These two mountains, with all their forests, thus overturned into the River, formed there a mighty dike which forced that stream to change its bed, and to spread over great plains recently discovered. At the same time, however, it undermined all those displaced lands and caused their gradual detrition by the waters of the River, which are still so thick and turbid as to change the color of the whole great St. Lawrence river. Judge how much soil it must take to keep its waters flowing constantly full of mire every day for nearly three months. New Lakes are seen where there were none before; certain Mountains are seen no more, having been swallowed up; a number of rapids have been leveled, a number of Rivers have disappeared; the Earth was rent in many places, and it has opened chasms whose depths cannot be sounded; in fine, such confusion has been wrought, of woods overturned and swallowed up, that now we see fields of more than a thousand arpents utterly bare, and as if very recently plowed, where a short time ago were only forests.

From this report it can be inferred that there were some major landslides along the St. Maurice River north of Trois-Rivières that carried large amounts of soil and large numbers of trees and other plants into the river. So much soil fell into the river that it changed the color of the river for months afterward as the landslide soil was being eroded. The landslides and land slumps must have been of such a lateral extent into the land away from the river that they left depressions that filled with water, forming new lakes. In other areas land probably slid into some of the smaller streams that flowed into the St. Maurice River, cutting off the flow of the water and therefore making the stream in the former downstream area disappear. This effect would have caused flooding in the area behind where the landslide had dammed the stream, causing water to spread over the lower-lying places. The report talks about mountains being leveled, but this is almost certainly an exaggeration of what actually happened. The area near Trois-Rivières is hilly but not mountainous, and the slump of one of these hills might have appeared to persons of the time as the disappearance of a mountain. The end of this report seems to indicate that there was a land slump about 1,000 arpents in size, which would correspond to about 850 acres. The description in this report bears many similarities to that of the Broken Lands of the Saguenay region that are discussed below, which is thought to have been another major land slump triggered by the 1663 earthquake.

The greatest number of landslides caused by the earthquake and its aftershocks may have been along the St. Lawrence River around Tadoussac. For example, Father Lalemant described landslides into the St. Lawrence River at Baie St. Paul and at Pointe Alouettes near Tadoussac:

*If one were inclined to follow the river bank all the way from Cap de Tourmente to that point [Tadoussac], he would see some marvelous effects of the earthquake. Near the Bay (called St. Paul's [Baie St. Paul]) there was a little Mountain, situated on the riverbank and a quarter of a league, or nearly that, in circumference, which was swallowed up; and, as if it had only taken a plunge, it came up again from the depths, to be changed into a little Island, and to turn a spot all beset with breakers, as it used to be, into a haven of safety against all kinds of winds. And farther down, near Pointe aux Allouettes [sic], a whole forest became detached from the mainland and slid into the river, where it presents to view great trees, straight and verdant, which sprang into being in the water, over night.*

The slide described in this report near Baie St. Paul corresponds today to a small point of land that juts out into the St. Lawrence River and is called Les Éboulements (the Landslides), thus preserving the story of its formation in 1663.

The largest known landslide due to the 1663 earthquake is thought to have taken place north of the town of Saguenay along the Saguenay and Shipshaw Rivers. Investigations of a major land slump in this area in 1971 showed that a larger, earlier land slump took place in the same area, and dating of this earlier slump showed that it was probably coincident with the occurrence of the 1663 earthquake. The extent of the suspected land slump due to the 1663 earthquake is not known for sure, but it extends several miles north along the Shipshaw River. The area was known as the Terres Rompues or Broken Lands (*Missiquini* in the local Native American language), along which was a Native American trail between the Chicoutimi and Saguenay Rivers. There is the Small Island of Broken Lands in the Saguenay River near the mouth of the Shipshaw River and the Point of Broken Lands on the Saguenay River east of the mouth of the Chicoutimi River. Large land slumps like that suspected in 1663 typically leave a surface terrain that is very irregular, with many small hills and depressions, and the name Broken Lands is an apt description of such a terrain.

Rivers to the northeast of Tadoussac were strongly affected by the earthquake. In the spring and summer of 1663, Fr. Henri Nouvel traveled with some companions along the St. Lawrence River, and he provided the following account of his observations of the Pontneuf and Betsiamites Rivers: "On the eleventh of the same month [May], we arrived at the river which the Savages call Kouakoueou. We saw in passing the ravages wrought by the Earthquake in the rivers of Port neuf; the water coming there-from is all yellow, and it retains this color far into the great river, as does also that of the Betsiamites. The Savages could no longer navigate these two rivers."

The yellow discharge from these two rivers was probably due to fine sand and clay that had slid into the rivers due to earthquake landslides. Between the landslides themselves and the trees on the landslides carried into the rivers, the rivers apparently were so blocked by debris that the Native Americans could no longer easily navigate the waters in their canoes.

Father Lalemant's report contains a short notation from an unknown source about his experience traveling along the St. Lawrence River in the summer of 1663. The source states that the river was still full of trees due to the earthquake landslides the previous winter: "The earthquakes were still continuing there, severe and alarming shocks having been felt ever since the fifth day of February; and yet we were well along in the month of July. The great trees hurled down into the River, together with whole hills and mountains, were still rolling about in a frightful manner in those waters, which Continued to cast them up again on the bank in strange confusion."

The effects of the earthquake along the St. Lawrence River were visible for a long time after the earthquake. Father Lalemant cites two letters written by Father Simon in December 1663: "He [Simon] certifies that he saw both shores of the St., Lawrence strewn over with uprooted trees, for three hundred miles, which distance he has traversed."

This description is probably fairly accurate, as the distance from the St. Maurice River (the most southwestern river with reported landslides) to the Betsiamites River (the most northeastern river with reported landslides) is about 200 miles.

Apparently, it was difficult to overstate the extent of the effect of the earthquake and strong aftershocks on the landscape of the region. Fr. Francois Le Mercier, S.J., wrote the *Jesuit Relations* of 1665, and in it he included this statement: "Two highly trustworthy Frenchmen who have traversed that whole coast of Malbaye, made the assertion that the Relation of the year 1663 had only half described the ravages wrought by the earthquake shocks in those regions."

The effects on the landscape of the 1663 earthquake and its subsequent aftershocks must have been indeed profound along that part of the St. Lawrence River.

## Soil Liquefaction Due to the Earthquake

There are several historical reports that suggest that liquefaction of the ground also took place due to the strongest earthquake shaking near the fault that slipped in the earthquake. In many cases the descriptions include elements such as smoke or ashes that do not occur during soil liquefaction but could have been fanciful misinterpretations of what was actually observed. Sister l'Incarnation gives a report that corresponds the best to the observation of liquefaction effects: "During the space of six hours it rained ash in so great a quantity that on the ground and in the boats there was an inch of thickness."

Sandblows can squirt sand and water several feet into the air, and a sand layer an inch or so thick is commonly observed on the ground following a sandblow. If a small canoe was on a riverbank next to a place where a sandblow erupted, it is quite possible that the spurting sand could have been deposited into the canoe. Thus, the description in this report could well have been of a sandblow that formed in the 1663 earthquake. The indication that the sandblow formed over a time period of six hours may be an indication that some of the strongest initial aftershocks were also associated with soil liquefaction. Unfortunately, Sister l'Incarnation does not state where this sandblow formed.

Father Lalemant also included some reports of possible liquefaction features in his report to Europe. He wrote,

> We learn from Tadoussacq that the stress of the Earthquake was not less severe there than elsewhere; that a shower of ashes was seen crossing the stream like a great storm.
>
> During this general wreck on Land, ice of five and six feet in thickness was broken, flying into fragments, and splitting open in various places, whence issued either great clouds of smoke or jets of mud and sand, which ascended to a lofty height in the air. Our springs either ceased to flow or gave forth only sulphurous waters. . . .
>
> Furthermore, opposite them they saw a great section of the earth borne upward and carried into the river; and, at the place whence it was separated by the yawning open of the earth, there burst forth globes of smoke and flame, at certain spaces from one another, and very

*dense clouds of ill-smelling ashes were cast upward; and, as these fell down, the deck of their ship was filled with them. The same traders observed, on their way, that from the inmost bowels of the earth Jets of water surged violently upward, with the magnitude of streams, as if from fountain pipes or leaden conduits.*

In the first report the "ashes" that were reported were probably fine sand particles that were erupted as part of a sandblow. The second report incorrectly surmises that smoke was erupted from the earth. No smoke issues from sandblows, although the squirting of a mist of liquid water into very cold winter air might well have yielded what looked like smoke or steam as the fine water particles froze in the very cold air. A comparable phenomenon is seen when one watches snowmaking machines at ski resorts, which often seem to release a kind of fog along with the snow that they are making. The second report talks about sulphurous waters coming out of springs, but this is probably fanciful. Very fine sand may have colored the water yellow, giving observers the mistaken impression that the water was tainted with yellow sulphur. The third report also seems to be referring to eruptions from sandblows with the same mistaken impressions about smoke and ash as in the earlier reports.

The only location of possible liquefaction effects like sandblows mentioned in any of these reports is Tadoussac. Recent investigations by geologists have found several mounds between the mouths of the Gouffre and La Malbaie Rivers that are the remains of sandblows that probably erupted during the 1663 earthquake and its strong aftershocks. Sandblows and other liquefaction features can form only at localities with very specific geologic conditions, and those are found only in some places in the river valleys of Quebec. The best evidence for sandblows from both the historical reports and the geologic evidence is between the Gouffre River and the settlement at Tadoussac. As discussed below, this is the area that is thought to overlie the fault that moved in the 1663 earthquake, and it is the area where the strongest ground shaking would have been experienced. It is also the area where the greatest number of landslides probably took place. The evidence all seems to align and indicate that this was the source region of this earthquake.

## THE EXPERIENCE OF THE EARTHQUAKE BEYOND QUEBEC

The February 5, 1663, mainshock and probably some of its largest after-shocks clearly had a profound impact on the landscape and settlements of Quebec, and in particular on the shorelines of the St. Lawrence River for many miles upstream and downstream of the settlement at Tadous-sac. The earthquake was also experienced at areas far away from the St. Lawrence region, as would be expected today for an earthquake of large magnitude in eastern North America.

The first report that Father Lalemant sent to France about the earth-quake was written in the summer of 1663. By that time he must have received many reports from different places about the wide expanse of North America over which the earthquake was felt. He wrote, "There are many things incidental to the Earthquake and various circumstances by

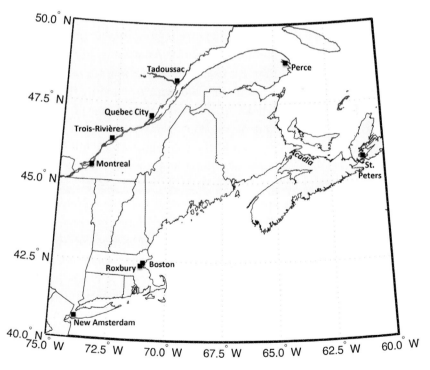

Known localities where the 1663 earthquake was experienced

which we are led to believe that all America was shaken by it. In fact, we have already ascertained that it extended from the borders of the Iroquois country to Acadia, which is a part of Southern America, — that is, a thousand miles; multiplying this extent, for each region, by five hundred and three miles, as the measure of the [St. Lawrence] river valley."

At the time of the earthquake, the Iroquois country extended from the eastern Great Lakes to the St. Lawrence River valley and south to Pennsylvania. Acadia was a region from New Brunswick to eastern Nova Scotia, not a part of "Southern America" as indicated by the clause that immediately follows the mention of Acadia. In fact, based on a modern understanding of how far strong earthquakes are felt in eastern North America, the 1663 mainshock likely would have been felt at much greater distances than the 500 miles (800 kilometers) mentioned in this report, although no felt reports from more distant sites such as Virginia are known to exist today.

Independent evidence implies that the earthquake was probably felt well to the northwest of the St. Lawrence region. In a letter from Sister l'Incarnation, there is a mention of Native Americans, perhaps Inuits, who lived near Hudson Bay (La Grande Mer du Nord) and who traveled south to trade at L'Isle-Verte or Tadoussac. Apparently these Native Americans stopped at Quebec City on their travels. Sister l'Incarnation's letter reads, in part, "Indians of a distant country have been pressed to retire to these quarters ... to avoid the trembling which followed them everywhere They have discovered a thing long sought after, to know the entrance of the great North Sea."

The most interesting part of this report is that these Native Americans indicated that they felt earthquakes no matter where they went. In his 2001 book, *Historical Earthquakes Felt in Quebec (1534–1925)*, Fr. Pierre Gouin, a French-Canadian Jesuit, interpreted this report as possible evidence that the mainshock was felt all the way to Hudson Bay and that these Native Americans felt aftershocks throughout their travels to trade at Tadoussac.

To the south of the St. Lawrence region, the earthquake and some of its strongest aftershocks were felt in the New England colonial areas and in the New Amsterdam colony. In New England information about the effects of the mainshock and some of its immediate aftershocks was provided by the Reverend Samuel Danforth of Roxbury, Massachusetts, now part of the city of Boston. Reverend Danforth, giving the Old Style date of the earthquake, wrote in his diary, "1662 Jan. 26 about 6 o'clock at night there happened an earthquake, wch shook mens houses and caused many to run out of their houses into the streets, and ye tops of 2 or 3 chimnyes fell off, or some part ym, likewise there was another earthquake about midnight. Also in ye morning once or twice ye earth trembled and mens houses were shaken."

He further reported another earthquake felt on January 28 at about 10:00 a.m. Two other Massachusetts observers, John Hull of Dorchester and Increase Mather of Cambridge, also wrote accounts of the mainshock and some of these aftershocks. For example, Hull's diary account of the earthquake reads, "In the evening, about six o'clock, was an earthquake, that shook much for near one-quarter of an hour;—there was shaking in several parts of the town, and other towns, two or three times the same week; but the former was general."

Mather reported in his diary, using Old Style dates, "In the year 1662, on the 26, 27, and 28 of January, the Earth was shaken at least six times in the space of three dayes. I remember that upon the first approach of the earthquake, the things on the Shelves in the House began to move. Many People ran out of their Houses with fear and amazement; but no House fell, nor was any damage sustained."

The Boston area is about 370 miles (600 kilometers) from the St. Lawrence River area where the earthquakes were centered. The chimney damage at Roxbury mentioned by Reverend Danforth provides some constraint on the magnitude of the mainshock, as is discussed later in this chapter. Mather reported no damage in Boston, although the ground shaking was great enough to move objects on shelves.

Another report of about damage in Boston itself due to the 1663 mainshock was described in an item included in the book *Rambles About Old Boston*, published in 1887 by E. G. Porter. He wrote about a building at Clark Street and Ship Street (later North Street) in Boston. This building, which had been demolished about 20 years before Porter wrote his book, had been known as Ship Tavern. Porter wrote this about Ship

Tavern: "It was originally two stories high, and built of English brick, laid with shell and clay mortar. There was an old crack in the front wall, said to have been caused by an earthquake in 1663, 'which made all New England tremble.'"

Not only had the building survived the 1663 earthquake, but it also experienced the 1727 and 1755 earthquakes. The latter two earthquakes were much more damaging in Massachusetts than that of 1663, and yet legend clearly attributed the crack in the front brick wall to the very early earthquake of 1663. The 1663 earthquake must have been memorable in Boston if some of its damage was cited 200 years later.

The earthquake was felt noticeably in the New Netherland colony in what is now New York. Peter Stuyvesant, the last Dutch governor of New Amsterdam (now New York City), wrote in his annals, "The year 1663 was a year of many disasters. Early in the year an earthquake shook severely the whole of New Netherland and of the adjacent regions."

More details about the earthquake were provided in a letter dated 6 August 1663 from Jeremias van Rensselaer of Rensselaerswijck in New Netherland to his brother, Jan Baptist, in Amsterdam in the Netherlands. Van Rensselaer wrote, "There is not much news to tell except that last winter we had an earthquake which was very strong further inland and did a lot of damage to the houses of the French."

None of the reports from New Netherland suggest that any damage took place in that Dutch colony, although the earthquake was reported as widely felt by the Dutch colonials. The Dutch in America were clearly aware that the earthquake was much stronger in French Canada than in their own area and that there was considerable damage in Canada.

There are important notations of the 1663 earthquake being felt at several places in eastern Canada. Father Lalemant wrote that the earthquake was felt on the Gaspe Peninsula and at Perce on the north shore of New Brunswick. A report from Nicolas Denys suggests that the earthquake also was felt in eastern Nova Scotia. Denys was the governor and lieutenant-general of Acadia during 1663 when the earthquake occurred. According to Father Gouin's book on Canadian earthquakes, at that time

Acadia extended from eastern New Brunswick to Nova Scotia. In 1663 Nicolas Denys and his family probably lived in St. Peters, which likely was on what is today Cape Breton Island in eastern Nova Scotia. In 1672 Denys wrote, "I experienced [the earthquake] nine or ten years ago. Yet this was so small an affair that it was scarcely noticed. It had only three little shocks, and had it not for some rattling of cooking utensils and table ware it would not have been perceived. There were some Indians who felt it. They were not even surprised."

The earthquake shaking was strong enough to rattle objects in the home of Denys, which was probably more than 370 miles (600 kilometers) from the epicenter. This level of ground shaking was great enough to suggest that St. Peters was not close to the eastern limit where the shaking for this earthquake might have been felt had land and human settlements existed farther to the east.

The full spatial extent over which the shaking of the 1663 earthquake was experienced is difficult to ascertain due to the relatively sparse number and extent of the settlements of eastern North America at this time. Strong earthquakes in the Charlevoix area in 1925 (magnitude about 6.2) and in the nearby Saguenay area in 1988 (magnitude 5.9) were felt well to the south of New York, and so the 1663 earthquake also should have been felt south and west of New York. The 1663 mainshock likely would have been felt well into what is today the U.S. Midwest and southeastern U.S. states. However, there are no known reports of this earthquake beyond New York. The next colonial settlements southwest of New York were in Virginia, where the earthquake likely would have been lightly felt, but there are no known reports of an earthquake in 1663 from anywhere in Virginia. The earthquake also likely would have been felt at what is today Labrador and Newfoundland. By this time colonial settlements were in existence in Newfoundland, but there are no reports known today about the 1663 earthquake being felt there. In the book *History of Canada* by W. Kingsford, published in 1887, there is a statement that the 1663 earthquake was felt to Labrador, although no evidence is given in that book to support this statement. What is today Labrador was not colonized by Europeans until after 1663.

## Earthquake Sounds, Earthquake Lights, Earthquake Electricity, and Animal Behavior

In addition to the earthquake ground shaking, there were other effects due to the mainshock that were reported. As noted in chapter 1, seismic waves in the earth can convert to sound waves in the air, and these sound waves can be quite audible if an observer is close enough to the fault where the earthquake took place. Father Lalemant reported in the *Jesuit Relations* that the earthquake was heard as well as felt at Trois-Rivières: "From Three Rivers they wrote the following account: 'The first and severest of all the shocks began with a rumbling like that of Thunder, and the houses were shaken like tree tops during a storm, amid a noise that made people think there was a fire crackling in their garrets.'"

The authors of this account are not stated. Father Lalemant described the earthquake as a "loud roaring," a "noise, which gave one the impression that the house was on fire." Roaring sounds are typically reported by those who experience strong earthquake shaking.

Another report by Father Lalemant in the *Jesuit Relations* gives some additional details: "Beside the roaring which constantly preceded and accompanied the Earthquake, we saw specters and fiery phantoms bearing torches in their hands. Pikes and lances of fire were seen, waving in the air, and burning brands darting down on our houses — without, however, doing further injury than to spread alarm wherever they were seen."

The first phrase here suggests that there were roaring sounds that accompanied the aftershocks as well as the mainshock. Although the rest of this report sounds fanciful, in fact it may well be referring to observations of earthquake lights. Earthquake lights are faint glows or faint streaks of light that are sometimes reported to accompany or perhaps precede strong earthquake shaking. The cause of earthquake lights is uncertain, although laboratory experiments have shown that rocks are capable of carrying electrical currents and discharging those currents to the atmosphere. In some cases earthquake lights have been photographed, and so their existence does have some observational evidence. Although the descriptions in Father Lalemant's report are rather imaginative, the images of the visual lights and glows underlying these descriptions are similar to descriptions of earthquake lights from other parts of the world as well as from later earthquakes in northeastern North America.

Later in the same document, Father Lalemant states, "Crashes, and more vehement dins than of cymbals, brazen cannon or thunders, burst forth from the bowels of the earth and deep caverns. From the same furnaces emanated fiery torches and globes of flame — now relapsing into the earth, now vanishing in the very air, like bubbles."

The first sentence of this passage appears to refer to the earthquake sounds associated probably with the mainshock and aftershocks, whereas the second sentence may be a description of earthquake lights that were observed.

In another section of Father Lalemant's long report about the 1663 earthquake, he summarizes a letter from Father Simon that was written to Simon's sister in December 1663. Father Lalemant's description of one item in Simon's letter reads, "He relates that a man so shuddered at the sudden Earthquake, although at other times he was brave, that his hair, bristling up with horror and standing upright, shook off his Fur-cap."

Electrical currents associated with lightning strikes are well known to cause human hair to stand on end, and this description might be an observation of the same phenomenon but in this case associated with a strong earthquake. The observation of earthquake lights strengthens the argument that the effects on the man's hair described by Father Simon did indeed take place and were caused by local electrical currents in the ground induced by the earthquake.

Reports of unusual animal behavior prior to earthquakes is a topic that often captures the imagination of the public, even if those reports cannot be verified scientifically. In the case of the 1663 earthquake and its aftershocks, the existing records contain no mentions of any type of animal behavior, unusual or normal, that preceded any of the earthquakes. There is only one report of animal behavior from any of the records, and that report is from an unnamed traveler whose accounts were reproduced by Father Lalemant. The account about the birds and earthquakes reads, "The neighboring districts constantly resound with the cries of these birds, except in time of earthquakes, 'such as were experienced here this year; for then, as I was informed by some Hunters, the birds preserved a wonderful silence.'"

This account suggests that the birds went quiet at the times of earthquakes. In this case the animals appeared to react to the earthquakes themselves, with no indication that their behavior changed prior to the earthquakes.

## AFTERSHOCKS OF THE 1663 EARTHQUAKE

The historical accounts from 1663 and later contain numerous references to the aftershocks that followed the mainshock. Aftershocks apparently started occurring even as the shaking of the mainshock was still abating. Father Lalemant reported that at Trois-Rivières the earthquake seemed to have been felt for a half hour:

> *This first shock continued fully half an hour, although its great violence really lasted only a scant quarter of an hour. There was not a person who did not really think the Earth was about to split open. We further observed that, while this earthquake was almost continuous, still it was not of the same intensity, sometimes resembling the rocking of a great vessel riding gently at Anchor, — a motion which caused giddiness in many. At other moments the disturbance was irregular, and precipitated by various sharp movements — sometimes of considerable severity, at other times more moderate; but most commonly consisting of a slight quivering motion, which was perceptible to one away from the noise and at rest.*

This is a good description of the initial aftershocks as experienced at Trois-Rivières. It states that the mainshock lasted about 15 minutes, a duration of initial shaking that was also reported by John Hull in Boston, as described above. In fact, the mainshock ground shaking must have been only a few minutes, as indicated earlier in this chapter and also reported for modern strong earthquakes. What likely was happening was that the first strong aftershocks started taking place on the fault as soon as the mainshock ended, and these aftershocks were perceived as continuations of the mainshock ground shaking.

During the first few hours after the mainshock, aftershocks likely took place in an irregular pattern, every few seconds to a few minutes. Most of the aftershocks would have been accompanied by weak ground shaking, but some would have had stronger ground shaking. In Father Lalemant's report there were some aftershocks that were accompanied by lower frequency ground motions ("rocking of a great vessel riding gently at Anchor"), whereas other aftershocks were accompanied by higher frequency ground motions ("the disturbance was irregular, and precipitated by various sharp movements"). It is likely that there were so many aftershocks during the initial half hour or so after the mainshock that they provided what seemed like continuous ground shaking at Trois-Rivières. After a half hour or so, the aftershocks apparently decreased in number such that there probably started to be noticeable pauses between episodes of ground shaking at Trois-Rivières due to the aftershocks. The people of the region experienced some notable aftershocks that night and the next morning, as is discussed in more detail below and as was documented above in the reports from Massachusetts.

The local reports indicate that frequent aftershocks continued to be felt in the hours following the mainshock. Various observers in Quebec City mention anywhere between 6 and 32 aftershocks being felt at that settlement during this first night and following morning. According to Marie de l'Incarnation, there were some aftershocks during the night of February 5, with a few notable events between 8:00 p.m. and 10:00 p.m. and the strongest aftershock early the next morning, between 3:00 and 4:00 a.m. As described above, additional information about the strongest aftershocks during the first night was provided by the Reverend Samuel Danforth of Roxbury, Massachusetts, now part of the city of Boston. In his diary from the time, Reverend Danforth indicated that there was an earthquake experienced about midnight and again in the morning. Perhaps the seismic events that Reverend Danforth reports at midnight on January 27 (O.S.) and in the morning on January 27 (O.S.) correspond to the aftershocks about 10:00 p.m. on February 5 (N.S.) and 3:00 to 4:00 a.m. on February 6 (N.S.) recorded by Sister l'Incarnation. This provides confidence that their reports are about the same aftershocks that were felt in both localities. Because the Boston area is about 370 miles (600 kilometers) from the Charlevoix area, where the earthquakes were centered, any seismic event from Charlevoix that was felt in Boston must have been above about moment magnitude 5.5.

All of these inferences about the initial aftershocks of the 1663 earthquake are consistent with what has been observed by seismologists in modern strong earthquakes throughout the world. The largest aftershocks often take place within minutes or hours of the mainshock, and the aftershock rate almost invariably is highest during the first hours following the mainshock. The average rate at which aftershocks occur (in other words, the number of aftershocks per hour) decreases rapidly immediately following the occurrence of a mainshock, after which the change in average aftershock rate becomes smaller. This is Omori's Law of aftershocks discussed in chapter 1. Thus, during the first half hour or so after the 1663 earthquake, it appears that the aftershock rate was so high that felt aftershocks seemed to take place in an almost continuous fashion. The rate of aftershocks slowed down after that such that there were pauses between the felt aftershocks, at least as perceived at Trois-Rivières, which is about 150 miles (250 kilometers) from the Charlevoix area. At this distance only aftershocks above about moment magnitude 4.0 would be felt, so the above report gives us information about how many aftershocks above this magnitude level took place during the first hour or so immediately following the mainshock.

The historical accounts provide some information on the duration of the aftershock sequence and how the rate of aftershocks varied with time. The highest rate of aftershocks and most of the strongest aftershocks took place during the first hours and days following the mainshock. However, the aftershock activity clearly persisted well after the first few days after the mainshock. Father Simon, perhaps writing in September 1663, reported that "a month thus passed [following the mainshock] with shocks gradually relaxing in Violence, except that five or six were more intense, and that they persist to this day, but are less violent and less frequent."

This report describes a very typical decay of aftershocks with time following a mainshock. Father Lalemant noted that "three circumstances, moreover, rendered this Earthquake very remarkable. The first was its time of duration, it having continued into the month of August, or for more than six months. The shocks, it is true, were not always equally severe. In certain districts, as toward the mountains in our rear, the din and the oscillating motion were unintermittent for a long time; in others as in the region of Tadoussacq, the shocks occurred ordinarily two or three times a day, with great force; and we noted that in more elevated places the motion was less than in the level country."

This report suggests that even in August 1663, six months after the mainshock, aftershocks at a rate of two or three a day were still being felt at Tadoussac, which is in the area where the fault rupture likely took place. Sister l'Incarnation also reported feeling aftershocks, but to September 1663. These reports were completed in time to be sent on the ships that were returning to Europe in the fall of 1663, which is why there is so much documentation on the aftershock activity in late summer and early fall of 1663. In fact, there is documentary evidence that the aftershocks continued into 1664 and later. In a letter dated 18 August 1664, Sister l'Incarnation indicated that the earth had trembled lightly a few times (presumably shortly before the letter was written), unlike the great shaking that she had experienced the year before. Other than this 1664 letter, there are no other indications of aftershock activity in the surviving written records from this decade. Aftershock activity at a low level probably did take place after 1664, with occasional stronger shocks also being experienced. An indication of this comes from a report by Fr. François de Crépieul, S.J., whose report from the Tadoussac Mission in 1673 indicated that he felt a notable local earthquake: "About this time [December 6, 1673] there was a very noticeable earthquake near us. I had still further opportunity, during our journey, to observe the extraordinary ravages of the terrible earthquake that took place some years ago in these wild regions."

## The Location and Magnitude of the 1663 Earthquake

Aside from the historical reports, which indicate the general area along the St. Lawrence River where the greatest effects of the earthquake were experienced, the best evidence for the location of the fault on which the 1663 earthquake took place comes from modern monitoring of the earthquakes of Quebec. The most seismically active area in all of northeastern

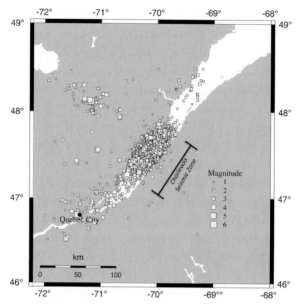

Earthquakes from 1975 to 2017 and location of the Charlevoix Seismic Zone

North America is called the Charlevoix Seismic Zone by seismologists. This zone stretches from Baie St. Paul, about 45 miles (73 kilometers) northeast of Quebec City, for about 45 miles (72 kilometers) northeast along the St. Lawrence River to just past Tadoussac. The Charlevoix Seismic Zone is thought by many seismologists to represent late aftershock activity associated with the occurrence of the 1663 earthquake. The modern earthquakes appear to be occurring on two parallel faults that steeply dip toward the southeast from beneath the St. Lawrence River to a depth of about 20 miles (30 kilometers). If the modern Charlevoix Seismic Zone is the aftershock zone of a past earthquake, that earthquake would have had a large magnitude and would have been capable of causing the significant effects on man-made structures and natural landscapes that are reported in the historical accounts.

Because no seismological instruments recorded the 1663 earthquake, it is impossible to make a direct measurement of the magnitude of this event. However, there are several lines of reasoning that can be used to infer the magnitude of the mainshock, obviously with some uncertainty involved. In the past seismologists have used the amount of damage near an earthquake fault and the total felt area of an earthquake to estimate its magnitude. These kinds of estimates can be made for modern earthquakes where the total damage, felt areas, and instrumental magnitudes have all been determined, and then the relationships between damage and magnitude and between felt area and magnitude can be applied to historical earthquakes. Unfortunately, for the 1663 earthquake the descriptions of the damage near the fault are too general and incomplete to be used for such an analysis, and the felt area of the mainshock is not known.

Fortunately, there are other ways to infer the magnitude of the mainshock from the existing historical reports and from the modern seismic data. The reports of some minor chimney damage at Roxbury, Massachusetts, can be used to estimate the level of earthquake ground shaking that occurred at Roxbury. Using this ground-shaking level at Roxbury and knowing the distance from Roxbury to the fault that had the earthquake, the magnitude of the earthquake needed to cause the Roxbury shaking can be estimated. This procedure suggests that the 1663 earthquake had a moment magnitude between 7.3 and 7.7. A different way to estimate the magnitude of the 1663 earthquake is to use the size of the Charlevoix Seismic Zone. The zone is about 45 miles (72 kilometers) long with an activity rate of a few earthquakes per week, and the length of this seismic zone probably reflects the length of the fault on which the 1663 earthquake slip took place. Modern earthquakes with a fault length of 45 miles or 72 kilometers have moment magnitudes between 7.3 and 7.6. Based on these numbers, a best estimate of the moment magnitude of the 1663 is about 7.5. This makes the 1663 earthquake comparable to the largest of the earthquakes that took place in the New Madrid, Missouri, area in 1811–1812. The New Madrid earthquakes are considered some of the largest earthquakes to have taken place in any stable continental region worldwide.

CHAPTER 5

# 1727: A "Great Earthquake" in Massachusetts

AFTER 1663 TO THE END OF THE 17TH CENTURY, THE RESIDENTS OF Massachusetts felt only occasional sharp jolts from small local earthquakes and the vibrating and rolling ground motions from a couple of stronger, more distant earthquakes. The latter were earthquakes in 1665 and 1668 with unknown epicenters. The 18th century started in the same way, but that changed on the evening of Sunday, October 29, 1727 (O.S.). The *Boston Gazette* of November 6 set the scene: "On the 29th past about 30 Minutes past 10 at Night, which was very Calm & Serene, and the Sky full of Stars . . ."

In a letter dated November 21, 1727, Henry Sewall of Newbury, Massachusetts, described his reactions to the seismic event that shattered that peaceful evening: "Thro' God's goodness to us we are all well, and have been preserved at the time of the late great and terrible earthquake. We were sitting by the fire and about half after ten at night our house shook and trembled as if it would have fallen to pieces. Being affrighted we ran out of doors, when we found the ground did tremble, and we were in great fear of being swallowed up alive; but God preserved us."

Paul Dudley, Esq., of Roxbury, Massachusetts, wrote a long letter to the secretary of the Royal Society that was dated November 13, 1727, describing in detail both his own observations and reports of others about the earthquake and its effects. He wrote how one person described experiencing the earthquake: "One of my Neighbours that was walking home at the very Instant, [he] tells me, the Noise first brought him to a stand,

and that during the Shake, the earth trembled so under him, that he was so far from attempting to continue his Walk, that it was as much as he could do to keep upon his Legs, and expected every Moment the Earth would have open'd under him."

John Blunt of New Castle, New Hampshire, penned a vivid description of what happened that evening:

*On the night between the 29 & 30 of October about 9 of the clock I retired to bed. (being my usual hour) but being that night otherwise different than commonly I took a book and read of it for about . . . an hour and then composed my bed for sleep but long had I not been asleep before I awoke, Awoke! Did I lay . . . : I Dreamt, oh Dream! Do I lay, no, no Dream neither, But to then that I lay I believe a mean between both, but never in such a strong . . . confirmation in all my Life: for as soon as I raised my head from my pillow and my Intellect again began to exert its operative faculty, Perceiving the Bed to Work like a boat & the house trembled as though it would immediately fall to pieces and the Terrible noise which was began compared to the strongest that I remember now . . . to . . . Rev. Landon to inquire what the matter was (who himself had just got out of his bed) replied, its a Terrible Earthquake with that I ran & got my clothes, then we ran out at the Door, but by the trembling of the Earth and the Dreadful noise accompanying it seemed as the foundations of the Earth now moved and the powers of heaven shaken the . . . land to come from the NW & pass along toward the SE (this from my own observation . . . one of our neighbors they plainly perceived the shaking of the earth about half a minute before they heard the noise . . . I cannot now give you a particular account to affects it had on the place & people, I cannot give, the chimneys of many houses have broken and the tops broken off to the roof of the houses and som Cellar walls tumbled in. It seems it was a great Deal more Terrible in the towns on Merrimack, especially Haverhill, Amesbury, Saybrury and Newbury.*

Rev. Mathias Plant of Newbury, Massachusetts, gave a similar account of the earthquake: "Oct. 29. 1727. being the Lord's-Day, about 40

Minutes past Ten the same evening, there came a great rumbling Noise; but before the Noise was heard, or Shock perceived, our Bricks upon the Hearth rose up about three quarters of a Foot, and seem'd to fall down and loll the other way, which was in half a Minute attended with the Noise or Burst."

Both Blunt and Plant reported that the ground movements started about 30 seconds before the noise of the earthquake. This is an unusual observation that has not been reported in other earthquakes either in New England or elsewhere. In any case the earthquake shaking was clearly quite strong and locally damaging. From the description by Blunt of his reactions and movements during the earthquake, the ground shaking must have lasted at least a few tens of seconds, long enough for him to get out of his bed, grab his clothes, and run out of his house. This was a strong earthquake that had significant effects in northeastern Massachusetts and nearby New Hampshire. Locals immediately started calling it "the great earthquake."

## DAMAGE TO STRUCTURES IN NORTHEASTERN MASSACHUSETTS AND SOUTHEASTERN NEW HAMPSHIRE DUE TO THE EARTHQUAKE

That the earthquake shaking was quite strong and caused damage to many structures is well documented in many written records that exist from this time period. Although most structures in the area surrounding the apparent earthquake epicenter at Newbury, Massachusetts, survived the earthquake, a number of reports attest to the damage that some structures sustained due to the strong ground shaking. John Blunt's report given above indicates that many chimneys sustained damage and that some cellar walls caved in. At Newbury, Stephen Jaques wrote in his diary that "It shook down bricks from yᵉ tops of abundance of chimnies, and some almost all the heads. . . . All that was about yᵉ houses trembled, beds shook, some cellar walls fell partly down. Benjamins Plumer's stone without his dore fell into his cellar. Stone walls fell in a hundred plasis."

Richard Kelley at Amesbury, Massachusetts, reported similar effects in his community in his diary: "The housen did shake & windows ratel and puter and dishes clatter on ye shelves & ye tops of many chimneys fell

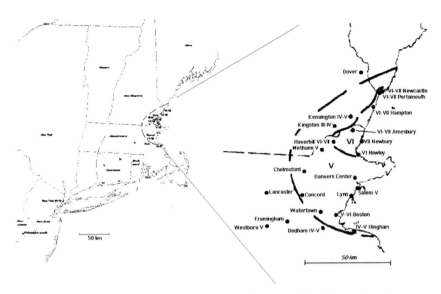

Towns in northeastern Massachusetts and southeastern New Hampshire that reported the 1727 earthquake MODIFIED FIGURE FROM WESTON GEOPHYSICAL CORP., 1976

of & maney ware so shattered as that people ware fain to take them down and new build them again."

The communities of Newbury and Amesbury are quite near each other, and so it is not surprising that the reported damage effects are similar in both communities. A letter to John Cotton from his unnamed brother in Haverhill describes the damage in that town: "As to the Damage done by them, I suppose you may have had a better Account than I can give, ... in our Town ... only shaking down Tops of Chimneys, shattering some Brick Houses, and shaking others so as to throw Pewter off the Shelves, make Andirons jump off the Hearth, throw down Stone Wall, &c. In our House it stop'd our Clock just half an Hour past 10. P.M."

There was also some damage caused by the earthquake to towns in New Hampshire just north of the Newbury and Amesbury area. Blunt's description of the damage was written in New Castle, New Hampshire, on January 23, 1728, and his description of damage is very similar to that of Jaques and Kelley. It is not clear whether Blunt's damage description

79

concerns what happened in New Castle or whether he is reporting the damage from the Newbury and Amesbury area. However, a letter dated November 20, 1727, by William Shurtleff of New Castle confirms some damage in his town: "Some Damage was done to the more brittle sort of Moveables, and some Bricks on the Tops of some Chimneys fell; but not an House was broken, nor a Creature hurt."

Shurtleff's account indicates that there were no injuries in his town due to the earthquake. There was also damage at Hampton, New Hampshire, which is stated in a sermon published in 1727 by Nathanial Gookin of that town: "The Houses trembled as if they were falling; divers Chimneys were Crack'd and some had their tops broken off."

Although towns somewhat farther away from Newbury and Amesbury reported the earthquake, generally they did not indicate that there was any local damage. This includes the towns of Methuen, Salem, and Danvers in Massachusetts and Portsmouth in New Hampshire, although some pewter was said to have been knocked off shelves at Portsmouth. The only known exception to this is Boston, where William Douglass wrote in a letter dated November 20, 1727, "The tremor may be said to have continued in Boston 1½ minute the tops of a few chimneys suffered and the Ladys sustained some damage in their china."

Most of the damage was to brittle objects like china that likely were knocked off of shelves and broken when they fell. It is not clear what kind of damage occurred to the chimneys since Douglass states that they only "suffered." Thomas Prince of Boston in a period sermon includes wording that is identical to that of Shurtleff. Thus, it is not clear if he is using those words to describe what happened in Boston or if he took those words to indicate the kinds of effects that the earthquake caused in nearby towns in the area. In any case the existing written records are ambiguous about how much and what kind of chimney damage may have occurred in Boston due to this earthquake.

The letter of Paul Dudley to the Royal Society states, "A Country Farmer tells me, he had forty or fifty Rods of Stone Wall thrown down by it." The location of this farmer's wall is uncertain. Dudley was in Roxbury, Massachusetts, but all of the other reports of fallen stone walls came from north of Boston. Thus, this note by Dudley cannot be interpreted to mean that stone walls in Boston itself were knocked down by the earthquake. Taken as a whole, the written records suggest that at most there was only very minor damage to a few chimneys in Boston.

The area over which the most significant damage occurred was summarized by Reverend Plant from Newbury in a postscript to his account of the earthquake and its effects that he wrote in his Minister's Record Book: "These frequent Repetitions of the Roaring and Shocks of the Earthquake were upon Merrimack River, and seldom extended above seven or eight Miles Distance from, or 20 or 30 up the said River; those Instances only excepted, which I have mention'd in the Relation; and the first Shock of it was greater with us than anywhere else in New-England; and the Tops of Chimneys, and Stone-fences, were thrown down only in these Parts."

Reverend Plant's report suggests that the damage to chimneys and stone fences was confined to Newbury, Amesbury, and immediately surrounding communities, consistent with the picture of damage from the surviving written reports from that time. Thus, although the earthquake was widely felt, the damage was confined to only a few towns in northeastern Massachusetts and southeastern New Hampshire.

## EARTHQUAKE EFFECTS FARTHER FROM THE EPICENTER

The epicenter of this earthquake must have been somewhere in the Newbury and Amesbury area, since those are the localities where the greatest amount of damage was reported. This earthquake was widely felt throughout southern New England and beyond, and there are many surviving reports that describe the experience of the earthquake in these places. These reports are useful for delimiting the southwestern extent to which this earthquake was felt. In eastern and central Massachusetts, contemporary reports of the earthquake survive for the towns of Concord, Chelmsford, Dartmouth, Dedham, Framingham, Hingham, Killingly, Lynn, Plymouth, Roxbury, Watertown, Westborough, and Wrentham.

Jabez Delano of Dartmouth, in a letter dated November 6, 1727, stated that the earthquake "shook both ye land and water, the Islands & sea, at that degree that several doors were shook of ye latch in our village, & 'tis said that Nantuket ye harth stone grated one again another, and

Modified Mercalli intensities at different localities due to the 1727 earthquake FIGURE FROM WESTON GEOPHYSICAL CORP., 1976

that Car, ye boat builder, Run out of his house, got in to a boat for fear ye Island would sink."

The earthquake was also reported at Northampton in western Massachusetts.

Primary records from a number of towns in Connecticut, namely Ashford, Greenwich, Guilford, New London, and Wethersfield, contain references to the earthquake, as does a period diary entry by John Comer of Newport, Rhode Island, where he states that it awakened many who were asleep. The *Weekly News-Letter*, a newspaper published in Boston, in its November 10, 1727, edition reported that the earthquake "was also at Guilford in Connecticut Colony, which is 160 Miles from this Place; It was about Ten o'clock, and was so violent that it shook down a chimney, threw open the Door of the Ministers House, toll'd a Bell, remov'd Blocks in the Chimney Corner, and a Chest about the Floor, and shook the Houses to a great degree."

In addition to the reports discussed above for New Hampshire, other towns with surviving written reports of the earthquake are Dover, Kensington, and Kingston. The November 3, 1727, edition of the *Weekly News-Letter* provides the following summary of the known area, as of that point in time, where the earthquake was experienced: "We hear already that this fearful Earthquake was felt about the same time, to the Northward as far as Dover; to the Westward as far as Lancaster, Haddam, Enfield and Woodstock, and to the Southward as far as Providence, Rhode-Island, Taunton, Rochester and Barnstable: How much further we have not been yet informed."

The November 16, 1727, issue of the same newspaper reported that the earthquake was felt as far east as Arrowswick (today Arrowsic, Maine). A period newspaper from Philadelphia dated November 2, 1727, reports, "We have advice from New York, that on sunday night (d. 29 Octob.) about ten a-clock they had a shock of an Earthquake, and about Two they felt a second shock which shook the pewter from off the shelves, and the China from off the cupboard-sheads & chimney pieces, & set all the clocks a running down."

There was also a published report indicating that the earthquake was felt in New Jersey.

The most extensive contemporaneous description of the felt area of this earthquake was written in the letter to the Royal Society by Dudley. A part of Dudley's letter reads,

*The last Thing I have to mention is the Course and Extent of the Earthquake. Boston, the Metropolis of this Province, lies in the Latitude of 42 Deg. 25 Min. North, and 4 Ho. 43 Min. to the Westward of London; as the Longitude between the two Places was settled by Mr. Thomas Brattle of this country, and Mr. Hodgson of London, many Years since: And making Boston a Center, we have a certain Account that our late Earthquake was felt in Kennebeck River to the Eastward, and at Philadelphia to the Westward, one hundred and fifty Leagues distant one from the other upon a W.S.W. and E.N.E. Course nearest: and no Part of the intermediate Country, that I can understand, escaped the Shake; the Colonies Rhode-Island, Connecticut, and New-York, that lie between us and Pensylvania being all affected, though not equally, particularly at Philadelphia they write, a small Shock. As to the opposite Line or Latitude, as we may call it, of the Earthquake, we have two noted stands to the Southeast, called Nantucket and Martha's Vineyard, about ninety Miles distant from Boston, and the first named lies about twelve Leagues into the Sea, distant from the main Land; both these Islands had the Earthquake. Our English settlements towards the NorthWest, don't yet exceed forty or fifty Miles from Boston; but they all of them had this Earthquake very sensibly; and how far it might reach beyond them toward Canada we cannot yet say. By this Calculation I believe it will be found, that our Earthquake was of a much greater Extent, than any yet taken notice of in History: As to the course of the Earthquake, or where it first began, I am not yet able to determine by all the Information I can get: For they write from Rhode-Island, Connecticut, New-York and Philadelphia, all to the Westward, that it was between the Hours of Ten and Eleven at Night. The same again is affirm'd from Piscataqua, Casco-Bay, and Kennebeck River, which are to the Eastward: So that as yet it seems to me, that the Earth, through the whole Extent aforesaid, was shaken very near at the same Time.*

The early records also give some indication of where the earthquake was not felt. William Douglass of Boston wrote in a letter dated February 13, 1728, that "by Vessels from Virginia Nova Scotia and Newfoundland I learn that the late Earthquake was not felt in these places."

The northeast-southwest felt extent of the 1727 earthquake can be documented to have been from Arrowsic, Maine, to Philadelphia, Pennsylvania. To the southeast the earthquake shaking was experienced at Nantucket Island, which is the most southeastern land extent where the earthquake could have been reported. There are no felt reports to the northwest of the earthquake, which is not surprising because that area was still only lightly settled at this time. Douglass summarized his understanding of the felt area of this earthquake in a letter dated November 20, 1727:

*We have accts of it so far NE as our settlements reach being about 130 miles from Boston, and so far SW as your accts from N. York and Philadelphia, towards the NE from Boston, it did gradually decrease so fast that it cannot be supposed to reach far into agitation on the waters Such as we had in our bay. Comparing all these accts together I find the centre of its Violence must be somewhere in the Wilderness NW of our Settlements, and that it gradually decreased towards the SW and SE, to the NE it must reach a great way because it was violent 130 miles NE of Boston.*

There is a discussion later in this chapter on the possible location of the fault that radiated the seismic waves of this earthquake.

## Soil Liquefaction, Groundwater Changes, and Landslides

One of the most remarkable features about this earthquake is the number of reports that describe sandblows and changes in groundwater patterns that were observed following the event. There are several firsthand accounts of these features, and contemporaneous newspapers and preachers included descriptions of them in their written publications. Not only did these features provide wonderment to the people at the time of the earthquake, but they also have been a source of fruitful scientific information in modern times. The latter topic is discussed later in this chapter.

Henry Sewall of Newbury provided one of the best descriptions of a sandblow in a letter dated November 21, 1727. In the letter he wrote, "We ran out of doors, when we found the ground did tremble, . . . and did not suffer it to break out, till it got forty or fifty rods from the house, where it brake the ground in the common near a place called Spring island, and there is from sixteen to twenty loads of fine sand thrown out where the ground broke, and several days after the water boiled out like a spring, but is now dry, and the ground closed up again. I have sent some of the sand that you may see it."

Sewall provides a keenly clear description of a sandblow, where a water-saturated sand layer below the surface erupted to the surface in the strong ground shaking of the mainshock. The water carried the sand to the surface, a fine sand as described by Sewall, where it left a deposit of the sand on the ground. Sandblows will sometimes continue to expel a flow of water after the earthquake shaking ceases, and Sewall tells us that this happened for several days after the earthquake. Although Sewall says that the water "boiled out" of the ground, in reality the water must have been quite cool since it would have been at the typical groundwater temperature.

Paul Dudley of Roxbury appears to have obtained possession of Sewall's letter with the above description, whether the letter was sent directly to him or transferred to him from another party. In any case, in his letter to the Royal Society, Dudley reproduced part of the text of the letter but then added some additional details:

*A Gentleman of Probity, from Newbury, a Town situate between thirty and forty Miles to the N.N.E. of Boston, writes word, that at forty Rods distance from his House, there was a Fissure of the Earth, and near twenty Cart-Loads of fine Sand thrown out where the Ground brake, and Water boil'd out like a Spring, and mixing with the Sand, made a fort of Quagmire; but at the Date of his Letter, which was the 21st current, the Spring was become dry, and the Ground closed up again. Since the Receipt of this Letter, I understand that the Ground where this Sand is thrown up, and round about it for a considerable Distance, is a solid Clay for twenty or thirty Foot deep, and nothing like Sand ever to be found there before; so that the Exhalation forced this great Quantity of Sand through a very deep Stratum of Clay.*

Dudley's description of how the sandblow must have formed is remarkably accurate. The overlying clay layer is needed to trap the water-saturated clay below the surface until the water pressure in the sand layer, due to the shaking, can reach a level where it is great enough to erupt through the clay layer.

Rev. Mathias Plant of Newbury also provided a direct observation of some sandblows and groundwater changes. His account reads, "In some Places (in the lower Grounds, about three Miles from my House; where I dwell) the Earth opened, and threw out some Hundred loads of Earth, of a different Colour from that near the Surface, something darker than your white Marl in England; and in many Places, opened dry Land into good Springs, which remain to this Day; and dried up Springs, which never came again."

Whereas the sandblow that Sewall observed was near his house, the sandblow described by Reverend Plant was a few miles away from where he lived. He describes it as being in the "lower Grounds," but where those were located is difficult to figure out because there are many low areas within a few miles of Newbury. He does not say that it was sand that was erupted onto the surface (he calls it "Earth"), but he indicates that it is darker than white Marl. A fine, light brown sand could have been expelled in the creation of the sandblow, and such a sand could fit Reverend Plant's description. His estimate of the amount of material that came out of the sandblow is greater than that of the sandblow described by Sewall, but it is still in the typical range of sandblow sizes that are observed from earthquakes in many different parts of the world.

Stephen Jaques of Newbury also reported sandblows that apparently formed in his town due to the earthquake shaking. He wrote, "The first night it broke out in more than ten places in yᵉ town in yᵉ clay low land, blowing up yᵉ sand, sum more, sum less. In one place near Spring Island it blew out, as was judged twenty loads."

An anonymous contemporary report from Newbury has yet another description of a sandblow: "In many places the Earth opened a foot or more & opened a running Spring in Sam Bartlett Land in the meadow ground and threw up in the low ground in Newbury several loads of sand."

This sandblow was on the land of Sam Bartlett in Newbury, whereas the sandblow described by Revered Plant was several miles away from Newbury and the sandblow described by Sewall was near his house. Thus, the 1727 mainshock caused multiple sandblows over a distance of at least several miles in the Newbury area. Strong earthquake ground shaking often causes multiple sandblows in areas that have the proper geologic conditions for sandblows to form, and so the evidence is strong that multiple sandblows formed during the 1727 earthquake.

In the letter from John Cotton's brother in Haverhill, he wrote that Haverhill did not experience the sandblows that were observed in Newbury: "As to the Damage done by them, I suppose you may have had a better Account than I can give, they say it has broke the Ground in many places in Newbury; in our Town I think no such thing has been observ'd." Although there was ground shaking strong enough to cause chimney damage in Haverhill, the apparently ground shaking was not strong enough to trigger any sandblows to form.

Curiosity about the sandblows appears to have been widespread. William Douglass of Boston, in his letter of November 20, 1727, wrote, "In Newburry a Spring of Water broke out in a plain, and brought up with it some fine grey sand like Pipe clay dryd and levigated, I tryd it in the fire it does not crackel flame fume or ascend any smell, this spring soon vanished and dry'd up."

It is not surprising that there was no reaction when Douglass put the sand into a fire because sandblow sand typically is very pure sand with little or no organic material. Thus, typically there is almost nothing that can combust in the sand from a sandblow. On the other hand, Jaques also threw some of the sand into a fire with what he reported to be a very different result: "When it was cast on coals in y$^e$ night, it burnt like brimstone." Whether this statement is based on an actual or a fanciful observation cannot be ascertained from the evidence that survives today.

The descriptions just presented indicate that there were substantial changes to the groundwater flow patterns in the areas where the sandblows formed. Reverend Plant's account of the sandblow a few miles away from Newbury also includes the observation that some new springs of water opened following the earthquake and some springs that had been flowing before the earthquake were dry after the event. In his letter to the Royal Society, Paul Dudley provided an especially detailed account of groundwater changes due to the earthquake:

*A Neighbour of mine, that has a Well 36 Feet deep, about three Days before the Earthquake, was surprised to find his Water, that used to be very sweet and lympid, stink to that degree, that they could make no Use of it, nor scarce bear the House when it was brought in; and thinking some Carrion was got into the Well, he searched the Bottom, but found it clear and good, though the Colour of the Water was turned wheyish or pale. In about seven Days after the Earthquake, his Water began to mend and in three Days more return'd to its former Sweetness and Colour. I am also very credibly inform'd, that several Springs and good Watering-Places were some of them lower'd, and others quite sunk and lost with the Earthquake. A worthy Divine in a Town about twenty Miles distant from Boston, assures me, that immediately after the Earthquake, there was such a Stink or strong Smell of Sulphur, that the Family could scarce bear to be in the House for a considerable Time that Night. The like is confirmed also from other Places.*

Unfortunately, from this account it is not clear whether the well that became undrinkable three days before the earthquake was in Roxbury or some other locations. It is a guess that the "worthy Divine" who lived about 20 miles from Roxbury was living somewhere north of Boston, where the ground shaking would have been stronger and more likely to cause changes to the local groundwater.

The 1727 sermon of Nathanial Gookin of Hampton, New Hampshire, has an interesting description of a sandblow and of changes in the groundwater system that were observed at the southern boundary of his town. In his sermon Gookin stated,

> *The Earth broke open, near the South Bounds of this Town (as it did in diverse places in Newbury) and cast up a very fine Blewish Sand. At the place of the Eruption, there now (above two Months after) continually issues out considerable quantities of Water; and for about a rod round it, the Ground is so soft, that a Man can't tread upon it without throwing Brush or some other thing to bear him up; it is indeed in Meadow Ground, but before the Earthquake it was not so soft but that Men might freely walk upon it. A Spring of Water, which had run freely for Fourscore Years, and was never known to Freeze, was much sunk by the Earthquake, and Froze afterwards like any standing Water.*

## MAINSHOCK DURATION

The reports of this earthquake generally agree that it took place about 10:30 p.m. on October 29. This was a time when many people were in bed asleep, but also many people were still awake. In eastern Massachusetts and southeastern New Hampshire, there are many reports that those who were asleep were awakened by the earthquake shaking.

A number of sources estimate the duration of the shaking due to the mainshock, probably some estimates by those who were awake when the earthquake started and some by those who were asleep when it began. As noted from John Blunt's description of the earthquake at the beginning of this chapter, the ground shaking due to the mainshock must have lasted at least a few tens of seconds, although Blunt gives no estimate of length of the shaking. There is only one report of the duration of the ground shaking from the Newbury and Amesbury area, that of Henry Sewall, who wrote, "Our house kept shaking about three minutes."

Further from the likely epicenter of the earthquake, estimates of the duration of the ground shaking due to the mainshock are found in a number of documents by direct eyewitnesses to the event. For example, Rev. Christopher Sargeant of Methuen, Massachusetts, states in his 1727 diary that the earthquake "Continued a Minute & half at least." J. D. Phillips of Salem, Massachusetts, quoted in *Salem in the Eighteenth Century*, published in 1937, wrote that the earthquake "lasted two minutes."

There are several estimates from primary sources of the duration of the mainshock shaking from Boston. William Douglass of Boston, in his letter of November 20, 1727, said that the mainshock "continued in Boston 1½ minute." Rev. T. Foxcroft, in a sermon dated November 23, 1727, stated, "The violence was soon over (I believe it scarce exceeded a minute & half)." J. Allen, in a period entry in a church record in Boston, recorded, "All of a sudden our Houses shook as if they were falling to pieces, and this was attended with a great Noise, which lasted about one Minute." Thomas Prince of Boston, in notes appended to a sermon in 1727, describes various aspects of the earthquake shaking and gives an estimate of how long each aspect occurred. From this report the total duration of the mainshock ground shaking appears to have been about two minutes. Paul Dudley wrote in his letter to the Royal Society, "As to the Duration of the Shock itself — Whatever others may print or have printed, I can by no means suppose it exceeded the Space of a Minute, if it was so long; I mean the First and Great Shock."

There are also several estimates from primary records of the duration of the ground shaking from localities to the south and west of Boston. Josiah Cotton of Plymouth, Massachusetts, in a 1755 letter wrote that the 1727 earthquake shaking "lasted about 2 or 3 minutes or I have entered it." Samuel Dexter of Dedham, Massachusetts, wrote in his diary that "it shook $y^e$ houses as if $y^{ey}$ $w^d$ have fell down for $y^e$ space I suppose, of a Minute or two." Rev. Ebenezer Parkman of Westborough, Massachusetts, wrote in his diary that "there was a very terrible Earthquake which lasted

Shaking Etreamly [probably "Extremely"] about a minute and a half — a trembling continued for a Considerable time Longer." Nehemiah Hobart of Hingham, Massachusetts, entered into his diary that "it lasted 2 or 3 minutes." Joshua Hempstead of New London, Connecticut, in a period diary entry wrote that "an Earthquake Shook the houses Continued about 1 minute & half."

Newspapers from the time also report estimates of the duration of the ground shaking in the mainshock. The *Boston Weekly News-Letter* of November 10, 1727, published a report from Guilford, Connecticut, that "the shock lasted about a Minute." From another newspaper report that was cited in a later history by Peter Kalm, an estimate of the earthquake shaking in Boston is that "the shock continued but about 2 minutes." The *Boston Gazette* of November 6, 1727, reported, "the Shock continued but about ten Minutes."

With a few exceptions the estimates of the duration of the mainshock ground shaking are between one and two minutes. These estimates are quite consistent with the estimated durations reported for modern earthquakes with moment magnitudes between 5.5 and 6.0. Furthermore, the duration of the mainshock ground shaking is similar throughout the region, an observation that also is consistent with scientific observations of modern earthquakes.

## Aftershocks of the 1727 Earthquake

One notable aspect the 1727 earthquake was the large number of aftershocks that were experienced following the mainshock. As is typical of aftershock sequences following mainshocks throughout the world, the greatest number of aftershocks and the predominance of the strongest aftershocks following the 1727 mainshock took place in the first few days after the mainshock. Unlike the 1663 earthquake in Quebec, the ground shaking due to the 1727 mainshock appears to have died away before the first aftershocks were felt, and this probably explains why the estimates of the duration of the ground shaking described in the previous section of this chapter are so consistent with the felt durations of modern earthquakes.

Rev. Mathias Plant wrote a vivid account of the 1727 aftershocks that were experienced during the first night in his town: "It continued roaring, bursting and shocking our Houses all that Night. Though the first was much the loudest and most terrible, yet eight more, that came that Night, were loud, and roared like a Cannon at a Distance."

Stephen Jaques of Newbury left a similar account of the immediate aftershocks: "It came very often all $y^e$ night after, and it was heard two or three times some days and nights, and on the Sabbath day nigh on $y^e$ twenty-fourth of December following, between ten and eleven it was very loud, as any time except $y^e$ first, and twice that night after but not so loud."

J. Allen in his diary summarized the immediate aftershocks as they were experienced in Boston: "In a very short time [after the mainshock] it return's upon us, tho' with far less Strength, and the Shocks were repeated seven Times in my hearing that Night; but there were many more at Salem, Ipswich, etc. Distant Rumbles were heard by us many times until the next Friday-Evening. Since that we don't know that we have heard it; but it has been heard at Newbury every Day since, and for more than three weeks."

N. Adams of Portsmouth, New Hampshire, was quoted in an 1825 history of that town as having written, "Several light shocks were felt during that night and almost every day for nearly a fortnight afterwards."

Rev. Ebenezer Parkman of Westborough, Massachusetts, provided several details about some of the immediate aftershocks that followed the mainshock: "And within 65 Minutes [after the mainshock] 5 more rumblings and quiverings might be perceiv'd. Especially the last of those 5. But yet this was not Like the First of all. In about 18 minutes more a Seventh, and near Two o'clock an 8th, and between 5 and 6 in the morning (perhaps 35 minutes after 5) there was a Ninth. First of all these, if not all the rest were heard (I am ready to think) all over New England."

These five accounts give a consistent picture of the aftershock activity that followed in the immediate hours after the mainshock. Whereas the residents of Newbury indicate that they felt almost continuous aftershocks during the night following the mainshock, only several of these were felt as far away as Portsmouth, New Hampshire, and Boston and Westborough, Massachusetts. Thus, most of the aftershocks felt at Newbury had small magnitudes and only a few were stronger and therefore more widely felt. The event at about 2:00 a.m. on the morning following the main-shock was probably the strongest of the immediate aftershocks, as it was reported to have been felt as far away as New York City. During the fol-lowing days frequent aftershocks continued to be felt at Newbury, with only a few of these being felt as far away as Boston.

There is a very complete record of the individual aftershocks that took place during the months and years that followed the mainshock on October 29 due to the efforts of two individuals. During the first several months following the mainshock, Rev. Mathias Plant of Newbury made entries in his parish records each time he felt an aftershock, sometimes with additional information about the strength of the ground shaking or the localities where the event was felt. Given the large number of after-shocks that he experienced, this apparently became a tedious task, for he stopped recording the earthquakes he felt from July 1728 to March 1729. At some point members of the congregation of Reverend Plant learned that he had stopped entering the aftershocks into his church record, and they prevailed on him to resume this practice, which he did. Except for the time period from July 1728 to March 1729, Reverend Plant has left an incredibly complete record of the aftershocks that followed this important earthquake in New England history.

The second important source of information about the aftershocks of this earthquake come from the church records of Reverend Parkman. Like Reverend Plant, Reverend Parkman kept a record of all of the seis-mic events that he felt. Because of the distance from Newbury that he lived in Westborough, Reverend Parkman felt only the strongest after-shocks, those above about moment magnitude 4.0 or so. Thus, whereas the record left by Reverend Plant provides information on all of the aftershocks that took place, the record left by Reverend Parkman indi-cates which were the largest of those aftershocks.

From all of the sources of information about the aftershocks of the 1727 mainshock, it can be documented that between the time of the mainshock on October 29 and the end of November, at least 78 after-shocks were felt at Newbury, with 9 of these having been felt as far away as Westborough. By the end of 1731, at least 160 aftershocks can be documented from Newbury, with 16 of these also being felt at Westborough. Furthermore, the aftershock data set closely follows an Omori's Law decay in the rate of occurrence of aftershocks with time. The greatest rate of aftershock activity occurred during the first few days following the mainshock, with a decreasing rate of aftershocks with time during the following months and years. By 1732 the Newbury area was experiencing an average of only about two earthquakes per year.

It is important to note that the Newbury/Amesbury area continues to experience regular earthquake activity even today. Since the mid-1970s, when the modern instrumental seismic network began operating in New England, the Newbury/Amesbury area has experienced a felt earthquake every three to five years. During the instrumental period the largest earthquake to date in this area was a magnitude 3.0 earthquake at Amesbury on January 10, 1999. This earthquake was felt locally in northeastern Massachusetts and southeastern New Hampshire, but it was not felt in Boston. These modern Newbury/Amesbury area earthquakes may be recent aftershocks of the 1727 earthquake. If so, they can provide important information about the location of the fault on which the 1727 earthquake took place. This topic is discussed in more detail later in this chapter.

## EARTHQUAKE SOUNDS
The sounds that accompanied the mainshock and aftershocks of the 1727 earthquake were almost as notable as the strong ground shaking, and many of the authors of accounts of the earthquake describe the earthquake sounds in some detail. The mainshock was particularly loud in the epicentral area, which likely added to the terror that spread through the local population when the earthquake struck.

Stephen Jaques of Newbury provided a vivid description of the sound of the mainshock: "It came with a dreadful roreing as if it was thunder, and then a pounce like grate guns two or three times close after one another." Richard Kelley of Amesbury, Massachusetts, wrote in his diary that the earthquake was "extrodenery loud."

John Blunt of New Castle, New Hampshire, indicated that the mainshock included "the Terrible noise which was began compared to the strongest that I remember." In his account he states that he heard the "Dreadful noise" even after he had left his house and run outside. N. Adams at Portsmouth, New Hampshire, wrote, "The sea was affected as well as the land, and roared in an unusual manner." Nathanial Gookin of Hampton, New Hampshire, noted that the earthquake was "attended with a Terrible Noise."

Peter Clark of Salem, Massachusetts, recorded in his diary that the mainshock was "accompanied with a terrible noise and shaking." Rev. Christopher Sargeant of Methuen, Massachusetts, noted in his diary that "it began like a most violent clap of thunder. Some say preceeded by a trembling of the earth."

In Boston William Douglass wrote a particularly descriptive account of what he heard. His letter of November 20, 1727, reads, "from the N (westerly) corner was hear'd first a noise like a storm of Wind at a distance gradually increasing to that of a roaring of a foul chimney afire, and at its height resembled the rattling of 20 or more carts unloading great stones (some say the days were observed to have some seconds before the noise was noticed)."

Paul Dudley, in his letter to the Royal Society, appears to have mixed in the Douglass report with his own impressions of the sounds of the mainshock:

*That our Earthquake was of the first Species is also proved from the Sound that accompanied it, since tremulous and vibrating Motions are proper to produce Sounds; which brings me to the third Particular, viz. the Noise or Sound that accompanied or immediately preceded our Earthquake. This indeed was very terrible and amazing; though I am apt to think it was thought more considerable by those within doors, than such as were without in the Air. Some of our People took this Noise to be Thunder; others compared it to the Ratling of Coaches and Carts upon Pavements, or frozen Ground. One of my Neighbours liken'd it to the shooting out of a Load of Stones from a Cart under his Window. For my own Part, being perfectly awake, though in Bed, I thought at first my Servants, who lodged in a Garret over my Chamber, were haling along a Trundle-bed: But, in truth, the Noise that accompanies an Earthquake seems to be Sonus sui generis, and there is no describing it. This Noise, as amazing as it was, in an Instant of Time, as one may say, was succeeded by a Shake much more Terrible. . . . 'Tis impossible to describe the Terror and Amazement that an Earthquake carries with it; and though I had never felt one before, yet I was thoroughly convinced what it was at the very Time.*

The Reverend T. Foxcroft of Boston included the following description of the sounds of the mainshock in his sermon of November 23, 1727: "They heard first a gentle Murmur, like a small ruffling Wind, and then a more noisy Rumbling, as of Thunder at some Distance: which seem'd to approach higher, and grew louder, till it roared terribly; and then we felt our Houses totter and reel."

Rev. Thomas Prince of Boston claimed, "It came on with a loud hollow Noise like the Roaring of a Great fired Chimney, but incomparably more fierce and Terrible. In about half a Minute the Earth began to heave and tremble." Samuel Sewall in Boston stated in a letter dated November 14, 1727, that "the crashing noise was very amazing to me."

The sound of the earthquake was reported from as far away from the Newbury/Amesbury area as Connecticut. Stephen Mix of Wethersfield, Connecticut, included in his sermon delivered in November 1727 that "it came on with a grave and heavy Sound . . . which might possibly be attended with a small Trembling, towards the ending of which Grave Sound, there seemed a very strong shock."

The descriptions of the sounds of the mainshock by those at different distances from the probable location of the fault where the earthquake slip took place are consistent with modern theories concerning the generation and propagation of seismic waves in an earthquake. As described later in this chapter, the residents of Newbury and Amesbury were probably living within a few miles of the fault that moved in the mainshock, and those residents described a roaring noise that was incredibly loud with little or no perceptible buildup. In Boston the noise grew in volume until it was the loudest when the strongest shaking was experienced. Boston is about 37 miles (60 kilometers) from Newbury, and so the time difference between the arrival of the P and S wave at Boston from an earthquake in

Newbury is about eight seconds. At Boston the first arriving P wave from the earthquake would be accompanied by a rumbling sound, whereas the loudest sounds would occur about 10 seconds later, when the S wave and surface waves would arrive. This is the pattern of the earthquake sounds as reported by all of the observers in Boston, although the time difference of one minute between the beginning of the rumble and the loudest sound, as reported by Thomas Prince, is too large to be consistent with the seismic waves. In Connecticut the volume of the sound would be expected to be much less than closer to the earthquake epicenter, and the sound would be expected to be dominated by lower tones. This is consistent with the rumbling, grave sounds that were reported from Wethersfield, Connecticut.

The aftershocks reportedly generated a wide variety of sounds in the Newbury/Amesbury area, as indicated in the report by Reverend Plant. He describes the aftershocks as "roaring, bursting, and shocking our houses." The smaller aftershocks would sound more like a boom or explosion, and hence the description of "bursting." Somewhat larger aftershocks would be louder, hence the "roaring" events. Still larger aftershocks, like the eight strong aftershocks that immediately followed the mainshock, sounded like even louder explosions. Reverend Plant wrote that "though the first was much the loudest and most terrible, yet eight more, that came that night, were loud, and roared like a Cannon at a Distance."

This description carries the unmistakable signature of a nearby aftershock that was locally strong, being accompanied by a loud, explosive sound.

In Boston only a few of the aftershocks were felt, but some of the documents from the time suggest that a number of aftershocks may have been heard there. J. Allen from Boston wrote, "Distant Rumbles were heard by us many times until the next Friday-Evening."

William Douglass described the aftershocks in Boston during the night and morning following the mainshock. He wrote in a letter dated November 20, 1727, "Some tell us of more small shakes tho' not generally perceived; but many rumblings as if at a distance from time to time were heard all the following part of the night."

Thus, it appears that some of the aftershocks may have been heard in Boston but not felt there. This reminds me of an aftershock survey in which I took part in California in 1979. I was a graduate student at the California Institute of Technology in Pasadena, and a magnitude 5.1 earthquake took place in the Mojave Desert about 120 miles east of Los Angeles. Several graduate students, including myself, rushed portable seismic instruments into the Mojave the day of the earthquake to monitor the aftershock activity. I was assigned a location just north of the fault where the earthquake took place, and my job was to operate a portable seismograph that needed regular attention. I spent the night out in the open in the desert operating the instrument. Every few minutes I felt an aftershock that also registered on my seismograph. I also heard frequent booms off in the distance to the south, of the order of one or two per minute. Sometimes the booms registered as seismic events on my seismograph, and sometimes they did not. My experience from 1979 suggests to me that the descriptions by Allen and Douglass sound realistic and that some in Boston were hearing some of the aftershocks that came from their north.

## EARTHQUAKE LIGHTS

The 1727 earthquake occurred at 10:30 p.m. on the night of October 29, several hours after the sun had set. The weather was clear that evening, and so the local inhabitants had a star-filled dark sky at the time of the earthquake. There are some reports of flashes of light that were seen at the time of the earthquake. The conditions would have been very good for observing such phenomena given the weather conditions and lack of artificial lighting. Unfortunately, all of the known accounts of earthquake lights associated with the 1727 earthquake are secondhand accounts, as no person who left a primary account of the earthquake mentioned having seen any light flashes or glows at the time of the earthquake. Nevertheless, the surviving accounts of earthquake lights are interesting and deserve being preserved as part of the story of this seismic event.

Rev. T. Foxcroft of Boston mentioned earthquake lights in his sermon of November 23, 1727. He said, "Some say, Before they were sensible of the Shock they saw Flashes of Light glance by their Windows."

Paul Dudley, in his letter to the Royal Society, included a note about earthquake lights that reads very much like the report by Reverend

Foxcroft: "Persons of Credit do also affirm, that just before, or in the Time of the Earthquake, they perceived Flashes of Light." Aside from the report of earthquake lights, the most interesting part of this report is that Dudley wants to assure the readers that those who reported the earthquake lights were people who could be believed.

Rev. Nathanial Gookin of Hampton, New Hampshire, wrote in his account of the earthquake, "When the shake was beginning some Persons observed a Flash of Light at their Windows, and one or Two say Streams of Light Running on the Earth, the Flame seemed to them to be of a Blewish Colour. These Flashes, no doubt, broke out of the Earth; otherwise it is probable, they would have been seen more general'y, especially by those who were abroad."

All of the phenomena described here are similar to those reported in earthquakes from other parts of the world. Reverend Gookin's supposition that the electrical phenomena came from inside the earth is probably a good one. There are electrical currents that are running all the time through the rocks of the earth, and the pressures associated with seismic waves can cause sudden changes in these electrical currents. The sudden changes in the electrical currents could cause visible radiation at the earth's surface that human beings might observe. The flashes of light are often not strong, nor do most last very long according to those who have reported them. The light can have different colors, including the blue color given in Gookin's report. In some cases earthquake lights are reported as a more general glow on the horizon that can last several minutes, but that was not reported here.

The most amusing secondhand account of an earthquake light comes from the November 16, 1727, edition of the *Weekly News-Letter* of Boston. It reads,

*Divers People in this & some Neighbouring Parishes observed just as the Earthquake began, A flash of Light at the Windows: A Young Man of this Town being then standing abroad near his Fathers House, at first heard a small Rumbling Noise: immediately upon which he sew a Flash of Light run along ypon the Ground 'till it came to the House, and then began the Shake. It appears that what he said of the flash of*

*Light was not a meer Fancy, by this, That a Dog which was then lying on its Course as the Light came to him gave a sudden yelp and leap, and thereby show'd that he perceiv'd it.*

It is impossible to know if this is an accurate account of what happened or if it is a fanciful embellishment of the actual occurrence. In any case the story of a flash of light running along the ground is reminiscent of similar tales that have been told following earthquakes in other parts of the world.

## ANIMAL BEHAVIOR

As for the accounts of the earthquake lights, there are no firsthand reports of animal reactions during or prior to the earthquake. The account of the dog and the earthquake light given in the previous section of this chapter indicates that the dog did not react to the initial earthquake shaking but only jumped when the earthquake light passed under it.

From Boston Rev. T. Foxcroft wrote that just before people felt the earthquake shaking, "others observ'd their Dogs give a sudden bark, as when affrighted. But before any cou'd look about them, to know the meaning of these things, they heard first a gentle Murmur, like a small ruffling Wind, and then a more noisy Rumbling, as of Thunder at some Distance." Reverend Foxcroft's description seems to imply that the dogs barked only seconds before the first vibrations of the earthquake were felt.

The letter of Paul Dudley to the Royal Society contains a mention of animal reactions to the earthquake. Dudley wrote, "Another [neighbor] that was riding home, says, that upon the Noise the Earthquake made, his Horse stood stock still, and during the Shake, trembled to that degree, that he thought he would haye fell under him. Our House-Dogs were also sensible and affected with the Earthquake; some of them barking, others howling, and making strange and unusual Noises."

This report suggests that the neighbor's horse reacted to the first arrival of the earthquake waves. The neighbor's dogs also apparently reacted to the earthquake shaking in various ways. None of these reports indicates that there were any unusual animal reactions prior to the earthquake by more than a few seconds, if that.

Rev. Nathanial Gookin of Hampton, New Hampshire, also mentions animal reactions in his sermon, although in only a very general way. His sermon reads, "It is hard to express the Consternation that fell, both upon Men and Beasts, in the time of the great Shock. The Bruit Creatures ran Roaring about the Fields, as in the greatest distress."

As for the accounts discussed above, the report by Reverend Gookin implies that the animals reacted to the earthquake shaking and noise, and not prior to the earthquake.

## MAGNITUDE AND POSSIBLE FAULT OF THE 1727 MAINSHOCK

From a scientific point of view, the historical records of the 1727 earthquake provide a surprisingly rich set of observations that can be used to estimate the seismological source properties of this earthquake. The temporal pattern of the dates and times of the many aftershocks that can be documented following the mainshock is quite consistent with an Omori's Law aftershock decay. Furthermore, from the descriptions of the felt and sound effects of many of the small aftershocks, it appears that the people of Newbury and Amesbury were very close to the epicenters of these events. These people must have been living adjacent to the fault if not directly over the fault that moved in the mainshock.

One report of an aftershock from the church book of Rev. Mathias Plant from Newbury states that the aftershock was felt more strongly in Haverhill than in Newbury. Thus, the fault for the 1727 mainshock must have been directly under or just to the west of the Newbury/Amesbury area in the direction of Haverhill. The aftershocks of a strong earthquake invariably spread over some spatial area, and the area of the fault rupture is proportional to the magnitude of the mainshock. For an earthquake of the estimated size of the 1727 earthquake, the aftershock would be expected to spread a few miles (several kilometers) in extent.

With the approximate location established of the fault where the mainshock took place, the reports of the damage and felt effects of the mainshock can help constrain the magnitude of the earthquake. The earthquake was significantly damaging in the Newbury/Amesbury area, with damage also reported from Haverhill in Massachusetts and Hampton and New Castle in New Hampshire. On the other hand, the towns of

Methuen and Salem in Massachusetts and Portsmouth in New Hampshire reported strong earthquake shaking but no damage, and with minor exceptions, such as in Boston, there are no damage reports outside of these few communities in northeastern Massachusetts and southeastern New Hampshire. The earthquake was felt as far southwest as Philadelphia in Pennsylvania and as far northeast as Arrowsic in Maine. It was felt to the southeast as far as Nantucket Island, which is the farthest extent of land in that direction. From the limited area with reported damage, the more distant reports of strong shaking and noises but no damage, and the largest distance to which the earthquake was felt, the magnitude of this event is estimated to be about 5.6 or so. The duration of the ground shaking of about one to one and a half minutes is consistent with an earthquake of this magnitude.

An inference about the location of the fault on which the 1727 earthquake slip took place can be drawn from the 1999 earthquakes at Amesbury. There were four small earthquakes that were felt in 1999, three on January 10 and one on January 14. The largest of these four earthquakes was the first one, with a magnitude of 3.0. From an analysis of the seismic waves radiated by the magnitude 3.0 earthquake of 1999, it was determined that the earthquake took place on a fault that is oriented in a northwest–southeast direction and took place at a depth about 1.2 miles (2 kilometers) below the town of Amesbury. The northwest–southeast trend for the fault projects the fault to the southeast toward the town of Newbury, parallel to but just southwest of the final course of the Merrimac River before it empties into the ocean. Although it has not been mapped by geologists, a fault oriented in the northwest–southeast direction could control this final course of the Merrimac River. Also, the 1999 earthquakes were heard as loud booms, consistent with the shallow depths of these four earthquakes as determined from seismological data. Interestingly, many public reports of the sounds heard in the 1999 earthquakes used the same kinds of descriptions of the earthquake sounds as are given in the extant records for the aftershocks of the 1727 earthquake. This provides corroborative evidence that the 1999 earthquakes can be considered part of the aftershock activity following the 1727 earthquake and that the 1727 earthquake must also have been centered only 1 to 2 miles (1.6–3.2 kilometers) below the surface of the earth.

Further support for the estimated location of the fault and for the magnitude of the 1727 earthquake can be drawn from the occurrences of the sandblows due to the earthquake. Research published in the journal *Geology* in 1991 by Dr. Martitia Tuttle and Dr. Leonardo Seeber described a study of several of the sandblows in the Newbury area that erupted in the 1727 earthquake. Geological investigations of these features confirm that they formed in the 1727 earthquake. Interestingly, the sandblows that were found by Drs. Tuttle and Seeber follow a northwest–southeast trend, similar to the direction inferred for the fault of the 1727 earthquake.

Another discovery by Drs. Tuttle and Seeber is that the 1727 earthquake was not the first earthquake to have caused sandblows in the Newbury area. These researchers discovered that an earlier earthquake, within the past 4,000 years, also caused sandblows at the same locations as those in 1727. Where the epicenter of this past earthquake was and what its magnitude was cannot be ascertained from the sandblow data. However, the sandblow data do confirm that at least one very strong earthquake affected northeastern Massachusetts in prehistoric times. Ground liquefaction effects like sandblows require a minimum strength of ground shaking for their formation, and this minimum level of ground shaking usually can be damaging to brittle structures such as brick chimneys and walls. Thus, had there been towns in the Newbury/Amesbury area during this prehistoric earthquake, they likely would have suffered damage similar to or worse than the damage they experienced in the 1727 earthquake.

CHAPTER 6

# 1744: Another Earthquake
# Shocks Massachusetts
# 1755: The Great Cape Ann Earthquake

## AN EARTHQUAKE ON JUNE 3, 1744

The damaging earthquake of October 29, 1727, was the beginning of several decades of earthquake activity that was centered in eastern

Contemporary woodcut illustrating the ground shaking in Boston in the 1744 earthquake

Massachusetts. Within a few months of the 1727 mainshock at Newbury, the high rate of initial aftershocks in late 1727 and early 1728 quickly decayed to a low, irregular pattern of activity with time. From 1728 into the early 1740s, earthquakes were felt in northeastern Massachusetts every few weeks to several months. Most of these were small earthquakes that were centered somewhere in eastern Massachusetts, and some were probably larger earthquakes that were centered at localities outside of eastern Massachusetts and perhaps outside of New England. For example, in 1737 there was an earthquake that struck near New York City and was felt throughout Massachusetts.

During this period after the "great earthquake" of 1727, a notable earthquake took place on June 3, 1744 (O.S.). The *Boston Weekly News-Letter* issue of June 5, 1744 (O.S.), summarized the event and its aftermath:

> *Last Lord's Day between 10 and 11 o'Clock in the Forenoon we were surprised with a violent Shock of an Earthquake attended with a loud rumbling Noise whereby People were put into a very great Consternation, and many who were attending the Divine Worship ran out into the streets fearing the Houses would fall upon them: A great many Bricks were shook off from several Chimneys in this and other Towns, and much of the Stone Fences in several Places in the Country was tumbled down by it. It was perceived to continue longer and be more severe in some Places than at others; and 'tis tho't by some to be felt near equal to that which we had in the Year 1727. How extensive it was we cannot yet learn, but by Information at present we are assured that it reach'd above 100 Miles. Another shock was felt at Salem, and others adjacent: Towns, about five o'Clock in the Afternoon of the same Day, which was considerable and again surprised the People very much. Three or Four smaller Shocks were perceived in the Night and Morning Succeeding.*

This and other accounts give no information about the damage in the 1744 earthquake, specifically which towns had chimneys that sustained some damage or how much damage took place to the chimneys. A history of Salem, Massachusetts, published in 1835 stated that bricks were shaken from chimneys and stone walls were thrown down. However, the primary source for this report is not stated, and it is not clear whether the reported damage took place in Salem or in some other place. A history of Dorchester, Massachusetts, published by William Orcott in 1843 reported, "A second earthquake shock visited Dorchester in 1744. It was not so severe as that of 1727; but it was enough to shake the meeting-house from top to bottom, and to cause a wall near by to fall. Several chimneys in Boston were also thrown down."

Once again, the primary source of this information is not stated. If true, this report indicates that the ground shaking due to the 1744 earthquake was strong enough to cause some chimney damage in Boston. The ground shaking was clearly frightening to the local population. The earthquake occurred at a time when many churches were in the middle of their Sunday morning services, and reports indicate that people ran out of churches in Salem, Newbury, and Canton. The 1835 town history of Salem states, "In the Hamlet parish at Ipswich (now the town of Hamilton), the shock came when the pastor, Rev. Mr. Wigglesworth, was preaching. The congregation was greatly alarmed; but he endeavored to calm them, remarking that 'there can be no better place for us to die in than the house of God.'"

The history does not say whether or not he was successful at convincing the congregation not to flee the church due to the shaking.

Similar to other earthquakes, there were notable sounds that accompanied the earthquake shaking. The *Boston Evening Post* of June 4, 1744, reported that the earthquake was "attended with a Noise much like the rattling of a Coach."

The *Boston Gazette or Weekly Journal* indicated that at Portsmouth, New Hampshire, the earthquake was "attended with a loud rumbling noise," although no damage was reported from that locality. Heath Peleg, in a period diary from Barrington, Rhode Island, wrote that the earthquake "came with a mighty noise." Reports from the *Boston Evening Post* indicated that the earthquake was felt for about a minute or more but its duration was shorter than that of the earthquake of 1727.

The epicenter of the 1744 earthquake cannot be very well established by the information about the earthquake that survives today. The *Boston*

*Weekly News-Letter* issue of June 5, 1744, excerpted previously, indicated that some aftershocks were felt in the Salem area, most notably in the late afternoon. The Salem history that was published in 1835 reports that there also were two small shocks felt in the morning sometime in May 1744.

The scant historical data provide only broad constraints on the location and magnitude of the June 3, 1744, mainshock. Whereas the greatest amount of damage in the 1727 earthquake apparently was centered at Newbury and Amesbury, the historical records suggest that the chimney damage in the 1744 earthquake was from Salem to Boston. The epicenter of the 1744 earthquake was probably somewhere in this vicinity. The historical reports all agree that both the strength and the duration of the ground shaking in the 1744 earthquake were less than those experienced in the 1727 earthquake. On the other hand, the 1744 earthquake was felt as far away as New York City and Long Island. All of these facts together suggest that the 1744 earthquake probably had a moment magnitude somewhere between magnitude 4.5 and 5.0.

## A Major Earthquake in the Early Morning of November 18, 1755

In the several years following the 1744 earthquake, only a few small earthquakes were felt in eastern Massachusetts, with the last occurring in 1751. If the residents of the region adopted an attitude that the worst of the earthquakes was over, they proved badly mistaken. After four years with no earthquakes reported felt in Boston, on November 18, 1755, a major earthquake struck with no warning at all. Although the records of the time state that no persons were killed by the earthquake, nevertheless the earthquake had a significant impact across a wide swath of New England.

A summary description of the earthquake is provided by N. Adams of Portsmouth, New Hampshire, as quoted in an 1825 history of the town: "The most severe and tremendous earthquake, which was ever felt in this country, took place on the night of the 18th of November, after midnight. The weather was remarkably serene, the sky clear, the moon shone bright, and a solemn stillness pervaded all nature, at the time it commenced."

Contemporary woodcut illustrating the ground shaking in Boston in the 1755 earthquake

Across a wide area of New England and beyond, the earthquake woke people from their sleep and caused them to rush about in a panic. An anonymous journal entry from Northampton, Massachusetts, states, "Some people supposed that the day of judgement had come, & were in great terror."

The day of the earthquake, Rev. Nathanael Henchman of Lynn, Massachusetts, preached a sermon from Matthew chapter 7, likely to a very full church.

John Hyde of Boston left a graphic account of the ground shaking that he experienced during the earthquake. His account, from a letter dated November 24, 1755, reads:

*November 18, 1755, being Tuesday, the Morning, I was awaked by the shaking of my bed, and of the house; the cause whereof I immediately concluded could be nothing but an earthquake, having experienced one before. The Trembling (for as yet it was scarce more) increasing I soon got out of bed, and went towards the window on the other side of the chamber, to observe the sky, or heavens. By the time I had got about half way across the room, which might be six or seven seconds from my first awaking, the shaking was a little abated; But this thought no sooner came into my mind, than I found how much I was mistaken; for instantaneously the shock came on with redoubled violence, and loud noise: the windows, doors, chairs, etc. being pro- digiously agitated; and indeed the whole house rocking and cracking to such a degree, that I concluded it must soon fall, or be racked to pieces, unless perhaps it should be swallowed up entire. Having first just looked out at the window, I hastened down stairs, unbolted and opened the door, I found the shock was something abated, and having looked out at the door a moment or two, returned to my chamber, and opened a window, at which I stood for the space of five or six seconds; the shaking and the noise were by this time much lessened, and still kept increasing as though all would be very soon become still and quiet.*

One interesting aspect of this description is the pattern of the initial shaking described by Hyde. He was awakened by trembling that was not strong, after which he arose from his bed and started to walk over to a win- dow. As he was walking, he thought the shaking was abating somewhat, but that suddenly changed. By his estimate, about six or seven seconds after he first noticed the earthquake, the strongest shaking arrived. This set of observations is easily explained by the seismic waves generated by an earthquake. The first wave to arrive is always the P wave, which is often described as a rumble. A second, later wave to arrive is the much stron- ger S wave, which is immediately followed by the strongest waves, the surface waves. The time difference between the arrival of the P wave and the S wave can be used to estimate the distance of the observer from the fault where the earthquake waves were generated. A greater time differ- ence between the P and S wave arrivals corresponds to a greater distance between the observer and the fault. In the description by John Hyde, the time between the P and S wave arrivals is about six or seven seconds or a bit more (depending on how long it took him to awake when the P wave first arrived). This would correspond to a distance to the fault of between 30 and 35 miles (50 to 58 kilometers). This observation is analyzed later in this chapter when the location of the 1755 earthquake fault is discussed.

[ 1 ]

PHILOSOPHICAL

TRANSACTIONS.

I. *An Account of the Earthquake felt in* New England, *and the neighbouring Parts of* America, *on the 18th of* November 1755. *In a Letter to* Tho. Birch, *D.D. Secret. R. S. by Mr. Professor* Winthrop, *of* Cambridge *in* New England.

Reverend Sir,

Read Jan. 13, 1757. I Beg leave to lay before you the best account I am able to give of the great earthquake, which shook New England, and the neighbouring parts of America, on Tuesday the 18th day of November 1755, about a quarter after four in the morning. I deferred writing till this time, in order to obtain the most distinct information of the several particulars relating to it, both here and in the other places where it was felt; and especially the extent of it.

Vol. 50.       B       The

First page of the 1757 publication in the *Philosophical Transactions* by Prof. John Winthrop concerning the 1755 earthquake

Prof. John Winthrop of Harvard University published a detailed and lengthy paper in the *Philosophical Transactions* that was read to the Philosophical Society on January 13, 1757. Professor Winthrop reported on the experience of one of his neighbors who was on the road in Cambridge when the earthquake struck. Winthrop wrote,

*By his account, as well as that of others, the first motion of the earth was what may be called a pulse, or rather an undulation; and resembled (to use his own comparison) that of a long rolling, swelling sea; and the swell was so great, that he was obliged to run and catch hold of something, to prevent being thrown down. The tops of two trees close by him, one of which is 25, the other 30 feet high, he thinks waved at least ten feet (and I depend on his judgment in this particular, because he judged right of the height of the trees, as I found by actual mensuration); and there were two of these great wavings, succeeded by one, which was smaller. This sort of motion, after having continued, as has been conjectured, about a minute, abated a little; so that I, who was just then waked, and, I suppose, most others, imagined, that the height of the shock was past. But instantly, without a moment's intermission, the shock came on with redoubled noise and violence; though the species of it was altered to a tremor, or quick horizontal vibratory motion, with sudden jerks and wrenches. The bed, on which I lay, was now tossed from side to side; the whole house was prodigiously agitated; the windows rattled, the beams cracked, as if all would presently be shaken to pieces.*

This description is somewhat confusing because Winthrop seems to blend his own experiences of the ground shaking into the description of the ground shaking from his neighbor. Even so, it is clear that the ground shaking experienced by Winthrop in his home was so great that he thought the building would collapse.

The Reverend Ebenezer Parkman of Westborough, Massachusetts, is one observer who reported his experiences of both the 1727 and 1755 earthquakes. On November 18, 1755, he wrote in his diary, "This Morning about a Quarter past 4 We were all Wak'd up by a very Terrible Earthquake. The shock seems to me to be as great and to last about as long as the great Earthquake October 29, 1727, but the manner of Shaking I think is different — That more horizontal, this partly vertical. My children rose and gather'd into my chamber, where we gave Thanks to God."

The *Boston Weekly News-Letter* issue of November 20, 1755, reported that people on ships also felt the earthquake: "Some Vessels being at this Time in the Bay under sail, felt the Effects of it, for tho' it was very Calm, they were suddenly put into such a Tremor as if they had run upon a Rock; The same Effects were felt on board the Man of War and other Vessels which lay at Anchor in the Harbour."

## DAMAGE TO STRUCTURES IN BOSTON DUE TO THE EARTHQUAKE

The 1727 and 1744 earthquakes had almost totally spared Boston, with only very minor damage reported in those earthquakes. On the other hand, the 1755 earthquake was a much different story in Boston. New England's largest city at the time, Boston suffered severe effects throughout the city, as described by Prof. John Winthrop in his 1757 report on the earthquake to the Philosophical Society:

> *The principal effects of the earthquake, for which I can find sufficient vouchers; for many strange things have been related, which upon examination, appear to be without foundation. Besides the throwing down of glass, pewter and other movables in the houses, many chimnies were levelled with the roofs of the houses, and many more shattered, and thrown down in part. Some were broken off several feet below the top, and, by the suddenness and violence of the jerks, canted*

*horizontally an inch or two over, so to stand very dangerously. Some others are twisted, or turned around in part. The roofs of some houses were quite broken in by the fall of chimneys; and the gable ends of some brick buildings thrown down, and many were cracked. . . . The vane upon the public markethouse in Boston was thrown down; the wooden spindle, which supported it, about five inches in diameter, and which had stood the most violent gusts of wind, being snapt off. A new vane, upon one of the churches in Boston, was bent at its spindle two or three points of the compass; and another at Springfield, distant about 80 miles from Boston, was bent to a right angle. A distiller's cistern, made of plank, almost new, and very strong put together, was burst to pieces by the agitation of liquor in it; which was thrown out with such force, as to break down one whole side of the shed, that defended the cistern from the weather.*

The *Boston Weekly News-Letter* of November 20, 1755, published the following account of the damage in Boston:

*The Tops of many Chimnies, and some of them quite down to the Roofs, were thrown down, and several of the Roofs upon which they fell were beat in: Many Chimnies also, for 6, 7, and 8 Feet below the Top, were loosned and turned several Inches on the main Body; and others, with the Brick Walls of some houses were disjointed, burst out and shatter'd:*

 *The wooden Post that supported the Spindle and Vane of Faneuil Hall Market was by the Shake broke off, and they fell to the Ground on the North Side: . . . And in the inside of many Houses, the Pewter, Earthern, Glass, China, and other Ware, were thrown off the Shelves, and other Places whereon they stood, and many Things were broke to Pieces.*

In *The Early History of New England* by Rev. Henry White, there is transcribed a period account from a letter by an anonymous source in Boston who wrote, "I observed the tops of many chimneys demolished, others cracked and much damaged — bricks, tiles, and slates scattered in the streets, and large quantities of mortar and rubbish almost every-where spread, and several houses suffered by large cracks and breaches in their foundations."

John Hyde's letter of November 24, 1755, described the damage throughout the city. A version of the letter was printed in the November 24, 1755, issue of the *Boston Gazette or Country Journal*, and various later authors apparently took their descriptions of the damage in Boston from Hyde's newspaper account. The description of the damage in the *Boston Gazette or Country Journal* reads,

> *The visible effects of the earthquake are very considerable in the town; to be sure much more considerable than those of any other earthquake, which has been known in it. Many chimnies, I conjecture (from observation) not much less than an hundred, are leveled with the roofs of the houses: many more, I imagine not fewer than 12 or 1500 are shattered, and thrown down in part; so that in some places, especially on the low loose ground, made by encroachments on the harbour, the streets are almost covered with the bricks that have fallen. Some chimnies, though not thrown down, are dislocated, or broken several feet from the top, and partly turn'd around, as upon a swivel; some are shoved on one side horizontally, jutting over, and just nodding to the fall; the gable ends of several brick buildings, perhaps of twelve or fifteen, are thrown down, and the roofs of some houses are quite broken in by the fall of the chimnies: . . . Many clocks were also stopped by being so violently agitated.*
>
> *These are the most considerable effects of the earthquake, which have fallen under my observation; for the shaking of pewter, etc. from the shelves seems hardly worth mentioning after them.*

In his 1757 report to the Philosophical Society, Professor Winthrop presented a detailed analysis of the damage to his own chimneys, which were badly broken by the earthquake shaking. His account contains a very precise set of observations, and his inferences about the earthquake shaking from those observations are fully compatible with today's understanding of earthquake seismology. This part of his account reads,

*Tho' the degree of violence was doubtless different in different places, yet, that I might make some estimate of it with us, I measured the greatest distance on the ground, to which any of the bricks, which were thrown off from the tops of my chimnies, had reached, and found it to be 30 feet, and the height from which they fell was 32 feet. Now since bodies fall thro' 16 feet nearly in 1" of time; and the times, in which they fall through other heights, are in the subduplicate ratio of those heights; it follows, that the velocity, wherewith those bricks were thrown off, was that of above 21 feet in 1" of time: for the subduplicate ratio of 32 to 16 is the same as the simple ratio of 30 to a little more than 21. But the velocity was less at less heights: for the key before spoken of, as thrown from off a shelf in a chamber in my house, was not thrown so far, in proportion to the height thro' which it fell, as the bricks were from the top of the chimnies; and in my lower rooms nothing was thrown down, but a small bell in the garret was made to ring by it. Hence it appears, that our buildings were rocked with a kind of angular motion, like that of a cradle; the upper parts of them moving swifter, or thro' greater spaces in the same time, than the lower; the natural consequences of an undulatory motion of the earth.*

Professor Winthrop correctly concludes that it was the oscillatory horizontal ground shaking that caused the damage to the chimney that he observed. Furthermore, he correctly infers from his measurement of the thrown distance of the bricks from the top of his chimney to the smaller distance that a key was thrown inside the house that the top of the house shook more strongly than the lower part of the house.

## DAMAGE TO STRUCTURES AWAY FROM BOSTON DUE TO THE EARTHQUAKE

Although the damage effects of the earthquake in Boston received the bulk of the attention in the records of the time, many other localities also sustained damage in the earthquake. These reports reveal how widespread was the strong ground shaking due to this earthquake. The future U.S. president John Adams wrote in his diary the following entry about the earthquake in Braintree, Massachusetts: "I was then at my Fathers in Braintree and awoke out of my sleep in the midst of it. The house seemed to rock and reel and crack as if it would fall in ruins about us. 7 chimneys were shatter'd by it within one mile of my Fathers house."

The diary of Lt. Samuel Thompson from Woburn, Massachusetts, contains an entry that reads, "1755, Nov. 18: There was a great shock of an earthquake . . . it knocked off the chimney here and in other places."

Later histories of several towns in the region provide details of local damage as reported in sources that were contemporary to the earthquake. In the 1917 history of Ipswich, *Ipswich in the Massachusetts Bay Colony*, there is a citation that states, "In ye Town of Ipswich much Damage was Done to Many Houses." The Reverend E. Bridge of Chelmsford was cited in *History of Chelmsford, Massachusetts*, published in 1917, as being awakened by the earthquake and saying that "two bricks fell from the tops of our chimneys."

In *History of the Town of Essex from 1634–1868*, published in 1868, a quote from R. Crowell of Essex, Massachusetts, reads, "On the 18th of November, between the hours of four and five in the morning, there was a great earthquake, which threw down stone walls and the tops of many chimneys, and bent the vanes on some of the steeples. It did much damage to many houses in this town."

An 1896 history of Salem, Massachusetts, from the *Essex Institute Historical Collections*, volume XXXII, contains a period entry that reads, "Tops of chimneys and stone walls were thrown down, and clocks stopped by the shake." A history of Gloucester, Massachusetts, published in 1891 entitled *Notes and Additions to the History of Gloucester* includes a period entry about the 1755 earthquake that states that the earthquake "shattered a great many chimneys in this town and in other towns." Similarly, *History of the Town of Hampton, New Hampshire*, published in 1893, has a citation from a contemporary record that reads, "several chimneys in this town were thrown down."

Farther northeast, along the coast in southern Maine, the earthquake shaking apparently was comparable in strength to that experienced in the towns of northeastern Massachusetts. The 1931 *History of York, Maine*, volume 1, cited a report by C. E. Banks of the local effects of the earthquake in York. In part this report reads, "Sleepers were awakened by violent rocking of beds, the falling of bricks from chimneys, pewter platters tumbling from the dressers, and the creaking of timbers as houses swayed with the vibrations of the quake ... chimneys bore the greatest injuries being generally broken at the roof hue and otherwise twisted out of position. The Ingraham brick house was badly shaken up, bricks being loosened and cracks in the walls started."

According to Rev. T. Smith of Portland, Maine, that city also sustained damage due to the earthquake shaking. He wrote in his diary that the earthquake "threw down near one-hundred bricks of our chimney, and did the same to many other chimneys in town."

South of Boston, the area that experienced damage may have extended into Rhode Island. A period entry in the diary of J. Arnold of Exeter, Rhode Island, includes a statement about "a very severe shock of an earthquake, to such a degree as to shake the top of chimneys down." Unfortunately, it is not clear from this entry as to whether the chimney damage was local in Exeter or was at some other locality, such as Boston. West of Boston, an entry in the diary of Seth Metcalf of Worcester, Massachusetts, reads,

*Remarks Upon the Year*
*November the 18 1755*
*About four in the morning there was A Very Surprising Shock of an Earthquake which was so Exceeding hard that it Shook Down the Tops of Chimneys and Steples to metenhouses.*

An entry for 1755 in the journal of an anonymous author from the town of Northampton, Massachusetts, mentions the effects of the earthquake in the following way: "The earthquake of 1755 was sensible felt in [Northampton], the tops of several chimneys were thrown down, & things were jarred from the shelves in cupboards, etc. Mrs. K said bricks tumbled from the chimney of her father's house."

The *Boston Gazette or Country Journal* of December 1, 1755, includes a report from New Haven, Connecticut, dated November 22 that describes the earthquake shaking and goes on to say that "many Tops of Chimnies were thrown down; but by the gracious Interposition of Divine Goodness, no considerable Damage was done."

This report is not clear about whether it is describing damage to the chimneys in New Haven or whether this is a general statement of the kinds and amount of damage experienced more widely throughout New England.

Taken together, the contemporary reports suggest that a widespread area experienced structural damage, primarily to chimneys, in the 1755 earthquake. That area appears to have extended from Rhode Island to Portland, Maine, and perhaps as far west as Northampton, Massachusetts, and New Haven, Connecticut. This damage area is quite vast compared to that of the 1727 earthquake, and in fact it is the largest damage area of any earthquake to date that has been centered in New England since 1700.

## FELT AREA OF THE 1755 EARTHQUAKE

Damage due to the 1755 earthquake spread over a very large area compared to the area that was damaged in the "great earthquake" of 1727. The area over which the 1755 earthquake was felt also greatly exceeded that of the 1727 event. In New York City many people were awakened by the earthquake, although no damage was reported. The *New York Mercury* edition of November 24, 1755, indicated that it received reports of the earthquake being felt in many places, with Oyster Bay, Newton, Jamaica, and Flushing on Long Island specifically being mentioned in the article. The earthquake also was felt in Philadelphia and in New Jersey, again with no damage.

In Annapolis, Maryland, the November 20, 1755, issue of the *Maryland Gazette* reported that "we had a Shock of an Earthquake, which was very sensibly felt by a great Number of People in Town, and round about it; and we have heard of its being felt in Prince George's county in many Parts, and on the Eastern Shore; . . . we have not heard of any Damage done by it."

According to the diary of a Dr. Holyoke, cited in a later history of Salem, Massachusetts, the earthquake was felt as far southwest as Winyah, South Carolina.

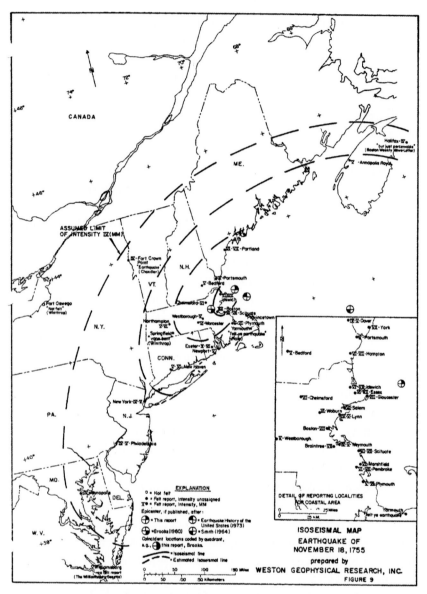

Map showing estimated locations and intensity VII, VI, V, and IV isoseismals (away from the epicenter, respectively) for the 1755 earthquake FIGURE FROM WESTON GEOPHYSICAL CORP., 1976

The earthquake was apparently felt across a wide area of Maritime Canada. The *Boston Weekly News-Letter* included a letter of January 19, 1756, that reads, "We hear from Nova Scotia, that the Earthquake on the 18th of November was felt at Annapolis Royal, and at Halifax, tho' but just perceivable in the last mentioned place."

Professor Winthrop, in his 1757 report to the Philosophical Society, added more information about the felt extent in this part of Canada:

*For the other limit toward the N.E. we are informed, that the earthquake was felt at Annapolis Royal in Nova Scotia, though in a much less degree than with us. It shook off a few bricks from the tops of some chimnies, but was not perceived by vessels on the water. And a letter from Halifax says, "The earthquake, which happened in the W. extended itself to this place, tho' scarcely perceived here." But it was not at all felt by our army, which lay encamped at Seganecto, about 100 miles N. from Halifax. Thus Halifax seems to have been very near the N.E. limit.*

It is difficult to reconcile the report of some minor chimney damage with the low level of ground shaking that apparently was experienced in Nova Scotia.

Several different sources indicate that ships at sea reported feeling the earthquake. As noted above, ships at sail as well as those in Boston Harbor reported experiencing the earthquake shock, and this is confirmed by entries in several ships' logs from this time period. The *Boston Gazette or Country Journal* edition of November 24, 1755, included an account from a ship captain that reads, "By a Person which came in Capt. Burnam, who arrived at Marblehead from Cadiz last Week, we learn that they felt the above Shock 70 Leagues E of Cape Ann, at ½ past 4, but concluded that they ran foul of a Wreck, or got upon a Bar, but on throwing over the Lead, found they could not sound in 50 Fathom of Water." A distance of 70 leagues corresponds to about 245 miles (390 kilometers), which means that the earthquake could be felt well east of the Massachusetts coast.

To the west the felt limit extended to the western shores of Lake Champlain and Lake George. Professor Winthrop, in his Philosophical Society report, stated that the earthquake was felt to a small degree by a contingent of the U.S. Army at Lake George in New York but that it was not felt at a British fort at Lake Oswego on the eastern shore of Lake Ontario.

Professor Winthrop's paper in the *Philosophical Transactions* mentions a report of the earthquake having agitated water at St. Martin in the Caribbean, and from that he concludes that the earthquake extended as far as 1,900 miles from the earthquake center. The St. Martin report is discussed in more detail later in the section on the possibility that this earthquake generated a tsunami that was experienced in the Caribbean.

## SOIL LIQUEFACTION AND GROUNDWATER CHANGES

In the 1727 earthquake several sandblows due to the strong seismic shaking erupted in the Newbury and Newburyport area, and they are well described in records from that time. Some reports of sandblows are also found in the descriptions of the effects of the 1755 earthquake. The November 24, 1755, edition of the *Boston Gazette or Country Journal* includes a statement that clearly refers to sandblows: "From other Parts of the Country we are informed, that several Eruptions were made in the Earth, which cast up several Quantities of Sand, of a fine Colour."

In his report to the Philosophical Society in 1757, Professor Winthrop provided a detailed description of the sandblows that formed due to the earthquake: "In some parts of the country, particularly at Pembroke and Scituate, about 25 miles S.E. from hence, there were several chasms or openings made in the earth, from some of which water has issued, and many cart-loads of a fine whitish sort of sand."

Rev. Charles Chauncy of Boston, in a description of the earthquake that he published in 1755 as part of a sermon that he delivered, provided many more details about the sandblows:

*In Pembroke, there were 4 or 5 chasms, or openings, made in the earth, from whence both water and sand were thrown out. In Situate, near the large dwelling house of Mr. Bailey, there was 7 openings of the ground, which still remain perceptible; one of them within 20 yards of the house, and the whole 7 within a few rods of it. From these have issued large quantities of water, and (at the lowest computation) 10 cart loads of a strange sort of earth, as fine as flower, and of a whiteish complexion. The house itself was most awfully shook; the chimney leveled with the roof; most of the ceiling fractured into small parts, and in many places separated from the sides of the rooms; a new case of drawers thrown down, and tho't to be irreparably shatter'd; Besides which 70 square feet of a firm cellar was burst from its former position, and another considerable part of it thrown to the ground.*

The cellar wall of Mr. Bailey's house might have been breached by a sandblow that erupted into the cellar, something that has been observed in recent earthquakes in other parts of the world. Jonathan Mayhew of Boston also provided a contemporary discourse on the liquefaction effects at Pembroke and Scituate, as well as a report on some ground deformation on Cape Cod and the formation of a chasm at Newington, New Hampshire, "of 60 rods in length and near 2 feet in bredth." Mayhew later published a correction to say that features that he reported in Pembroke were, in fact, features that had formed in Scituate. His correction also stated that the reported ground deformation effects on Cape Cod and at Newington, New Hampshire, were without foundation. Professor Winthrop concurred that the report of a long chasm in New Hampshire was a mistaken report.

The details in Professor Winthrop's and Reverend Chauncey's descriptions are so accurate that they could appear in a science textbook even today. Because sandblows only form where there is strong earthquake shaking above some known threshold, the facts that the reported sandblows were in towns south of Boston and there was much damage reported from Boston and towns to its north show that there clearly was very strong earthquake shaking that spread over a very wide area. Unfortunately, modern attempts to find the liquefaction features near the Bailey house have not located the exact features described in the Chauncey description. Scientists today would like to find and study those features both to learn more about the strength of the 1755 earthquake shaking and to search for any evidence of older sandblows that would indicate earlier strong earthquakes in the area.

One type of soil liquefaction effect is lateral spreading, where soil slides sideways down very gentle slopes due to a water-saturated sand layer beneath the surface soil. Although there is no direct evidence of lateral spreading due to the 1755 earthquake, there is some indirect evidence that some lateral spreading may have taken place in Boston. In his account of the earthquake and its effects, T. Prince wrote in a manuscript shortly after the earthquake, "I observed the tops of many chimneys demolished, others cracked and much damaged, Birches, Tiles and States scattered in the Streets, and large Quantities of Morter and Rubbish almost everywhere spread, especially in the streets near the Dock, and Alleys between the Warehouses, where most damage seemed to have been done; and several houses have suffered by large Cracks and Breaches to the Foundations."

The report of John Hyde of Boston cited earlier in this chapter adds one important detail about the damaged structures in Boston, namely that "especially on the low loose ground, made by encroachments on the harbour, the streets are almost covered with the bricks that have fallen." The phrase "encroachments on the harbour" apparently refers to man-made land atop what were the sands and silts of which the Boston peninsula had been composed when it was first settled by the English. The concentrated damage in these shoreline encroachments may have been due to some minor lateral spreading, which would explain the cracked foundations of the buildings there. The soft soils of the shoreline probably also enhanced the local earthquake shaking, which would have contributed additionally to the large amount of damage in this area.

The strong ground shaking apparently caused observable changes in the local groundwater system, something that was very important to the local inhabitants who relied on wells as their sources of drinking water. The letter of November 24, 1755, by Hyde includes a summary of the changes to the groundwater system that took place: "Some pumps are suddenly dried up; the convulsions of the earth having choked the springs that supplied them, as altered their course."

Mayhew, in a talk delivered at the West Meeting House in Boston on December 18, 1755, included the following statement about groundwater changes: "And springs, it is said, are opened in several parts of the country, which continue flowing; and some old ones dried up."

Other than water flowing out of the sandblows that were observed at Scituate, no specific localities with groundwater changes are given in the surviving records from the time of the earthquake.

## EARTHQUAKE DURATION AND EARTHQUAKE SOUNDS

Many reports about the 1755 earthquake mention the long duration of the earthquake shaking, often with an indication that the earthquake began with a noise that grew into the strongest ground vibrations. A report in *The Early History of New England* by Rev. Henry White gives a detailed description of the shaking:

> *It was first introduced with a noise like several coaches rattling over the pavements, or rather like a noise of many chart-loads of paving stones thrown down together. I was sensible it came from the north-west, and that side of my house felt concussion. The first motion was a strong pulsation, which threw my house upwards; immediately after, a tremor succeeded, which half a minute abated a little, but then instantly a quick vibration, with sudden jerks, followed; and this, by my best observation, held nearly a minute, before a second abatement, which went off gradually, in about half a minute more, so that the whole duration, from the first pulse to the end of the shock, seemed to be about two minutes: the greatest force, I apprehend, was about a minute after it began and had that vibration, with those sudden jerks continued one minute longer.*

John Hyde of Boston, whose description of the initial shaking and earthquake noise is given earlier in this chapter, also discussed the duration of the earthquake as perceived by himself as well as by others. In his letter of November 24, 1755, he wrote, "People, I perceive, differ very widely respecting the whole duration of the earthquake, from the first apparent symptoms of it, till it was entirely over, some supposing it to have been six or seven minutes, some four or five, and others scarce more than one. According to the best computation I am able to make, which is from what I did during the continuance of it, removing from one place to another, as related above, I think it could be but little more, and certainly no much less, than two minutes."

This estimate of the duration of the earthquake shaking is very much in keeping with other large earthquakes experienced in northeastern North America.

The *Boston Weekly News-Letter* of November 20, 1755, has a description of the earthquake sounds and earthquake shaking as experienced by those who were outdoors at the time of the shock. This account reads, "It is said by some People who were at that Time travelling on the Roads, ... they heard the Noise of its approach a short Time before the Shock came, and when it did come, the Ground under them rose and fell like the waves, and that the Course of it was from about N.W. to S.E. and continued about two minutes."

James Freeman of Boston, in his diary from the time period, wrote about feeling the earthquake, "At 1st a rumbling noise like low thunder, yt was immediately follow'd wh violent shaking of ye earth & buildings." He goes on to write that the ground shaking lasted from one to two minutes according to different persons. The captain of the H.M.S. *Hornet*, which was moored in Boston Harbor at the time of the event, estimated that the ship was shaken for about two minutes. The Reverend Ebenezer Parkman of Westborough, Massachusetts, who also had felt the 1727 earthquake, compared the two earthquakes: "The shock seems to me to be as great and to last about as long as the great Earthquake October 29, 1727, but the manner of Shaking I think is different — That more horizontal, this partly vertical."

A. Thomas of Marshfield, Massachusetts, recorded his account of the earthquake in his family Bible. He compared the noise of the earthquake to the roaring of the sea, and he estimated that the earthquake shaking lasted "by all the calculation that I can make about one minute and a half, & then we seemed to think it was going off, but ye repeated shock was more terrible." Thomas thought that the earthquake was dying away before it came with the strongest force of the entire shock.

This behavior of the earthquake is also well documented in the 1757 report by Professor Winthrop to the Philosophical Society, in which he attested,

*The night, in which this earthquake happened, was perfectly calm and serene. . . . The earthquake began with a roaring noise in the N.W. like thunder at a distance; and this grew fiercer, as the earthquake drew nearer; which was almost a minute in coming to this place, as near as I can collect from one of my neighbours, who was then on the road in this town. He tells me, that, as soon as he heard the noise, he stopt, knowing that it was an earthquake, and waiting for it; and he reckoned he had stood still about 2', when the noise seemed to overtake him, and the earth began to tremble under him. . . . By his account, as well as that of others, the first motion of the earth was what may be called a pulse, or rather an undulation; and resembled (to use his own comparison) that of a long rolling, swelling sea; and the swell was so great, that he was obliged to run and catch hold of something, to prevent being thrown down. . . . This sort of motion, after having continued, as has been con-jectured, about a minute, abated a little; so that I, who was just then waked, and, I suppose, most others, imagined, that the height of the shock was past. But instantly, without a moment's intermission, the shock came on with redoubled noise and violence; though the species of it was altered to a tremor, or quick horizontal vibratory motion, with sudden jerks and wrenches. . . . When this had continued about 2', it began to abate, and gradually kept decreasing, as if it would be soon over: however, before it had quite ceased, there was a little revival of the trembling and noise, though no-ways comparable to what had been before: but this presently decreased, till all, by degrees, became still and quiet. Thus ended the great shock.*

Professor Winthrop goes on to discuss estimates of the total duration of the earthquake shaking. He notes that the estimates ranged from one minute to seven minutes, with most estimating two or three minutes. His own best guess is that the earthquake shaking that he experienced lasted about four to four and a half minutes.

Estimates of the duration of the ground shaking at localities in other parts of the region are similar to those from Boston. E. Stilles wrote in his diary in Newport, Rhode Island, that the earthquake lasted two minutes. In *The History of the Late Province of New York from Its Discovery to the Appointment of Governor Colden in 1762*, a contemporary report states, "About two minutes after four in the morning, a rumbling noise was succeeded by jarring vibrations for four or five minutes. The shocks appeared to be not undualatory but horizontal."

The report goes on to state that there was no damage in New York City. C. Colden of New York City, in a letter dated December 9, 1755, wrote about the earthquake sound, "I plainly heard the noise like that of carts on pavements, going to the eastward, and now and then a noise like the explosion of a great gun at a distance."

The earthquake was also experienced quite noticeably at Philadelphia, Pennsylvania. A letter by an anonymous author in Philadelphia to Mr. Peter Collinson, dated December 1, 1755, indicates that the earthquake was not heard in Philadelphia but was felt quite distinctly there. The letter includes the sentence, "Some people think they felt its continuance five or six minutes, but I think it did not exceed two, nor was it less." The *Pennsylvania Journal and Weekly Advertiser* of November 20, 1755, mentions a "severe Shock of an Earthquake, which lasted nearly two minutes." The November 27, 1755, edition of this same newspaper reported that the earthquake was felt in New York for three minutes, but it caused no damage there.

## AFTERSHOCKS

Many of the surviving accounts of the 1755 earthquake mention aftershocks that were felt, although dates and times of only a few of the aftershocks are given. The account of John Hyde mentions a smaller shock about an hour and ten minutes after the mainshock, and Professor Winthrop agrees, noting that this later event, "though comparatively small, was generally perceived, both as to its noise and trembling, by those who were awake." The *Boston Evening-Post* of November 24, 1755, put this aftershock at about three-quarters of an hour after the mainshock. He reports other aftershocks in 1755 on November 22 at 8:27 p.m. and on

December 19 at 10:00 p.m., which he judged to be the smallest of the aftershocks that were felt in Boston.

More aftershock activity was experienced by those in communities to the north of Boston than were felt in Boston itself. *The History of Ancient Newbury* by Joshua Coffin, published in 1845, cited the diary of Richard Kelley of Amesbury, Massachusetts, which describes the mainshock on November 18 and then adds, "There was a shock every day till the twenty-second." A later entry indicates "two or three shocks about 10 P.M." on December 19. A period manuscript entry by W. Bentley of Salem, Massachusetts, suggests that a total of five earthquakes were felt, although the time period of the events is not given. *History of York, Maine*, published in 1931, includes a period entry that states, "and for the next four days slight rumblings ensued." Some of these might have been felt by a few persons in Boston, because the November 24, 1755, issue of the *Boston Evening-Post* notes that "about three quarters of an Hour after the Amazing Shock, there was a fainter one, and some Persons imagine they have felt several since." *History of the Town of Hampton, New Hampshire*, published in 1893, includes a period report that reads, "Shocks were frequently felt during the next fortnight. The most considerable one occurred in the evening of Saturday of the same week, about half-past eight o'clock. One who experienced it, calls it 'a very great shock.'"

The Saturday evening aftershock noted at Hampton is clearly the one mentioned by John Hyde on November 22 that was felt in Boston. The period diary of C. Chauncy of Boston describes the three shocks that were felt in Boston through November 22. He then wrote, "These are all the shocks we have had in this town, tho' elsewhere they have been more numerous. In some places they have felt 5 or 6; in others 10 or 11; & in others still, at least 20."

Apparently, it was the residents from Salem, Massachusetts, to Hampton, New Hampshire, and to York, Maine, who felt the largest number of aftershocks during the first couple of weeks after the mainshock.

## EARTHQUAKE LIGHTS
The historical records contain only one report of possible earthquake lights associated with the mainshock, and this is a secondary source of

information. The single report comes from John Hyde, as it was also printed in the November 24, 1755, edition of the *Boston Gazette or Country Journal*. It reads, "Some persons likewise speak of observing a glimmering light at the beginning of the shock, which lasted for some time. But I have no remembrance of this, though I observed with care, and now endeavor to recollect whatever was remarkable respecting a phenomenon so unusual in this part of the world, and so justly terrible in all."

The earthquake took place in the early morning hours when few people were awake, but the weather was clear and calm, so those who were awake would be likely to have seen any earthquake lights that were visible. Hyde himself did not observe any light at the time of the earthquake, as he notes in his account. Professor Winthrop does not mention an earthquake light nor does any other firsthand account. Thus, the occurrence of earthquake lights at the time of this shock is possible but not confirmed by the historical accounts that are accessible today.

## ANIMAL BEHAVIOR

The primary historical sources that were written shortly after the earthquake occurred contain very few references to the reactions of animals to the earthquake. The *Boston Weekly News-Letter* of November 20, 1755, states that "Horses, Cattle, and other Creatures by their unusual Agitation and Noise" reacted to the earthquake. The 1931 *History of York, Maine*, contains a report from the time that talks about animals "neighing" and "the howling of dogs and the startled cockle of fowl" due to the earthquake. These descriptions are rather generic in nature. They do not specifically state when the animals started reacting relative to the time of the earthquake, nor do they explain where or how many animals reacted to the earthquake shaking.

The most remarkable animal reactions to the earthquake were observed by sailors at sea. The 1757 report by Professor Winthrop to the Philosophical Society contains the following description of the effect of the earthquake on fish at sea: "One very uncommon effect of this concussion is related by several of our seafaring men, that almost immediately after the earthquake, large numbers of fish of different sorts, both great and small, came up to the surface of the water, some dead, and others dying."

The November 24, 1755, issue of the *Boston Evening-Post* contains a somewhat more detailed description of the fish behavior: "A fishing Vessel being at Sea, about 17 Leagues from Land, during or immediately after the Shock, observed the Fish to come up to the Surface of the Water in vast Numbers."

In other parts of the world, dead fish have been reported on the sea surface following the occurrences of large undersea earthquakes. Thus, not only is the observation of dead fish following the 1755 shock consistent with observations of other undersea earthquakes, but also it implies that the epicenter of the 1755 earthquake probably was offshore.

## A POSSIBLE TSUNAMI?

According to the report to the Philosophical Society by Professor Winthrop, the November 18, 1775, earthquake that rocked New England and beyond caused a small tsunami that was reported from the island of St. Martin in the Caribbean. The account by Professor Winthrop reads,

> An account, which we have lately received from the West-Indies, agrees very well with the supposition, that our earthquake proceeded south-eastward. The account is, that "on the 18th of November, about two o'clock in the afternoon, the sea withdrew from the harbor of St. Martin's, leaving the vessels dry, and fish on the banks, where there used to be three or four fathom water; and continued out with a considerable time; so that the people retired to the high land, fearing the consequence of its return; and when it came in, it arose six feet higher than usual, so as to overflow the low lands. There was no shock felt at the above time." As this extraordinary motion of the sea happened about 9h after our great shock, it seems very likely to have been occasioned by the same convulsion of the earth.

Although this is a very convincing account of a tsunami that was experienced at St. Martin, the attribution of the source of the tsunami to the Massachusetts earthquake is puzzling because no tsunami was reported anywhere in New England or Nova Scotia due to the earthquake on November 18.

In 1968 in the *Bulletin of the Seismological Society of America,* an investigation of the St. Martin tsunami report by Dr. Robert Rothman provided a satisfactory alternative explanation of the Caribbean tsunami. Dr. Rothman found primary accounts that stated that the tsunami at St. Martin was observed on November 1, 1755, about 2:00 p.m. A tsunami was experienced at several islands in the Caribbean on the afternoon of November 1, and the source of this tsunami was the great Lisbon earthquake (magnitude about 8.5) of November 1, 1755. That earthquake generated a devastating tsunami along the coast of Portugal, and it was strong enough to have generated a tsunami that would have been prominent across the Atlantic Ocean. Apparently, Professor Winthrop was confused about the date of the Caribbean tsunami and mistakenly attributed it to the November 18 earthquake in New England when, in fact, it occurred on November 1 and was due to the great earthquake that took place along the Portuguese coast.

## MAGNITUDE AND POSSIBLE FAULT OF THE 1755 EARTHQUAKE

The magnitude of the 1755 earthquake has been estimated by different scientists based on the total estimated felt area of the earthquake, on the spatial area where there was damage due to the earthquake, and on the estimated distances from the earthquake epicenter where different levels of ground shaking were experienced. These studies have reported moment magnitude estimates for this earthquake anywhere between 5.6 and 6.6, with a best estimate of about 5.9–6.0. Although this is a moderate magnitude by worldwide standards, it is sufficiently large to have caused the extent and variety of damage that is described in the contemporary accounts from 1755.

Most early investigators of the 1755 earthquake put the location of the fault on which the earthquake took place either onshore near Boston or offshore east of Cape Ann. During recent decades an offshore location has been favored because it best explains the extent of the area where damage took place, from south of Boston, Massachusetts, to Portland, Maine, and because it explains the fish deaths that were reported following the earthquake. My favored epicenter for this earthquake is located about 25 miles (40 kilometers) east-northeast of Cape Ann in an area that has had more than 10 earthquakes during the past 40 or so years. The recent seismicity that is in this offshore region might be very late aftershocks of the 1755 earthquake. Unfortunately, because this earthquake likely was centered at an offshore location, it is not possible to carry out studies of the local surface geology to look for the fault on which this earthquake took place. For this reason there is little understanding of the potential of future strong earthquakes on the fault that slipped in the 1755 earthquake.

# CHAPTER 7

# 1791: The Earthquakes of Moodus, Connecticut

PERHAPS THE MOST STORIED EARTHQUAKES IN THE NEW ENGLAND region and even beyond are those that have been experienced at a place called Moodus, Connecticut. Moodus is a village that is part of the town of East Haddam and is situated about 25 miles south-southeast of Hartford. The name Moodus comes from the Algonquian word *Machetmadosset* or *Machitmoodus*, transliterated into English as *Machemoodus* or *Machimoodus*, all of which mean "Place of Noises" or "Place of Bad Noises." A local hill called Mount Tom is the place where the noises seem to be centered. The records from the colonists who settled the area contain numerous references to earth noises and tremors that have been experienced in the area of Mount Tom. The legends of the Moodus noises have a long and colorful history, and one place where those legends survive today is at the local high school, Nathan Hale-Ray, whose sports teams are known as the "Machimoodus Noises."

At the time of the coming of European settlers to this part of Connecticut, the Mount Tom area had been a gathering point of Native Americans of at least three Algonquian tribes: the Wagunks, the Mohegans, and the Nehantics. Members of the Pequot and Narragansett tribes were also said to have visited the area. What attracted the Native Americans to this place were the occasions when the local hill, Mount Tom, would speak with sounds that ranged from booms to cracks to pops. Next to Mount Tom is a hill with a small cave. Today this hill is called Cave Hill, and it is said to be a place where the sounds can be heard especially clearly.

According to one legend of the Wagunks, the sounds came from pitched battles between good and evil forces in the underground. Another legend of the local Native Americans is that the noises that emanated from the earth were made by a god named Hobomoko, who sat on a sapphire throne in the earth and issued the sounds to communicate his demands to the people who lived in the area. The Wagunks based a religion on the noises, and medicine men of the tribe would listen to the varied sounds that came from the earth and interpret them for the local peoples. When the hill spoke, powwows would be held among the medicine men, chiefs, and others of the local tribes to decide what kind of offering or sacrifice was needed to appease the angry god who lived below. The Mount Tom area was a place where the Native Americans set aside all conflict due to their respect of the sacredness of the ground below which Hobomoko lived.

New legends about the Moodus noises arose after the first Europeans settled the East Haddam area in about 1685. By the year 1700 about 30 families had established homesteads at East Haddam. At the confluence of the small Salmon River with the much larger Connecticut River, the area was a natural place for permanent settlement. The first written reference to the Moodus noises dates from the year 1702. The earliest detailed account of the noises was written in a letter to a friend in Boston by the Reverend Stephen Hosmer of East Haddam. In the letter, which is dated August 13, 1729, and transcribed in the 1906 book entitled *Historic Towns of the Connecticut River Valley*, Reverend Hosmer wrote,

*As to earthquakes, I have something considerable and awful to tell you. Earthquakes have been here, as has been observed for more than thirty years. I have been informed that in this place, before the English settlements, there were great numbers of Indian inhabitants, and that it was a place of extraordinary pawaws, or in short, that it was a place where the Indians drove a prodigious trade in worshipping the devil. Also I was informed, that many years past, an old Indian was asked the reason of the noises in this place, to which he replied, that "the Indians' God was very angry that the Englishman's God was come there." Now, whether there be anything diabolical in these things, I know not; but this I know, that God Almighty is to be seen and trembled at, in what has been often heard among us. Whether it be fire or air distressed in the caverns of the earth, cannot be known; for there is no eruption, no explosion perceptible, but by sounds and tremors, which sometimes are very fearful and dreadful. I have myself, heard eight or ten sounds successively, and imitating small arms, in the space of five minutes. I have, I suppose, heard several hundred of them within twenty years; some more, some less terrible. Sometimes we have heard them almost every day, and great numbers of them in the space of a year. Oftentimes I have observed them to be coming down from the north, imitating slow thunder, until the sound came near, or right under, and then there seemed to be a breaking, like the noise of a cannon shot, or severe thunder, which shakes the houses and all that is in them. They have in a manner ceased since the great earthquake. As I remember, there have been but two heard since that time and these but moderate.*

In this letter the great earthquake is the one that struck Newbury, Massachusetts, in 1727 and was strongly felt in central Connecticut. Reverend Hosmer and the inhabitants of East Haddam likely also felt a few of the aftershocks of the 1727 earthquake. However, many of the events mentioned in this letter clearly describe seismic shocks of a very local origin and not simply the dispersed seismic waves from some distant earthquake source. It is also clear from this letter that the Moodus noises were a frequent occurrence during this time period and that the European colonists must have been experiencing them right from the beginning of their settlement in this area.

Another description of the Moodus noises was written in 1831 or 1832 by an unknown source and is also transcribed in *Historic Towns of the Connecticut River Valley*. It reads,

*The awful noises about which Mr. Hosmer gave an account continue to the present time. The effects they produce are various as the intermediate degrees between the roar of a cannon and the noise of a pistol. The concussions of the earth, made at the same time, are as much diversified*

*as the sounds in the air. The shock they give to a dwelling house, is the same as the falling of logs on the floor. But when they are so violent as to be felt in the adjacent towns, they are called earthquakes. During my residence here, which has been almost thirty-six years, I have invariably observed that an account has been published in the newspapers, of a small shock of earthquake, in New London and Hartford. Nor do I believe, in all that period, there has been any account published of an earthquake in Connecticut, which has not been far more violent here than in any other place.*

The residents of the area who were of European descent were almost invariably Christians, and so they would not have accepted the explanations of the Native Americans about the source of the sounds. Rather, they developed their own theories to explain the strange auditory and vibratory emanations from the earth. One theory to explain the noises was proposed by a Dr. Steele, an Englishman who became acquainted with the phenomenon. Dr. Steele claimed that the noises were emanating from a large carbuncle that was within the earth somewhere beneath Mount Tom. The carbuncle was supposed to be a white stone fossil that glowed in the dark. Dr. Steele also claimed that he had a method to remove the carbuncle from the earth. About 1765 he came to the Moodus area, where he obtained a blacksmith shop for his work. To avert prying eyes, he boarded up the windows and closed all holes through which one might look into the shop. He reportedly worked at night, with evidence of fires and forging coming from the shop. Eventually he emerged to announce that he had indeed removed the great carbuncle, although he had also discovered several smaller carbuncles that he could not remove. He felt that the smaller carbuncles would cause some small noises but that he had removed the source of the loudest noises and strongest shakes. With that he left the Moodus area for England, allegedly taking the great carbuncle with him. The time period following Dr. Steele's departure was marked by only a few episodes of Moodus noises, and none was as violent as those that had been experienced previously. For this reason some of the local people came to regard Dr. Steele as a wizard who had indeed arrested the Moodus noises, while others thought him a person who had communicated with the devil. Sadly for Dr. Steele, he lost his life when his ship sank in the Atlantic, taking him and the mysterious carbuncle to the bottom of the ocean. Mr. J. G. C. Brainard, the editor of the *Hartford Mirror* at the time, published in his newspaper a long poem commemorating the appearance and then disappearance of Dr. Steele and of his work at Moodus.

Many of the people who lived in the Moodus area were convinced that there was some connection between the earthquakes and the cave on Cave Hill. One local claimed that the cave ran all the way to Long Island Sound to the south. The noises were sounds of the wind and tidal flows through this long subterranean passage. Another local argued that the cave hosted underground gases and minerals that sometimes combined explosively to produce the sounds from beneath the earth. The noises generally seem to come from the Cave Hill/Mount Tom area, and so it has been common for the locals to somehow connect the local cave to the sounds and vibrations that have come from the earth.

One legend about the Moodus noises was published in 1896 by Charles Skinner in a book entitled *Myths and Legends of Our Own Land*. It was a combination of the earlier legends of the Native Americans and the fascination of witchcraft by the colonial settlers. The story is that a group of witches from Haddam who practiced black magic clashed with a group of witches from Moodus who practiced white magic in the cave beneath Cave Hill. The cave was lit by the light of a large carbuncle that was hanging from the ceiling. Also in the cave was a king called Machimoddi, perhaps a personification of Satan himself, who ruled the cave from a solid sapphire throne. To stop the witches from fighting, the king would raise his wand and extinguish the light of the carbuncle. This would cause peals of thunder to rock the chambers and expel the witches out into the sky. Needless to say, this legend managed to incorporate the elements of almost all the earlier fanciful stories to explain the Moodus noises.

## EARTHQUAKES AS THE CAUSE OF THE MOODUS NOISES

Although the legends and myths about the Moodus noises have generally invoked supernatural explanations for the sounds that are heard and the vibrations that are felt, there also has been a longstanding thought that the Moodus phenomena are somehow connected with natural earthquake activity in the earth. Reverend Hosmer first posed this possibility in 1729, and written reports since then have compared the Moodus noises and shakes to earthquakes that have occurred in other parts of the region.

An article in the July to December 1853 issue of *National Magazine*, volume III, was entitled "'Moodus Noises;' or, Connecticut Earthquakes." This article described the history of the Moodus noises as experienced by the residents of the area, with a focus on the experiences during the 18th and 19th centuries to the time that the magazine article was written. In 1897 the journal *Science* published a report about a recent outbreak of the Moodus events that states, "There was a sound like a clap of thunder, followed for some two hours by a roar like the echoes of a distant cataract. A day later there was a crashing sound like heavy muffled thunder, and a roar not unlike the wind in a tempest. The ground was shaken, causing houses to tremble and the crockery to rattle, 'as though in an earthquake.'"

Throughout the 20th century it was the common practice of those who compiled catalogs of the earthquakes in the New England area to include the shakes that originated from the Moodus area as earthquakes. Not every boom and shock is listed, but rather the common practice has been to include those earthquakes that were felt in multiple communities around the Moodus area, thus giving good confirmation that an earthquake had indeed taken place.

The final scientific confirmation that connected the mysterious Moodus noises to natural earthquake activity was obtained in the 1980s. In the mid-1970s Weston Observatory of Boston College had installed six seismic stations around Mount Tom in order to look for small earthquakes in the Moodus area. This microearthquake monitoring network was funded to learn more about the local seismic hazard to a nearby nuclear power plant that was operating across the Connecticut River from Moodus at East Haddam. Seismic data from the Moodus network was used to detect local Moodus earthquake activity and to locate the earthquakes that were detected in order to relate those earthquakes to local faults that had previously been mapped in the vicinity of Moodus.

During the first couple of years that the Moodus microearthquake network was operating, nothing was recorded from the local area.

However, that changed in August 1981 when the first significant swarm of microearthquakes began. Over a span of four months, Weston Observatory located 177 earthquakes and in addition detected several hundred microearthquakes (very small earthquakes) that were too small to be located. The largest earthquake in this swarm had a magnitude of 2.1. Local residents near the epicenters reported that they heard some booming noises around the times of the events and that they felt the largest of the events. In June 1982 a second swarm of microearthquakes began. Once again local residents reported hearing noises from the earth and sometimes feeling vibrations of the ground associated with the louder of the noises. Weston Observatory was detecting many microearthquakes on its Moodus seismic network and was able to locate 120 of these events, the largest of which had a magnitude of 2.9.

In order to correlate the noises heard by the residents with the microearthquakes detected by the seismic instruments, Weston Observatory asked several local residents to record the precise times when they heard the noises. The times reported by the residents matched up perfectly with the times that the seismic instruments recorded microearthquakes. The earthquakes were originating from beneath Mount Tom, and the seismologists soon learned that only the larger of the microearthquakes were being heard. The seismic instruments were detecting microearthquakes down to magnitude -2, but only those events above about magnitude -1 were being heard by the local residents. For events above magnitude 0, local residents reported feeling ground vibrations along with hearing the earthquake sounds.

During the 1982 swarm there was a resident named Cathy Wilson who lived on Mount Tom in a house that was almost exactly over the spot in the earth from which the earthquakes were originating. Wilson kept a very detailed log of when she heard the noises, and the dates and times when she reported events matched up perfectly with the earthquakes detected by the Weston Observatory seismic instruments. Wilson further helped the scientific inquiry by spending some hours one afternoon in her yard with a cassette tape recorder, on which she recorded a number of the Moodus noises. While she was in her yard, a magnitude 2.3 event took place, and the boom from that earthquake was clearly picked up by the tape recorder. At times on the tape, she mentions popping and cracking sounds that she was hearing, but those sounds cannot be heard on the tape. At other times the sounds do register on the tape and sound like a boom or distant thunder. Weston Observatory scientists also heard some of the Moodus noises on a later day when they installed a portable seismographic instrument at the Wilson house. The descriptions of the earthquake noises that were provided by residents from the Moodus area in the 1980s were virtually identical to those that had been written during the previous centuries.

The 1982 swarm lasted two months and again comprised several hundred microearthquakes. Another Moodus earthquake swarm took place from February to June 1986 and had over 100 detected events. A fourth earthquake swarm occurred from September 1987 to April 1988. Between the end of the 1982 swarm (in July of that year) and the beginning of the next swarm in June 1986, only a few microearthquakes from the Mount Tom area were detected by the Weston Observatory seismographic instruments. In all of the swarms, the times that the local residents reported noises were invariably confirmed as small earthquakes by the seismic instrumentation. Higher-pitched sounds, described as "cracks," "pops," or "pistol shots," were associated with mircoearthquakes below about magnitude 0, whereas events that were described as "booms" or "distant thunder" corresponded to earthquakes above that magnitude. Earthquakes above about magnitude 1.0 usually were compared to underground explosions or claps of loud thunder and often had brief ground shaking in addition to the noise.

Scientific studies of the seismic data explain many of the details of the Moodus noises and microearthquakes. The Moodus microearthquakes of the 1980s originated from a very small volume at a depth of about 0.5 mile (0.8 kilometer) to 0.8 mile (1.3 kilometers) below Mount Tom and only about 500 yards (457 meters) in lateral extent. Because the earthquakes occur so close to the surface of the earth, the high-pitched cracking of the rock that takes places in the smaller earthquakes is able to propagate as seismic waves upward to the surface of the earth with little absorption by the intervening rock. At the earth's surface the seismic waves convert to sound waves, thus giving rise to the Moodus "noises." The larger of the Moodus earthquakes are associated with larger cracks that produce lower-frequency sounds. This same principle works in musical instruments such as a piano, where the short strings produce the higher-pitched sounds (treble) and the longer strings produce lower-pitched sounds (bass). The cave on Cave Hill likely focuses the sounds coming from the earth below and is thus a place where the earthquake sounds can be heard especially clearly. Ironically, the Moodus earthquakes do not seem to align on a single fault; rather, they seem to originate from a rock volume that may be characterized by a number of small faults. In the Moodus swarms in the 1980s, there were many more microearthquakes with smaller magnitudes than there were events with larger magnitudes. This same pattern is seen in earthquake activity the world over, and it helps confirm that the Moodus seismicity is natural earthquake activity that is not unique to Moodus.

## THE 1791 MOODUS EARTHQUAKE

Although scientific evidence now confirms that the Moodus noises are nothing more than the audible sounds of small earthquakes beneath Mount Tom, there was one much larger earthquake of note that was probably centered in the Moodus area. On the evening of May 18, 1791, residents of the Moodus area were startled by a noise and shake that was much greater than anything they had experienced previously. N. H. Heck, in the *Earthquake History of the United States, Part I*, published in 1958, wrote, "1791. May 16. East Haddam, Connecticut. Two heavy shocks caused collapse of stone walls and chimneys. Latched doors were thrown open. A fissure several rods long appeared in the ground, and rocks weighing several tons were moved. At Killingsworth, fish were observed leaping out of the water. Shock was felt from Boston to New York. About 30 lighter shocks followed during the night."

This simple summary entry describes an earthquake that apparently was destructive in the East Haddam area. Unfortunately, there are only a few surviving accounts of this earthquake, and there are just a couple of accounts from the time period of the earthquake that actually mention any damage from it. One account is contained in a letter written in 1815 by Rev. Henry Chapman of East Haddam to Benjamin Silliman, which

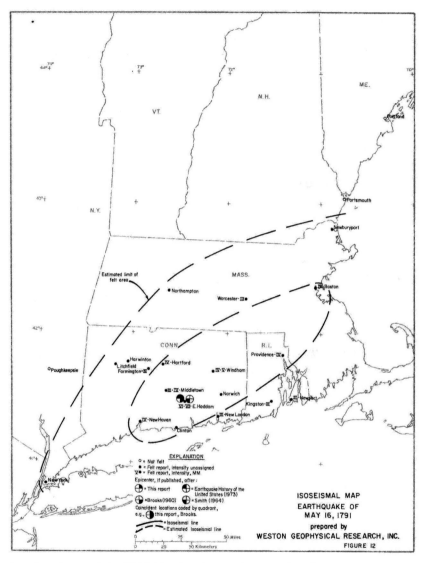

Isoseismal map of the 1791 Moodus, Connecticut, earthquake FIGURE FROM
WESTON GEOPHYSICAL CORP., 1976

is reproduced in a journal written by Silliman. Information on the 1791 earthquake came from the register of a local, unnamed gentleman from the East Haddam area. Reverend Chapman indicates that the gentleman had kept the register for about 30 years (i.e., from about 1785 to 1815). In his letter to Silliman, Reverend Chapman cites the following passage from the register:

*It began at 8 o'clock, P. M., with two very heavy shocks in quick succession. The first was the most powerful; the earth appeared to undergo very violent convulsions. The stone walls were thrown down, chimneys were untopped, doors which were latched were thrown open and a fissure in the ground of several rods in extent was discovered. Thirty lighter ones succeeded in a short time and upwards of one hundred were counted in the course of the night.*

*The shock was felt at a great distance. It was so severe at Killingsworth [now Clinton] about twenty miles distant, that a Captain Benedict who was walking the deck of his vessel, then lying in the harbor at that place, observed the fish to leap out of the water in every direction as far as his eyes could reach.*

*The atmosphere was perfectly clear and pleasant and the moon, which was near its full, shone remarkably bright. On the night of the 17th six more were observed. The atmosphere was still clear and warm.*

Silliman reproduced in his journal a similar description of the earthquake that was contained in a letter to Benjamin Trumbull written about 1800. The book *A Statistical Account of Middlesex County*, written by D. D. Field and published in 1819, states that apertures and fissures in the earth were observed near the Moodus River Falls and that there were disturbances in the banks of the Salmon and Moodus Rivers following the earthquake.

The only other mention of damage due to the earthquake in contemporary accounts was contained in the June 1, 1791, edition of a Boston newspaper called the *Columbian Centinel*. This account reads,

*Connecticut*

*Windham, May 21. Last Monday evening, about half after ten o'clock, two shocks of an Earthquake were felt in this town. The first was very considerable; it was preceded by a very rumbling noise, like distant thunder, and appeared to come from the south-west; the shock greatly agitated the buildings in this place, but we cannot learn as any damage was sustained. At East Haddam, it is said to have been much heavier; insomuch that the tops of several chimnies were thrown to the ground. The second shock happened a few minutes after the first, but was not near so heavy.*

This account, like many others from the time, put the earthquake at about 10:30 p.m. rather than 8:00 p.m. as contained in the register cited by Reverend Chapman. There is some confusion in the surviving records about the times of the two earthquakes that took place that evening.

Other newspapers from the time period mention the earthquake. The May 23, 1791, issue of the *American Mercury* published at Hartford, Connecticut, states that "on Monday evening last, about half after 10 o'clock two shocks of an Earthquake were felt in this town, and adjacent country — the air was very clear and serene at the time. The first shock was pretty severe, a few minutes before the other, and attended with a rumbling noise, like distant thunder, seemingly passing from the westward to the eastward."

At Boston the May 23, 1791, edition of the *Boston Gazette and Country Journal* reports "a considerable shock of an EARTHQUAKE" as being felt about 10:40 p.m. in that city as well as at "Worcester, Providence and Norwich." The May 20, 1791, edition of the *Herald of Freedom* newspaper in Boston called the earthquake "a slight shock" in that city. At Newburyport, Massachusetts, the *Essex Journal and New-Hampshire Packet* issue of May 25, 1791, contains a report about the earthquake in Connecticut and mentions that in New Haven, the shock "was so severe as to cause much noise among Pewter on the shelves." This newspaper does not mention the effects of the earthquake in Newburyport itself. There were also reports of the earthquake being felt in Rhode Island, New York City, and Albany, New York.

A few surviving accounts of the earthquake describe the duration of the ground shaking. The *Middlesex Gazette* of Middletown, Connecticut, edition that was published on May 21, 1791, included the following account of the earthquake from New Haven: "At about half past ten o'clock, on Monday evening last, the shock of an Earthquake was felt in this and the neighboring towns. It was preceeded by a rumbling sound, like that occasioned by the passing of a wheel-carriage. The tremor was violent, but continued only a few seconds . . . two shocks of an earthquake were felt. The first was severe and is judged to have continued about 12 seconds of time. The other was moderate, and of shorter duration."

Ezra Stiles, in a period diary written at Farmington, Connecticut, has the following entry: "16. At $8^h$ 25' just after getting into bed, happened an Earthquake of strong Concussion, but short in $Dur^a$ perhaps a quarter of a minute or rather not above ten seconds."

The *Connecticut Courant* issue of May 23, 1791, published at Hartford, contains a report of the earthquake: "Last Monday night about half past 10 o'clock, an earthquake was felt in this town. The shock was preceded and accompanied with a rattling rumbling noise usual on such occasions. The shock however followed the sound in a few seconds and was rather of the jarring than the waving kind. It lasted but a few, perhaps 8 to 10 seconds. After an interval of about 4 minutes, a second, but feeble shock was felt."

Unlike the stronger earthquakes described in other chapters in this book, the May 16, 1791, earthquake was neither as violent nor as long. The contemporary accounts indicate that the shaking in the 1791 event lasted only about 10 to 15 seconds and that the farthest extent of the felt ground shaking was Boston to the northeast and New York City to the southwest. As is typical for earthquakes in the New England region, the shock was preceded and accompanied by sounds like carriages on rough roads or like a rumbling thunder. The strength of the ground shaking weakened noticeably away from the epicenter. There was a weaker shock a few minutes later, and the people living at Mount Tom apparently heard a number of earthquake noises throughout the night following the earthquake.

## The Location and Magnitude of the 1791 Moodus Earthquake

The epicenter of the 1791 earthquake was clearly in Connecticut, as most of the felt reports came from that state and only mild shaking apparently took place outside of Connecticut. Furthermore, the only reports of ground shaking strong enough to move objects came from the Moodus area, and the historical accounts also suggest that a swarm of small earthquakes that could have been foreshocks and aftershocks took place at Moodus around the time of this large shock. Based on this evidence, the epicenter of the 1791 earthquake must have been at or very near Moodus.

The limited felt area of the 1791 earthquake constrains the magnitude of this shock. Past seismological studies have concluded that the magnitude of the 1791 earthquake based on its felt area was no more than about 4.5 to 5.0, with the more likely magnitude being somewhere at the lower end of this range. This presents something of a problem because an earthquake of magnitude 4.5 or so is not thought to be strong enough to damage stone fences or break chimneys. Furthermore, the limited area where the damage was reported is a strong indication that the earthquake was no larger than magnitude 5.0. Thus, there is some difficulty reconciling the reported damage effects of the earthquake with its probable magnitude. Even though this is the smallest of the earthquakes that are described in detail in this book, its apparent association with the long-active Moodus area makes it a most interesting seismic event.

CHAPTER 8

# 1884: An Earthquake at New York City

WHEREAS THE STRONG EARTHQUAKES OF THE 17TH AND 18TH CENTU-
ries in northeastern North America had been damaging in parts of New
England or in Canada, with few exceptions New York City received only
mild shaking from these events, with no damage. That New York was
mostly spared the ravages of very strong earthquake ground shaking in its
early history was a blessing because during this time period the city and
its surrounding area were growing into the most populated and richest
urban metropolis in the United States. New York experienced a number
of local earthquakes throughout its earlier years that were only minor
shakes with no damage. The only exception to this was one earthquake, on
December 19, 1737, that was strong enough to damage some chimneys
in the city.

Like Montreal in 1732 and Boston in 1755, it was on August 10,
1884, that New Yorkers took their turn to experience a damaging earthquake. The experience was a new one to most who lived in the city. A
story from the August 11, 1884, edition of the *New York Times* encap-
sulated the reactions of many locals: "An amusing incident happened at
the Occidental Hotel, at the Bowery and Broome-street. A number of
persons were dining in the restaurant. The building all of a sudden began
to shake until the chandeliers swayed to and fro. People left off eating
and looked at the chandeliers and then at each other in astonishment
until a middle-aged, well-dressed man got up and hastily put his hat on,
declaring at the same time in a loud voice: 'That's an earthquake. I'm from
California, and I know it.'"

All over the city, people were startled and confused by the sudden unsteadiness of the ground due to the earthquake shaking. The August 11, 1884, issue of the *New York Times* described it this way:

> *At 2:06:50 o'clock, by New-York time, when the clouds overhead were blackest, and the air below was moist and sticky, a sharp earthquake shock passed through the city, causing the most substantial buildings to quiver. The shock came suddenly, and with the least warning. Persons walking in the streets and wandering through the parks were suddenly startled by a low rumbling sound, apparently beneath their feet, which appeared like muffled thunder in the bowels of the earth, while the ground seemed to quiver gently, like the billowy motion of a great wave. Men stopped suddenly and listened with fear to the deep grumbling beneath them, and stood transfixed for what seemed at least five minutes to the more timid.*

Although this earthquake was far from catastrophic, it did cause some damage throughout the New York metropolitan area and even beyond. Even more so, it drove home the point to many New Yorkers that they were not immune to the possibility that a major earthquake could strike their city. The newspapers of the time provide a rich set of descriptions about the effects of the earthquake both far and wide.

## Damage to Structures in New York City and Nearby New Jersey Due to the Earthquake

In 1884 New York City was an urban center with many thousands of buildings, some founded on the hard rock of parts of Manhattan and some of the other boroughs and some founded on soft soils near the rivers and on Long Island. Variations throughout the city of the quality and type of building construction, combined with some sections of the city being more prone to amplifying the earthquake ground shaking than other sections of the city, meant that damage to buildings was scattered throughout the city. Indeed, most of the buildings in New York survived the earthquake shock with no damage.

As with all earthquakes from this time period and even today, the buildings that sustained the most significant damage were unreinforced masonry structures, typically made of bricks or stone cemented together by mortar with little or no other structural support. The most commonly damaged unreinforced masonry structures are brick chimneys, and that seems to have been the case in this earthquake as well. For example, the August 13, 1884, issue of the *New York Times* reported, "In Rossville, Staten Island, bricks were thrown off the chimneys of several houses."

For nearby Perth Amboy, New Jersey, the *New York Sun* of August 11, 1884, gave the following description of the damage there: "This afternoon chimneys were toppled over and dishes rattled in the closets. A heavy stone bridge over Englewood Creek was overthrown."

Two chimneys were reported wrecked at Matawan, New Jersey, just south of Perth Amboy.

Other damage may or may not have been due to failures of weak masonry from structures. Both the *New York Sun* edition of August 11, 1884, and the *New York Times* edition of the same date contain a report that a stone was thrown to the ground from a church steeple by the earthquake shaking. The description of this event from the *Times* reads, "A large stone forming part of the steeple of the church at Seventh-Avenue and St. Johns Place, Brooklyn, fell to the ground with a crash, terrifying pedestrians who were promenading the streets in the neighborhood."

The *New York Sun* contains a description of damage to an old house that may not have been in good condition, although the construction type of the house is not given. The report states, "The top floor of 528 West Forty-third street fell in. It was an old-fashioned house. Nobody was hurt."

The August 12, 1884, issue of the *New York Times* indicated that "the walls of the Presbyterian Sunday-school at Jamaica were cracked in two places, the openings being from 1 to 2 inches in width and extending from the roof to the foundation."

This type of damage makes the most sense if the building suffered some differential settlement on different parts of its foundation. Another type of damage was reported in the *New York Sun*, which contains the information that at Red Bank, New Jersey, "some small buildings were moved from their foundations."

There were also a number of reports in the New York newspapers of nonstructural damage to buildings in New York City and nearby New Jersey due to this earthquake. For the most part these reports are concerned with broken windows or with cracks in plaster walls and ceilings. For example, windowpanes were broken at a synagogue at Hestor and Ludlow Streets in New York City and at Atlantic Highlands and Elizabeth in New Jersey. Cracks in plaster walls and ceilings were reported at several places, including in New York City at the Eldridge Street police station and at a house at 137 Lewis Street. A horse car on Avenue B near Fifth Street that was filled with passengers was reportedly thrown from its tracks. There also was much damage to the contents of buildings, primarily objects that were broken because they were thrown from shelves. This was especially true at hotels, where china and glassware broke when it fell to the floor. A number of mirrors were also reported broken due to the earthquake shaking. This was especially true at the seaside hotels in New Jersey along Sandy Hook Bay. Objects were reported thrown from shelves in Jersey City and Brooklyn, and a clock was reported stopped at Fire Island.

Finally, although not a report of damage, per se, the following account from the *New York Times* demonstrates the power of the ground shaking that was experienced on Coney Island: "The large two-ton safe in the office of the Manhattan Beach Hotel was moved about three inches along the floor, scraping the plaster off the wall against which it rested and denting the floor considerably. This house was shaken up to a considerable extent, but no actual damage resulted, nor, as far as could be learned, was there any damage done at any part of the island."

The *Times* stated that a safe at Paul Bauer's Hotel on Coney Island also was shifted by the ground shaking.

## Damage Outside of New York City and Nearby New Jersey Due to the Earthquake

Although the largest number of damage reports and the most severe damage came from New York City and nearby New Jersey, there were some reports of damage to structures away from this area. These reports were almost exclusively of damage to chimneys, and in many cases the chimneys might have been damaged due to a poor state of repair, and some of the reported damage may have been preexisting and not due to the earthquake. The New York City newspapers mention damage to chimneys in East Norwich, Brookeville, and Mount Vernon, New York; Newtown, Plainfield, and the Delaware River area of New Jersey; and Easton and Philadelphia, Pennsylvania. Almost all of these reports were for single chimneys in the towns. The chimney that was damaged in Philadelphia was described as "rickety" and therefore was probably susceptible to damage in even light earthquake shaking. In addition to these reports of chimney damage, at Greenpoint, New York, two brick buildings were claimed to have been separated by the earthquake shaking.

A few localities away from New York City and New Jersey reported other kinds of damage. At Hartford, Connecticut, windows were said to have been broken and plaster walls cracked. At Danbury, Connecticut, a bookcase was reported to have been knocked over by the earthquake shaking. Bottles were said to have been knocked from shelves in Trenton, New Jersey.

## Variations in the Strength of the Ground Shaking in New York City and Nearby New Jersey Due to the Earthquake

In addition to the reports of damage to buildings or their contents due to the earthquake shaking, the contemporary newspapers in the greater New York City area contain numerous descriptions of local variations in the strength of the earthquake ground shaking from place to place. For example, the August 11, 1884, edition of the *New York Times* stated in one article, "It was felt at its greatest strength, probably, along the New-Jersey and Long Island coast, but nowhere is any serious damage reported."

Another article in the same issue reported, "The shock seems to have been most severely felt in Brooklyn and the lower part of Manhattan Island, which confirms the theory of Gen. Jackson, that the earthquake came from the direction of the Narrows and passed a northeasterly course. In the large buildings down town the shock was most severely felt in this city."

Many of the reports from the Sandy Hook area of the New Jersey coast indicate that the earthquake shaking was quite severe there. The August 11 edition of the *New York Sun* reported, "The severest shock was reported from Seabrook, N.J., where the depot was shifted to one side, shaking up the contents and alarming the sole inmate."

That same edition also contained a report from Long Branch, New Jersey, that read, "Some persons who were bathing allege that they felt a sensation like a slight electric shock pass from head to foot. . . . In several places along the coast persons were made seasick by the shock."

The *New York Tribune* issue of August 11, 1884, provides some additional details concerning the apparent location of the earthquake epicenter based on the felt effects in the city: "As to the direction of the wave all seem to agree that it came from the south, but some think it was a little to the west of south. It passed upward toward the north, or north by east."

This same issue of the *Tribune* indicated regarding the vibrations on Manhattan that the "two ends of the Island felt them most severely." This edition of the *Tribune* reported that no one felt it along the East River but that along the North River the earthquake shaking was strong:

*Along the North River front the experience of the inhabitants was somewhat different. Along the lines of Greenwich and Washington sts. the shock was severely felt. People sitting at dinner in upper stories were rudely disturbed, and the contents of soup-bowls or coffee-cups were spilled over the table. On the made ground nearer the water-front, along West-st., the disturbance was either felt slightly or not at all. Superintendent Wiley at the buildings of the New-York Steam Heating Company, at Greenwich and Cortland sts., said that he felt no disturbance in the building, but that people came rushing to the place, thinking that there had been an explosion of the company's pipes, or that some heavy building had fallen.*

Both the *New York Sun* and the *New York Tribune* stated that the earthquake was felt especially severely at the West End of Manhattan. The August 11, 1884, issue of the *New York Sun* provided the following summary of the distribution of the strongest earthquake shaking on

Manhattan Island: "The bed rock on which Manhattan Island rests rises to the street level in many places in the upper part of the city, and in the houses whose foundation rests on the rock the shock was particularly forcible."

It was reported that the residents of Harlem were frightened by the earthquake, and Harlem is one of the city districts that is built largely on the bedrock of Manhattan. The earthquake was also said to have been felt in Yonkers, which is also on the bedrock north of Harlem. People on Randall's Island felt the shock lightly, and it was also reported felt on Blackwell Island, which is today Roosevelt Island. The "Hebrew quarter" of Manhattan around Ludlow and Essex Streets also shook strongly enough to frighten the local residents.

People who were out and about away from buildings in Central Park apparently were less likely to have noticed the earthquake. The *New York Sun* reported, "The people who had gone early to Central Park felt less shock than those who were indoors, but they were perhaps more frightened, as they had neither boilers nor elevators to which to attribute the phenomenon."

On the other hand, just west of Central Park the story seems to have been somewhat different. The *New York Tribune* stated, "A gentleman living on Seventy-third-st. west of the Central Park said that he was looking from the window at the moment of the earthquake, and people on the sidewalk seemed to reel like drunken men and clutch at the railings."

The *New York Times* reported that three ladies standing on 125th Street were thrown to the pavement by the earthquake, although they were not injured. In Manhattan the shock was felt at Broadway and Park Place but apparently was not noticed at Greenwich and Cortland. The Western Union office at Day and Broadway experienced the earthquake. The shock was reported felt at the Iron Steam Boat and Sea Beach ferry piers along the Manhattan waterfront. Across the water at Bergen Hill in New Jersey, the earthquake was said to have been "severe." On Governor's Island the shaking was felt strongly and awakened soldiers who were sleeping.

The news reports are rather striking about the variations in the felt effects of the earthquake on the various islands throughout the area. The strongest shaking appears to have originated in Raritan Bay or Sandy

Hook Bay somewhere between New York City and the beach areas of nearby New Jersey. The newspapers suggest that parts of Brooklyn were strongly shaken by the earthquake, particularly at Rockaway, Gowanus, the south side of Jamaica, Coney Island, and Bay Ridge, with pockets of local very strong shaking. The *New York Sun* reported that "at Sheepsbend Bay village the shock was more severe than on Coney Island." People who were out on the streets of Brooklyn felt the ground suddenly vibrate, and some reported that it felt like an "electric shock" that came from the ground. A baseball game in Brooklyn was suddenly abandoned due to fright at the earthquake shock. According to the *New York Tribune*, "The shock was perceived all along the hill or ridge running northeast from Greenwood to Prospect Park, which is known as South Brooklyn. This part of the city is not much built up and a part of it is heavily wooded, while in front of many houses in the principal street old forest trees are still preserved."

Brooklyn City Hall swayed noticeably and church bells spontaneously rang in the city due to the shaking. It was stated that people indoors felt the earthquake quite sensibly whereas people in the street barely perceived it at all. A *New York Times* article indicated that the earthquake was felt less strongly at Bath Beach. Another article in the *Times* indicated that the earthquake was felt more strongly on higher ground.

The shore areas of western Long Island felt the earthquake strongly. The *New York Sun* indicated that "along the Atlantic coast from Rockaway Beach, through Far Rockaway, Pearsall's, Jamaica and Long Beach the shock was unusually severe." Farther to the east on Long Island, the earthquake was less pronounced. Fire Island reported the earthquake as a slight shock. People who were on ships at sea near the city also felt the earthquake. The *New York Times* edition of August 12, 1884, included the following report from the captain of a ship at sea:

> *Capt. Strum, of the brig Alice, which arrived yesterday from Turk's Island, reports that the earthquake shock of Sunday afternoon was felt quite plainly on his vessel, although she was then about seven miles east of the Highlands. The Captain says that the shock occurred at 2:10 P.M., when he was below. He felt a heavy shock, accompanied by a*

*rumbling noise, and it seemed as if the vessel had struck a submerged wreck. The shock and rumble continued long enough to have passed over a wreck. The pumps were sounded, but the brig was not found to be leaking. The Captain did not know what to make of this strange experience. He thought it might possibly have been an earthquake, but, as the shock was severer than any before, he concluded that the Alice must have struck something. The members of his crew, who had all felt the shock, were of the same opinion at first. The Captains of several other vessels which arrived yesterday reported having felt the earthquake shock.*

There were ferries plying the waters of the area at the time of the earthquake. One newspaper report indicated that people on the ferries did not feel the earthquake, whereas another stated that the earthquake was felt mildly on the ferries. There also were some accounts of the surfaces of local water bodies showing the effects of the earthquake shaking. The *New York Sun* reported that the Hudson River at Yonkers was disturbed but not farther downstream at Manhattan. On the other hand, the *New York Tribune* stated that the waters of the Hudson River were ruffled by the earthquake, as was the surface of the Wallabout Canal in Brooklyn.

The local newspapers contain several reports of people being knocked from their feet by the earthquake shaking. A man living on 40th Street at Ninth Avenue reported that his wife was thrown from her feet by the shock. A woman in Jersey City stated that she had just lain down when the earthquake threw her from her bed. The shock also awoke a number of people who were sleeping at the time of the event.

The newspaper accounts all agree that people on the higher floors tended to feel the earthquake shaking more strongly than people on the ground floors. This is a common report in all earthquakes in past times as well as today. It occurs because a tall building acts like an inverted pendulum when shaken sideways by the earthquake ground motions, and sideways shaking is invariably the strongest in an earthquake. In an inverted pendulum the top moves a lot farther than the bottom when the bottom is shaken. All tall buildings are somewhat flexible, and so they bend a little when shaken at their base. This is how the inverted pendulum effect occurs and why the shaking increases on higher floors in such buildings. It is also the reason that tall buildings can be felt to sway a little in strong winds.

The behavior of the Brooklyn Bridge illustrates how different structures reacted to earthquake shaking. Discussing the Brooklyn Bridge, the *New York Tribune* stated, "The shock was not felt upon the Bridge, the policeman on duty said, but in the Bridge office and engine room it was severely felt." The bridge was said to have been crowded with people at the time of earthquake, but there was no panic, as the shock seemed to have passed unnoticed there.

## EFFECTS OUTSIDE THE GREATER NEW YORK CITY AREA AND TOTAL FELT AREA OF THE EARTHQUAKE

Although the most serious effects of the earthquake were reported from New York City and nearby parts of New Jersey, the earthquake was felt widely beyond the area that obviously was closest to the earthquake epicenter. Similar to what was seen in New York City itself, in some of these more far-flung areas, the shaking was said to be heavy, whereas in other areas it was reported as light. As already noted, the shock was quite noticeable in Philadelphia, Pennsylvania, and nearby Trenton, New Jersey. In Philadelphia, where a chimney was reportedly damaged, the Delaware River was said to have been disturbed by the earthquake shaking, as described in more detail later in this chapter. In Trenton the newspapers claim that bells were rung by the earthquake. Albany, New York, felt the shock, with greater effects on the west and south sides of the city. Persons there who were sleeping were said to have been awakened by the shock. Hartford, Connecticut, also experienced the earthquake rather strongly, with crockery rattled and door bells rung by the ground vibrations. In Providence, Rhode Island, it was reported that a child was thrown from a chair by the earthquake shaking. In Boston, Massachusetts, a person reported being awakened by the shock. It was reported from Boston that chandeliers swayed, radiators rattled, and some people experienced mild seasickness as the seismic waves passed through this city.

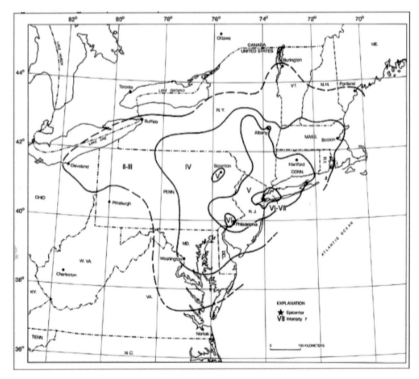

Isoseismal map of the 1884 New York City earthquake FIGURE FROM *SEISMICITY OF THE UNITED STATES 1568–1989* (REVISED), USGS

Effects similar to those in the major cities were reported in the newspapers from many of the smaller cities and towns throughout New Jersey, eastern Pennsylvania, southern New York, and Connecticut. Bells were said to have rung in New Haven, Connecticut, and Wilkes-Barre, Pennsylvania, where children were reportedly thrown off their feet by the earthquake. Newbury, New York, and Waterbury, Connecticut, indicated that sleepers were awakened. Experiences of seasickness were reported from Poughkeepsie, New York, where some crockery fell, and Saratoga, New York, although many did not notice the earthquake in the latter city. At Atlantic City, New Jersey, water pitchers were said to have been overturned by the ground shaking.

The newspapers state that the earthquake was felt from Maine to Maryland to Ohio. Felt reports of the earthquake came from Portland,

Maine; Brattleboro, Vermont; Baltimore, Maryland; Washington, DC; and Cleveland, Ohio. In Baltimore the ground shaking was reported as "light." The earthquake was said to have been felt in Toledo, Ohio, but not in Cincinnati, Ohio, or Pittsburgh, Pennsylvania. The newspapers contain no reports of the earthquake being felt in Canada.

## Deaths and Injuries Reported Due to the Earthquake

This is the first known earthquake in the northeastern U.S. for which deaths attributed to the earthquake are included in the historical accounts. One of the deaths was reported on August 16 from Kingston, New York, in the August 17, 1884, issue of the *New York Times*, which bore the headline "KILLED BY THE EARTHQUAKE." The article reads, "Henry Brown, aged 72 years, died here this morning. Last Sunday afternoon Brown was in his wood shed at the time of the earthquake shock. He trembled violently and shivered like as aspen leaf. He sat down under a tree nearby, thoroughly frightened. He got up to walk, but his legs refused to carry him far. At night when he went to bed his whole nervous system appeared shattered. Despite medical assistance he never rallied. He retained consciousness up to the evening before his death, suffering terribly."

The August 12, 1884, issue of the *New York Times* contains the following report from Plainfield, New Jersey, of another death attributed to the earthquake: "Mrs. Charles Scheler, who had been sick for two weeks with the chills, was so affected by the earthquake shock here yesterday afternoon that she died in a few hours."

The *New York Sun* included a report from Hartford, Connecticut, indicating that a man there was killed by the earthquake. No other details are given, but the *New York Times* also had an item about a death in Hartford due to the earthquake. The circumstances surrounding this death are explained in the *Times* as follows: "At the County Jail the prisoners were wild with fear and attempted to burst in the doors to escape. Their howlings could be heard for some distance. A prisoner named Doyle endeavored to break out, and died from fright occasioned by the earthquake."

The *New York Times* contained a story of an injury that can be attributed to the earthquake. That story reads,

*On Sunday, during the funeral of Lewis Ingler, Jr., the young man who committed suicide at Amityville, Suffolk County, an extraordinary scene occurred. As the minister was about to kneel to pray the shock of earthquake shook the house, a large mirror which reached from the ceiling to the floor was cracked from the top to the bottom, and the walls of the room were cracked in two places. The flowers were shaken from the coffin, and the silver handles on the sides of the casket rattled. The minister and several of the mourners fainted. When the shock was first felt nearly every one in the parlors remained motionless. Then there was a stampede to get outside, and one lady jumped through an open window and sprained her leg so that she had to be carried to her home. The women who fainted were carried outside to the open air. The minister was unable to go on with the service, and the mourners and others remained outside while the pall bearers re-entered the house and carried the coffin out to the hearse. A broom handle can be laid in the cracks in the walls.*

The *New York Sun* includes a story from the earthquake that has a happy outcome. This story from Long Branch, New Jersey, reads, "A man who for a long time had been suffering from a weakness of the back was cured of his ailment by the shaking up he received."

## Earthquake Duration

The newspapers of the time contain a number of different estimates of the duration of the earthquake shaking, ranging from as short as one and a half seconds to as long as two minutes. The *New York Sun* discussed the reports of the earthquake received by the main Western Union office in New York City. Part of this discussion summarized the average duration of the earthquake shaking in the city as follows: "Reports were also received from many of the sub-offices about New York. The reports as to the duration of the shock are diverse, but the average seems to be about ten seconds."

One article in the *New York Times* estimated that the duration of the earthquake was about 10 seconds. Another article in the *Times* discussed the duration of the earthquake in the following manner: "The entire duration of the shock was not above 20 seconds at the outside, and in some points in the city it was estimated by good judges, that it did not last more than about seven seconds, but the seconds to those who experienced the shock were drawn out into minutes, and it seemed a long time before the earth became solid once more and men found their legs and their voices at the same time."

On the other hand, the *New York Tribune* reported that the earthquake lasted about half a minute in the city.

The diversity of the estimates of the duration of the shaking is partly explained by the variations in the site conditions where the earthquake was experienced. Some sites tend to amplify the ground shaking, in which case people at those sites would feel the ground shaking for a longer period of time than those at a site where no such amplification takes place. Another reason for the different estimates is because some buildings shake more than other buildings due to their design and construction. Those buildings that are more sensitive to earthquake shaking will shake at lower levels of ground vibrations. A third explanation is provided in the *New York Sun*, where there is an item that states, "One cool-headed scientist, upon the first perceptible motion, took out his stopwatch and timed the vibrations. He reported that the shock began, as nearly as could be determined, at 2:06:59: that the first shock lasted just ten seconds, and that the 'quieting down' as he described it, took nearly fifty seconds more."

This description is quite compatible with modern seismic records that are taken near strong earthquakes. After earthquake shaking begins, there is a relatively shorter time period when the strongest shaking takes place, followed by a much longer gradual decay in the strength of the ground shaking until it is no longer sensible (the subsiding waves are called coda waves by seismologists). Thus, this "cool-headed scientist" probably accurately measured the strongest shaking lasting about 10 seconds, with the total sensible waves lasting another 50 seconds, for a total of 60 seconds of felt ground shaking. This means that those who reported 10 or so seconds of ground shaking were describing the strongest waves, whereas those who claimed the ground shaking lasted half a minute or more included the decaying coda waves in their estimate of the earthquake duration.

Differences in estimates of the duration of ground shaking can vary depending on the observer. One estimate of the ground-shaking duration at Long Beach, New Jersey, was 7–10 seconds, whereas another estimate was 30 seconds. How long reported ground shaking lasts can change significantly even over short distances, as is clear from the reports of the 1884 earthquake. At Coney Island the ground shaking was estimated to last 10 seconds by one observer, but another observer on nearby Rockaway Beach thought the ground shaking lasted half a minute. Red Bank, New Jersey, reported about one minute of shaking, whereas a report from nearby Long Beach gave the earthquake duration as 7–10 seconds. Similar discrepancies in the duration that the earthquake was felt are seen at greater distances from the earthquake source. At Trenton and Princeton, New Jersey, and in Philadelphia, Pennsylvania, the earthquake was described as lasting 10–15 seconds, although elsewhere on the Delaware River the shaking was said to have lasted half a minute. At New Haven and Danbury, Connecticut, the earthquake was reported to last between half a minute and one minute. Providence, Rhode Island, reported feeling the earthquake for 30 seconds, whereas a scientist at Harvard University in Cambridge, Massachusetts, across the Charles River from Boston, timed the earthquake shaking at 10 seconds.

## Multiple Shocks in the Mainshock, Foreshocks, and Aftershocks

Although many of the reports mention only a single earthquake shock, there also are a number of reports that mention that the earthquake appears to have been two distinct sets of vibrations separated by a few to several seconds. Locations where the strongest shaking was experienced, the southern parts of New York City and the shore areas of New Jersey across the bay, generally mention only one earthquake shock. It is sites that were at farther distances from the earthquake source region where two distinct shakes were reported.

An example of this comes from a *New York Sun* item that states, "Prof. J. K. Rees of Columbia University said, 'I was at my residence, 15 East Seventy-ninthstreet, and to me the manifestation was magnificently distinct. There was the low, rumbling noise preceding, and then two separate waves. They were of about equal length, equal strength, and equal continuation.'"

The *New York Tribune* contained a description of the two shocks as experienced at West Caldwell, New Jersey: "Two slight earth quake shocks were felt in this vicinity this afternoon at 2:09. The two shocks were separated by an interval of a few seconds and lasted about twenty seconds."

Close to the earthquake epicenter, the time difference between the arrival of the faster P waves and the slower S waves is very small, and the shaking is strong enough that people sense that they experience only one continuous shake from the beginning of the P waves to the end of the S waves. At farther distances the P and S waves are separated by a greater time interval, and a lull between the P waves and the stronger S waves may be perceived. This would give the impression of the earthquake consisting of two distinct earthquake shocks. Cities and towns where the earthquake was reported as two or more distinct shocks include Atlantic City and Highlands, New Jersey; Port Jervis and Albany, New York; and Boston, Massachusetts.

At a distance between the near-epicentral area of the earthquake and the areas farther away where the P and S waves are experienced separately, there is an area where the sensible shaking seems to increase in intensity from the initial, weaker seismic P waves and to the somewhat later and stronger seismic S waves. The *New York Tribune* had a good description of this phenomenon: "In Printing House square around THE TRIBUNE building the shock was pronounced. . . . The first instant the jar was faint and distant, but as it increased into a heavy rumble pedestrians rushed from the sidewalks into the middle of the street and gazed with expressions of fear and wonder at the tall buildings."

Of course, aftershocks can also be expected after a strong earthquake, and there apparently was at least one felt aftershock following the 1884 mainshock. When this aftershock occurred is a little uncertain. The mainshock took place at 2:06:50 p.m. according to Prof. J. K. Rees from Columbia College, and so the earthquake was felt at 2:07 p.m. throughout the New York City area, with more outlying areas feeling the S waves at 2:08 p.m. Several localities indicate that an aftershock was felt between about 2:15 p.m. and 2:30 p.m. The *New York Sun* stated that there was another earthquake felt at 2:15 p.m. This earthquake was shorter and not as sharp as the one less than 10 minutes earlier. At Matawan another shock was reported about six minutes after the mainshock, which would also be close to 2:15 p.m. The *New York Times* stated that another earthquake shock was felt at about 10 minutes after the mainshock. At Poughkeepsie, New York, another shock was reported at 2:30 p.m. On the other hand, Boston reported another earthquake at 3:00 p.m. Whether this was an aftershock of the New York City event at 2:06 p.m. or a separate felt earthquake that took place near Boston within an hour of the New York City earthquake is not known. However, the latter possibility cannot be ruled out. Atlantic City reported three distinct shocks. The times of the three shocks there are not reported. However, this report would make sense if the people of Atlantic City felt the separate P and S waves of the mainshock and then the aftershock about seven to ten minutes later. It also would make sense if they felt the separate P and S waves and then some strong surface waves after the S waves.

There are some reports of two or more possible aftershocks that occurred the day after the mainshock. The *New York Evening Post* reported that the people of Burlington, Vermont, felt two shocks, one at 2:30 p.m. and one at 5:30 p.m. The former was probably the mainshock at 2:06 p.m., and the latter is not reported in any other publication. The *New York Times* of August 12, 1884, contained the following paragraph:

> *It was said that another shock of earthquake was felt in the villages along the south side of Long Island yesterday afternoon. It was not so heavy as the shock Sunday, but was sufficient, together with the rumbling which accompanied it, to create an excitement. The Courthouse at Far Rockaway was shaken for several seconds, and the glasses and crockery on hotel tables rattled and some fell over, causing the guests to start from their seats. The shock was felt about 12:30 P.M. A few minutes later the big hotel at Rockaway Beach was shaken, the doors and windows rattling loud enough to be heard at a considerable distance. Open doors in other buildings were closed by the shock.*

Whether there were two different aftershocks or simply one shock with different times reported at Far Rockaway and Rockaway is not known from the available evidence. In any case this aftershock was reported from the same general area that seems to have felt the mainshock most strongly.

There are several different reports of possible foreshocks to the Sunday afternoon mainshock, although all of the reports come from different localities with no agreement about when the earlier events took place. According to the August 11, 1884, edition of the *New York Sun*, Paterson, New Jersey, reported two earlier shocks on August 10, one at about 11:15 a.m. and one at about 1:45 p.m. The latter lasted about 10 seconds. No other publications contain any information about earlier shocks on the day of the mainshock. The August 11, 1884, edition of the *New York Times* includes a dispatch from Providence, Rhode Island, that an earthquake had been felt there about 5:00 p.m. on the Monday before the August 10 mainshock. The same issue of the *New York Times* stated that New Yorkers had reported feeling an earthquake on Sunday, August 3. The August 11, 1884, issue of the *New York Sun* contained the following description of an earlier earthquake: "'About ten days ago,' Mr. Hinman added, 'we thought we felt a slight shaking of the building, and immediately concluded it was an earthquake shock. There was a rumbling noise and then a tremor. The fact would have been forgotten if this shock had not taken place. We forgot about it, as we thought some one might be moving a heavy piece of furniture on the floor below us. The building moved about an eighth of an inch that time.'"

Whether this is the same event as the one described for New York on August 3 or in Providence on August 4 is uncertain. In any case it appears that there may have been one or more possible foreshocks about a week or more before the August 10 mainshock.

## Earthquake Sounds

Sounds that accompanied the earthquake were widely reported from throughout the area where the earthquake was felt. In many ways the descriptions are remarkably similar. Where detailed observations are reported, it appears that most observers reported that the earthquake sound was the first thing that they noticed, with the shaking becoming noticeable a few seconds later. An example of this is the description of the earthquake sound and shaking by Prof. J. K. Rees of Columbia College in the *New York Sun*, which is given earlier in this chapter.

Another example comes from the *New York Tribune*, which stated, "Nowhere was the shock felt more severely than in the large hotels. The experiences in all of them were about the same. First came a heavy rumbling sound, increasing in volume, and then a vibration of the building. The swaying motion was much more violent in the upper than in the lower stories, although plainly perceptible on the ground floors and in the basements. There it was not so much felt by the guests as might have been expected."

The *Tribune* article went on to provide reports of the noise and shaking from the Fifth Avenue Hotel (where the rumbling noise was extremely loud), the Hoffman House, the Victoria Hotel, and the Gilsey House.

The descriptions of the earthquake sounds followed by the earthquake fit perfectly with the theories and observations of seismic waves in modern seismology. The fastest traveling wave, the P wave, converts easily to a sound wave in the air, and so this is almost certainly the source of the initial sounds that are reported felt. The slower S waves contain the strongest shaking, and that is why the strongest shaking comes after the first earthquake sounds are heard. Whereas the P-wave shaking is primarily up and down, the S-wave shaking is strongly horizontal and is primarily responsible for the sideways swaying motions and tremors that are felt in the buildings. It is the up-and-down ground motions that best transmit the earthquake sounds to the air.

The loudest earthquake sounds appear to have come from the south coastal areas of New York City and the beach areas of New Jersey across the bay. For example, at Far Rockaway, New York, a "loud report" was heard, while at Jersey City, New Jersey, there was a "loud rumbling sound." Prisoners at the Castle Garden Prison along the waterfront thought they heard a "clap of thunder" when the earthquake was first noticed. At localities away from the New York City area, where the earthquake was centered, the descriptions of the earthquake noise commonly state that it was a "low rumbling sound," which was compared to "distant thunder," a "loaded beer wagon," a "sewing machine," a "wagon on a macadam road," and a "heavy truck on a cobblestone road." Places where the rumbling sounds of the earthquake were heard included Albany ("faint but distinct"), Harlem (where the rumbling noise "grew to a roar"), Hudson, Marlborough, Newbury, Peekskill, and Poughkeepsie in New York; Dover, Jersey City, Key East, Morristown, and Plainfield in New Jersey; Harrisburg and Wilkes-Barre in Pennsylvania; Greenwich and New Haven in Connecticut; Providence in Rhode Island; and Boston in Massachusetts. A low rumbling noise was also heard by ships at sea. In contrast, Atlantic City and Camden in New Jersey and Kingston in New York reported that the earthquake was not accompanied by any sound.

Both the strength of the sounds and the timbre of the sounds depend on the distance of the observer from the focus of the earthquake. At close distances the sounds are loud and can contain higher pitches as well as deeper-pitched sounds. At farther distances the sounds are softer and the deeper-pitched sounds dominate. At even farther distances from the earthquake focus, the sounds are very low rumbles and may be barely audible, if at all. The reports from the 1884 event very much agree with this general pattern.

## Earthquake Lights

This earthquake occurred during the middle of a summer's day, and no earthquake lights are reported in any publication that discusses the earthquake.

## Animal Behavior

A number of the newspaper accounts from the New York area describe the reactions of animals to the earthquake. Many of the accounts concern the reactions of horses, which were in great use at this time for transporting goods and people. Examples of the reaction of horses were reported in the *New York Sun*, which stated, "The horses of Hook and Ladder 9 on Elizabeth street broke from their stalls and ran plunging in alarm to the door, when the firemen caught and held them. . . . A horse of Engine Company 4 was drinking at a trough in the company's house in Fulton street, when the rumble came. It reared with fright and ran, trembling, from its stall."

Stories of frightened horses that were pulling wagons resulted in at least one injury. These accounts, which come from the *New York Sun*, read, "Open street cars bowling along East Broadway at the time of the shock, fully loaded with passengers, were jolted up and down, and the horses staggered and neighed with fright.... A horse drawing a light wagon was so frightened by the noise and the shaking movement under his feet that he became unmanageable on Ocean avenue and ran into the side of a house. The wagon was overturned and its occupant was thrown to the ground and severely bruised."

From the *New York Times* comes the story of a couple driving a light wagon drawn by a team of horses when the earthquake came. The account describes how the horses reacted: "When the shock came the horses began to stagger and tremble, and one of them fell to the ground but got up again as soon as the quaking ceased."

The *New York Sun* also reported that a horse on a coach was thrown down by the earthquake.

One report from the *New York Sun* suggests that cattle reacted in a similar manner as horses to the earthquake. This account reads, "Thirty cattle owned by Patrick McIntyrn of Dutch Kills were out in the lots close by his house, and at the first rumble they rushed for the stable with tails erect."

Whereas horses and cattle appear to have been frightened by the earthquake shock, the newspaper accounts suggest that dogs and cats were not frightened in the same way. The *New York Tribune* reported, "No dogs howled or barked, no terrified cats crept for shelter to the protector man."

On the other hand, the *New York Times* stated, "Dogs stood transfixed while the deep noise rumbled on and barked dismally when it ceased."

One cat suffered fatally because of its lack of reaction to the earthquake. From the *New York Times* comes the following story:

*I was sitting in a room at my home, no. 2,114 Lexington-avenue, directing invitations to the third mid-summer dinner of the Thirteen.*

*I had written 12 invitations, and had started on the thirteenth, which was to President Arthur. I heard a rumbling sound, and then the house began to shake. I thought it was a cyclone, and looked out of the window, but saw the leaves were not stirring. Just then a heavy pier glass on one side of the room fell forward to the floor and broke into a thousand pieces. My black cat, Cornelius, who was 13 years old, was stretched out on the floor where the mirror struck, and didn't have time to get out of the way. He was stuck so full of splinters of glass that he looked like a porcupine. He died later in the evening in great agony. I buried him at dead midnight under a upas tree in my back yard.*

One fanciful animal story was used to explain the earthquake. It comes from the *New York Tribune* and describes the thoughts of a local orator who explained the earthquake this way: "The city was built on a ledge or rock, one portion of which extended out to Hell Gate, where a big whale attempting to pass at low tide, ran aground. The shocks were caused by the heavy blows of his tail in his struggles to free himself and were communicated along the ledge and felt all through Harlem."

## Soil Liquefaction, Groundwater Changes, and Landslides
Although the earthquake shock apparently was strongest along the coast of southern New York City and parts of New Jersey that are adjacent to the bay, there are almost no reports of liquefaction effects due to the earthquake. The *New York Times* described one locality where apparently there was some land settlement due to the earthquake: "Two large crevasses opened in the level ground between the Brooklyn Reservoir and the East New-York Boulevard near Clason-avenue. One was about 12 feet long, 10 deep, and 10 inches wide at its widest part; the other 10 feet long and deep and 8 inches wide. The gravelly soil was crumbled and fell in, nearly filling portions of both openings."

## A Seiche on the Delaware River?
The August 11, 1884, issue of the *New York Sun* contained some rather unusual descriptions of earthquake effects along the Delaware River. One report from Bordentown, New Jersey, reads, "Those who were at the

riverfront say that the Delaware bulged up, sending large waves over the Pennsylvania and Jersey shores."

A report from Philadelphia states,

*The shipping was affected by the shock. The large ships loading petroleum in the Schuylkill River snapped their hawsers, and were only prevented from going ashore by the united efforts of their crews. Several large steamers were thrown strongly against the wharves in the lower section of the city, and the crews were thrown out of their bunks. Huge waves, backed up by the rising tide, overflowed many of the wharves, and considerable property was flooded thereby. In several instances where persons were watching the river from the docks they found themselves suddenly overtaken by huge waves, and were thoroughly soaked with water. Deeply laden steamers lying in the Delaware trembled without apparent injury during the existence of the shock.*

A smaller version of disturbance on the Delaware River apparently happened in the Trenton, New Jersey, city reservoir. The *New York Times* contained an August 10 report from Trenton that stated, "The water in the city reservoir was agitated, and a small tidal wave was noticed on the Canal and feeder."

These reports sound fanciful given the lack of similar effects in the New York City area. However, an explanation for this phenomenon is that the seismic waves from the earthquake created a seiche on the Delaware River, and it was the seiche that caused the unusually strong waves in the river. A seiche is a standing wave that sets up in a confined water body like a lake or river, causing strong oscillations of the water that can run up onto the otherwise dry shore. Seiches in lakes are compared to tsunamis along ocean shores, as the effects of seiches are similar to those of tsunamis but usually on a much smaller scale. Both reports of seiche-type behavior described above come from the Delaware River, which may have been favorably oriented for a seiche to develop due to the strong earthquake centered in the New York City area.

A seiche also may have been generated on the Housatonic River in Connecticut. The *New York Sun* contained the following description of unusual water waves on the Housatonic River near Bridgeport, Connecticut: "The waters of the Housatonic River were greatly agitated by the shock, causing large waves to recede from each shore, meeting in the center of the river and forming a curious spectacle."

## Location and Magnitude of the 1884 Earthquake

Because of the importance of estimating the seismic hazard of the New York City area, the epicenter and magnitude of the 1884 earthquake have been the subjects of focused research by seismologists. The best estimates of the epicenter of the earthquake have put it somewhere in the Rockaway

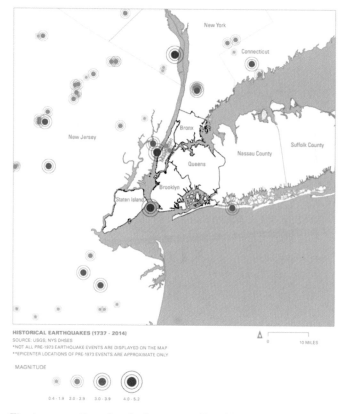

HISTORICAL EARTHQUAKES (1737 - 2014)
SOURCE: USGS; NYS DHSES
*NOT ALL PRE-1973 EARTHQUAKE EVENTS ARE DISPLAYED ON THE MAP
**EPICENTER LOCATIONS OF PRE-1973 EVENTS ARE APPROXIMATE ONLY

MAGNITUDE

0.4 - 1.9   2.0 - 2.9   3.0 - 3.9   4.0 - 5.2

The larger earthquakes in the greater New York City area from 1737 to 2017 FIGURE FROM NEW YORK CITY EMERGENCY MANAGEMENT

Park area of Long Island. The epicenter might have been in Jamaica Bay just north of Rockaway Park or in the Atlantic Ocean just south of Rockaway Park. In either case the earthquake location is in an area that is effectively impenetrable to detailed geologic investigations, and so the fault on which the earthquake likely took place is unknown. Estimates of the magnitude of the earthquake based on its damage area and total felt area range from 5.0 to 5.3, with the most recent study favoring the latter number. This is approximately the range of magnitude estimates that have been made for the size of the December 1737 earthquake, which was also probably centered somewhere in the greater New York City area.

# CHAPTER 9

# 1904: The First New England Earthquake Studied by a Geologist

THE EASTERN TIP OF MAINE IS KNOWN FOR MANY THINGS. IT IS CALLED Downeast by the people in Maine, because during the time of sailing ships the predominant westerly winds would carry the ships downwind to this part of the Maine coast. The Downeast region borders on the Bay of Fundy and on Passamaquoddy Bay, which experience some of the greatest swings in water level between high and low tides anywhere in the world. At one time a project was proposed for Passamaquoddy Bay to construct a series of gates that would be used to generate electricity. The gates would open at low tide to let water into the bay. At high tide the gates would close, trapping the water in the bay. The water would then be released from the bay through electrical generators. When the water from the bay had emptied back into the ocean at low tide, the gates would be lowered and the entire cycle repeated. In the end the economics of this project did not make sense and it was not built.

The Downeast region is well known for fierce winter blizzards that accumulate large amounts of snow. It is known for pleasant summers with little of the great summer heat typically experienced at more inland areas. President Franklin Delano Roosevelt loved to spend summer days on Campobello Island, just offshore from Downeast Maine, because of its mild weather. And the Downeast region is also known for earthquakes. A steady rate of small earthquakes have been recorded from the region in the decades since modern seismic instrumentation has operated in New England and Maritime Canada. Historical records indicate that this earthquake activity extended back throughout the time that Europeans have been settled in the region.

Damaging earthquakes that took place in 1817 and 1869 were probably centered somewhere in the Passamaquoddy Bay area. A strong earthquake that took place on March 21, 1904, was certainly centered somewhere in this area. The 1904 shock was one of the strongest earthquakes to have occurred in New England in historical time. Newspapers provide a rich record of the effects of the 1904 earthquake throughout northeastern North America. The *Rockland* (Maine) *Opinion* of March 25 reported the earthquake in this way: "The severest earthquake shock that has been felt within the memory of living people occurred last Monday morning, a few minutes past 1 o'clock. Most honest people were asleep, of course, but few continued their slumber during the disturbance."

The *Rockland* (Maine) *Daily Star* of March 22, 1904, summarized the event as follows: "The two earthquake shocks a few minutes after one o'clock yesterday morning were the severest and longest ever experienced in this section, and were more terrifying than the memorable seismic disturbance in August 1884 which was felt throughout New England. The shocks were felt from St. John, N.B., to Taunton, Mass. In Portland and other Maine cities the shocks were felt very perceptibly."

Among the older residents of eastern Maine, a common comparison of the 1904 shock was with the earthquake of 1869. The reports generally suggest that the event in 1869 was stronger. The March 21, 1904, issue of the *Daily Gleaner* of Fredericton, New Brunswick, mentions both earthquakes but is unclear as to which was stronger: "One of the most severe, if not the greatest, earthquake shock felt here for many years was experienced at a few minutes past 2 o'clock, this morning. In 1869, the year of the Saxby Gale, at 4 a.m., the whole province was shaken by seismic vibrations causing consternation."

However, the same issue of the *Daily Gleaner* contains the following report on a later page: "The shock this morning was not as severe as that which Dr. Bailey plainly recalls in 1869, when articles were shaken off the shelves at U.N.B. and a tall chimney in the city was razed."

The *Saint John Globe* issue of March 21, 1904, published at St. John, New Brunswick, reports, "Dr. J. H. Frink said that the shock shook his house so violently that all were awakened. Dr. Frink said that the shock was hardly as severe as that of 1869, which he distinctly remembered. Then dishes were rattled and in some houses knocked from the shelves and broken."

## DAMAGE DUE TO THE EARTHQUAKE

Damage to buildings due to the shaking from the 1904 earthquake appears to have been confined to brick chimneys, brick walls, windows, and interior plaster, which are the most easily damaged parts of typical construction of that time in the region. There are no reports of concentrations of damage in any one town; rather, there are isolated reports of damage in a number of towns in eastern Maine and southern New Brunswick.

For example, a report by S. W. Kain in volume XVII of the *Bulletin of Natural History Society of New Brunswick*, published in 1904, summarizes the effects in St. Stephen: "It would seem as if the shock was felt in St. Stephen more severely than in any other part of the province. Several chimney tops were thrown to the ground, some bricks were loosened from the walls of the Methodist church, and a number of panes of glass were broken in the Chipman Memorial Hospital. A locomotive in the C.P.R. roundhouse started forward and had to be stopped by the driver in charge. One correspondent, in a letter to Prof. W. F. Ganong, says: 'The pictures were hanging cornerwise the next morning.'"

The *Calais* (Maine) *Weekly Times* of March 24, 1904, contains a report from St. Stephen that states that chimneys at the residences of Collector Graham, Mrs. Kierstead, Hugh McKay, and F. Lebby were severely damaged. In addition, the newspaper accounts from the time state that one or more chimneys were reported damaged at Augusta, Bethel, Calais, Deblois, East Rumford, Eastport, Ellsworth, Gardner, Lubec, Milbridge, Southwest Harbor, and West Pownal in Maine. In some cases the newspaper reports indicate that there was damage to chimneys of oil lamps, and so at least some of the reports mentioned above of damage to "chimneys" could actually refer to oil lamp chimneys and not chimneys on houses. An example of this ambiguity can be found in the March 21, 1904, issue of the *Gazette* from St. John, New Brunswick. There is a report from Boston in that issue that states, "At Augusta, Maine, chimneys were shaken down and crockery was smashed." The same issue has a report from Augusta that reads, "and in the southern portion of the city there was a terrible jar, chimneys on lamps being demolished and bric-a-brac broken. No serious damage happened."

Another problem with the newspaper reports is that they may mistake preexisting damage due to age and disrepair of some chimneys as being caused by the earthquake. An indication that some of the reported chimney damage may not have been caused by the 1904 earthquake comes from the March 23, 1904, issue of the *Bar Harbor Record* from Bar Harbor, Maine, which says, "Henry Gordon appointed himself a committee of one to investigate the chimneys along his route and found a dozen or more that were either affected by this earthquake or the one of 75 years ago. He wouldn't take his oath which. At any rate there's lots of work for the masons."

In one case a news report confirms that some reported chimney damage was indeed preexisting and not caused by the earthquake. The March 22, 1904, issue of the *Rockland Daily Star* contains a story about this problem in Rockland, Maine, revealing that "someone started the story that the Carnegie Library building had been damaged by the shocks, from the appearance of one of the chimneys yesterday morning with considerable of the mortar missing from the bricks. This was not caused by the earthquake according to one of the trustees of the library, who said that the condition of the chimney was known to the board and that contractors had been notified some days ago, and were requested to remedy it."

Thus, although the newspapers report chimney damage at a number of towns spread throughout Maine, in fact the true damage was probably limited to a smaller area.

One way to assess the area with the strongest ground shaking is to identify those communities that had more than one kind of damage reported. For example, at Calais, Maine, not only were several chimneys reported damaged, but also there were reports of broken windows, cracks in plaster walls, and store goods knocked down from shelves. At Eastport, Maine, there were reports of bricks thrown from several chimneys, stove pipes shaken from their positions, and bric-a-brac thrown from shelves.

Ellsworth, Maine, also reported broken windows, plaster shaken from walls, and china knocked from shelves in addition to the chimney damage. In New Brunswick, in addition to the reported damage at St. John, there were broken windows and chimney damage reported at St. Stephen. These towns apparently experienced the strongest shaking in the earthquake. Other towns where the shaking was strong enough to throw things from shelves were Moncton and St. Martins in New Brunswick. Also, Marysville, New Brunswick, reported that part of one brick wall was thrown down. In Maine things were thrown from shelves in Seal Cove, Fairfield, Gardner (the top of one chimney was reported damaged), Bingham (also clocks were stopped by the earthquake), Winthrop, Roque Bluffs, Orono, Bath (where bells were reported to have rung), and Winthrop. At West Gouldsboro a windowpane was said to have been shaken from its sash. At South Surrey one house was reportedly shaken from its foundation. These towns were likely farther from the earthquake epicenter than the towns mentioned above, but nevertheless they were close enough to the epicenter to experience some losses due to the earthquake shaking.

## TOTAL EARTHQUAKE FELT AREA

Because the earthquake occurred just after 1:00 a.m. in Maine (just after 2:00 a.m. in Maritime Canada), most people were in bed and probably asleep when the earthquake took place. Well away from the earthquake epicenter where the ground shaking would have been too weak to waken most sleepers, it is likely that there would have been few felt reports even if the earthquake could have been felt. Thus, it is probable that the total felt area for this earthquake is underestimated from the surviving reports. Nevertheless, the felt reports at large distances from the epicentral area do give an idea of how widely this earthquake was experienced.

Several summary reports give indications of the spatial extent of felt ground shaking. S. W. Kain, in his 1904 *Bulletin of the Natural History of New Brunswick* article, wrote, "This earthquake was markedly felt in New Brunswick, Nova Scotia and New England, and naturally excited much interest throughout the region where it was felt."

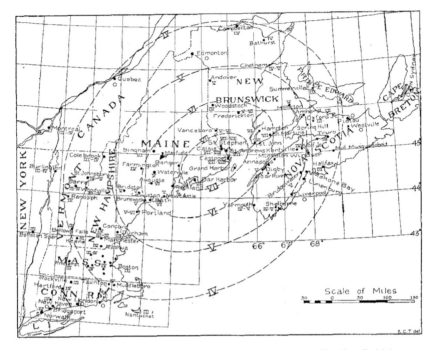

Isoseismal map of the 1904 earthquake published by Harry Fielding Reid in
1911 FIGURE FROM THE *BULLETIN OF THE SEISMOLOGICAL SOCIETY OF AMERICA*

N. H. Heck and R. A. Eppley, in their 1958 *Earthquake History of the United States*, summarized the felt area of this earthquake in the following way: "1904. March 21. This shock was felt throughout the greater part of New England and the provinces of New Brunswick and Nova Scotia. It was strongest in the vicinity of Calais and Eastport, Maine and St. Stephen, New Brunswick, where it overthrew some chimneys. It was felt as far west as the Hudson River, 340 miles; Montreal, Canada, 300 miles; and to southeastern Connecticut, 380 miles, respectively, from its center. The felt area was about 150,000 square miles."

The most detailed study of the area where the earthquake was more noticeably felt was produced by H. F. Reid, a member of the Geology Department at Johns Hopkins University in Baltimore, Maryland. Professor Reid was a well-known geologist who participated in the scientific investigation that studied the famous San Francisco, California, earthquake of 1906. One result of the 1906 earthquake was the founding in 1910 of the Seismological Society of America, commonly referred to in modern times as the SSA. Even today, one of the most important products of the SSA is its technical publication of scientific research on earthquakes and their effects, called the *Bulletin of the Seismological Society of America*. Dr. Reid's paper on the 1904 earthquake in Maine was one of the first papers published in the SSA *Bulletin*. In that paper Dr. Reid produced an isoseismal map of the 1904 earthquake by assigning intensity values to a large set of damage and felt reports from different towns throughout the region. Regarding the extent to which the earthquake was felt, Professor Reid wrote, "It was not noticed in Quebec at a distance of about 220 miles; but was reported from Montreal, about 300 miles from the origin, at Ballston Spa, N.Y., 340 miles, and South Norwalk, Conn., 380 miles from the origin."

Dr. Reid's intensity map shows an oval isoseismal that outlines the intensity IV area for the earthquake. The intensity IV isoseismal extends from the Connecticut–New York border to the St. Lawrence River near Montreal to the eastern border of New Brunswick and then across central Nova Scotia. This is the area over which those who were asleep were most likely to have been awakened by the earthquake shaking.

There are some other reports that further define the extent of the felt area of the earthquake. In Fredericton the *New Brunswick Daily Gleaner* reported that the earthquake was felt from "Ontario to Halifax [Nova Scotia]." On Prince Edward Island the March 23, 1904, issue of the *Summerside Journal* indicates that "some citizens of Summerside state that they also felt a shock early on Monday morning that made the houses tremble." The shock was also reported at Tignish on Prince Edward Island, with a report in the March 24, 1904, issue of *L'Impartial* that states, "On Sunday night, an earthquake made itself felt in the northern part of America. Here, at two in the morning, several persons were conscious of a shock for beyond 15 seconds."

The March 22, 1904, issue of the *Sydney Daily Post* of Sydney, Nova Scotia, carried a report from Halifax that indicated that the seismic event "does not seem to have been experienced in this city [Halifax]." The March 21, 1904, issue of the *Biddeford Daily Journal* of Biddeford,

Maine, ran the following report from Hartford, Connecticut: "Not all places in Connecticut apparently felt the earth tremor. The police of New Haven, New Britain and Bridgeport say that not only did they not notice anything out of the ordinary, but they have failed to find any one who detected the shock. At South Norwalk, however, only 14 miles west of Bridgeport, the shock was heavy."

The scattered felt reports from southwestern Connecticut, Quebec, and eastern Nova Scotia suggest that all of these areas were somewhere near the outer reaches of the area over which the earthquake was felt. Had the earthquake occurred during the daytime when people were awake, it is possible that some additional felt reports at greater distances from the area of strongest ground shaking might have been received.

## MAINSHOCK DURATION, NUMBER OF SHOCKS, AFTERSHOCKS, AND A POSSIBLE FORESHOCK

A number of the reports of the 1904 earthquake contain estimates of the duration of the shaking. However, the duration of the mainshock shaking is not easy to estimate. In part this is because of the variety of durations reported for the mainshock, but also in part it is because some reports indicate that the earthquake was composed of two or even three distinct shocks. The P and S waves from an earthquake are sometimes experienced as separate shocks, especially at large distances from the fault where the earthquake slip took place. Reports of three shocks are more difficult to explain for a single earthquake, but they would make sense if a strong aftershock took place almost immediately after the mainshock. For the 1904 earthquake the surviving reports provide sometimes conflicting accounts as to how many shocks were experienced and what the time differences were between the shocks.

In his 1904 article in the *Bulletin of the Natural History of New Brunswick*, Kain wrote, "There is very considerable difference of opinion as to the interval between the two shocks. Some observers say two minutes, some three, some four. Mr. H. E. Gould, of Sussex [New Brunswick], who was awake reading at the time, tells me the first shock took place at 2:04 a.m., lasting about fifteen seconds, and that after an interval of four seconds a second shock was felt lasting about ten seconds. Mr. C. F. Tilley made a like estimate of the time. I was not awake at the time, and so knew nothing of the matter till this morning."

An interval of two to four minutes is much too long for the time difference between the P and S waves at the localities where the earthquake was felt. On the other hand, a time interval of about 19 seconds (fifteen seconds duration of the first shock plus four seconds for the time between the first and second events) could represent the time between the P and S waves of the earthquake if Sussex was located about 200 kilometers from the earthquake hypocenter. The same article provides a report from Dr. G. M. Duncan of Bathurst, New Brunswick, who gave the following account: "It lasted about twenty seconds. Judging by the position of my bed, and the wave-like motion of my bed, I concluded that the shock was from southwest to northeast. This was followed in about five minutes by a slight tremor quite distinct. It was less distinct in Youghal, fifty miles off."

In this account the event about five minutes later must have been an aftershock, and the mainshock apparently was composed of only a single shock that lasted about twenty seconds. A report from Mainstream, Maine, in the March 21, 1904, issue of the *Lewiston Evening Journal* published at Lewiston, Maine, also states that there were two shocks about five minutes apart.

In a 1905 article on the 1904 earthquake that was published in the *Proceedings and Transactions of the Nova Scotian Institute of Science*, volume XI, J. E. Woodman cited a report in the March 21, 1904, edition of the *Halifax Herald* from Halifax, Nova Scotia, that the ground shaking at Moncton, New Brunswick, lasted "ten or fifteen seconds." He also cited a reply from Shelburne (probably Nova Scotia) to a questionnaire about the earthquake that indicated that the shaking "lasted about fifteen seconds." No second or later shocks are indicated in either of these two reports. In contrast, the Woodman article states that persons at Digby, Nova Scotia, felt the earthquake "quickly followed by another," and for those at the nearby town of Bear River, "two periods of vibration were felt." At this distance from the earthquake fault, these might have been the P and S waves from the mainshock rather than two separate earthquakes.

According to Woodman, the felt shaking at Bridgetown, Nova Scotia, reportedly lasted about 10 seconds. On the other hand, Woodman's article contains the answers to a questionnaire from Annapolis, Nova Scotia, that indicates that three shocks were felt and the earthquake lasted about 20 seconds. Answers to the same questionnaire from Truro, Nova Scotia, report "two principal disturbances," each lasting about 10 seconds and separated by about 5 seconds for a total duration of about 25 seconds. This report contains a good description of the ground shaking: "It seemed as though someone took hold of side of bed and shook it violently, lifting it up and down; as though it were taken hold of on the west side. Everything was still, and then in a few seconds the same thing happened again. It woke a person in this house and another in the next house."

In Maine the surviving reports contain variations in the number of shocks and the duration of the earthquake similar to those reported from New Brunswick and Nova Scotia. The March 21, 1904, issue of the *Bangor Daily News* indicates, "While in some places two shocks were felt many reports have come in of three shocks which was no doubt the case."

The same issue of this newspaper contains a report from Ellsworth, Maine, that states, "The people of the city were somewhat panic-stricken by two distinct shocks about 1:05 this morning. The streets were soon filled with people who thought that an explosion had taken place." It also has a report from Rochester, New Hampshire, that the earthquake lasted about 10 seconds. The *Bath Daily Times* on March 21, 1904, indicates that at Bath, Maine, "there were two distinct shocks, one, the first and most severe, lasting about quarter of a minute and the last, accompanied by a slight trembling, only a few seconds."

In both Canada and the United States, the 1904 mainshock was felt as one or two distinct shocks apparently followed a few minutes later by a somewhat weaker third shake. Some localities that were likely close to the fault on which the earthquake took place experienced additional shocks. The March 21, 1904, issue of the *Bangor Daily News* contains a report that Bar Harbor, Maine, felt seven shocks. The *Bar Harbor Record* of March 23, 1904, contains a report from West Gouldsboro, Maine, that states, "The earthquake did no serious damage in the village except to nerves. This village seems to have had a larger share than most towns, as fourteen distinct shocks were felt Monday morning followed by more shocks during the day, also Tuesday and Tuesday night, the last one occurring at 12:30 p.m. Wednesday."

The same issue of this newspaper reports for Southwest Harbor, Maine, that "about one o'clock Monday morning the inhabitants of Southwest Harbor were awakened by an earthquake shock which was followed by three other slight shocks at intervals of from three to twenty minutes. A loud rumbling noise accompanied the shocks." It also contains the statement, "At five o'clock last night [March 22] the earth quaked again [at Bar Harbor]."

One interesting report on this earthquake comes from the March 24, 1904, issue of the *Republican Journal*, which was published in Belfast, Maine. This report states, "People who were awake before the shock say there was a slight tremor at just 1 o'clock which gradually died away and was followed by the principal shock, which was sufficient to awaken even the soundest sleeper. The duration of this is variously estimated at from 10 to [unreadable] seconds. The third shock was much lighter, but was fully as severe as those felt in 1870 and 1897. It rattled dishes, windows etc., and was accompanied by the rumbling, but was only of 2 or 3 seconds duration. Two others followed, each lighter than its predecessor."

This is the only description that has been found of a possible small foreshock that took place a few minutes before the mainshock. There were apparently three aftershocks felt at this locality, and so it must have been close enough to the earthquake fault to experience some of the smaller aftershocks that followed the mainshock.

Several other localities in Maine reported multiple shocks. The *Bar Harbor Record* of March 23, 1904, includes the following report from Sullivan Harbor, Maine: "The shocks continued all night at intervals and all through the day until eleven o'clock Monday night, which up to the present writing was the latest shock reported."

The March 26, 1904, issue of the *Machias Republican* from Machias, Maine, contains reports about the aftershocks of the earthquake from a number of different Maine towns. The report from West Columbia states, "Lighter shocks continued for four hours." The report from Cooper states, "A number of slighter shocks followed but none were as severe as the first." The March 22, 1904, issue of the *Machias Union* at Machias, Maine, contains the following report from Columbia Falls, which is near West Columbia: "A heavy earthquake shock was felt here Monday morning at one o'clock, which shook the buildings and sounded like heavy thunder. This was followed in a few minutes by two other distinct shocks, but the movement was slight although there was a heavy rumbling sound for some time. At three o'clock there was two other slight shocks."

The *Fairfield Journal* of March 22, 1904, states that at Fairfield, Maine, "There were several different shocks here, one occurring at about 1 o'clock and the others following in quick succession."

The March 21, 1904, issue of the *Lewiston Evening Journal* published at Lewiston, Maine, reported that at Dexter, Maine, "Four distinct shocks were felt." This same newspaper issue has a report from North Anson, Maine, that indicates that the first shock was at 1:05 a.m., a second shock occurred at 1:08 a.m., and some people felt a third shock about a half hour later.

The *Moncton Daily Times* issue of March 24, 1904, from Moncton, New Brunswick, includes a report that states, "Ora W. Knight, widely known in scientific circles in Maine, says there were nine shocks in the Monday morning earthquake, but six of them were very slight. The first occurred at 1.05 Maine time, the second at 1.07 and the third at 1.29, the others at intervals later." Professor Knight was on the faculty at the University of Maine and lived in Bangor, so this is likely where he experienced the earthquake shocks.

Whereas a number of localities in Maine report multiple aftershocks, the same is not true for reports from towns in New Brunswick. With the exception of the two or three shocks at and shortly after 1:05 a.m. on March 21, the only other possible aftershock that was reported in Canada occurred about 5:00 a.m. on March 21, with felt reports at Adamsville, Fredericton, and St. Stephen in New Brunswick. Because the Canadian reports give a specific time for this earthquake but an earthquake at 5:00 a.m. is not mentioned in the U.S. papers, it is possible that there was an earthquake centered in Canada at this time and the event was not an aftershock of the 1:05 a.m. earthquake. The surviving historical records are not able to confirm or deny that a separate earthquake occurred in Canada.

## Soil Liquefaction, Groundwater Changes, and Landslides

There were only a few reports of groundwater changes associated with this earthquake. One man at St. Andrews, New Brunswick, reported that his well was muddied by the earthquake. A person at Fredericton, New Brunswick, claimed that the earthquake caused his well to go dry. No reports have been found in any existing sources of soil liquefaction or landslides due to the 1904 earthquake. According to Kain's *Bulletin* article about this earthquake, at St. John, New Brunswick, "the shock was felt most severely in buildings erected on clay and gravel areas," indicating amplification of the ground shaking in some parts of the city due to local soft soil conditions.

## Earthquake Sounds

The newspapers from the time period contain numerous reports of the sounds that accompanied the earthquake. For the most part the descriptions are general for a town or city, although some descriptions are given by specific individuals. Louder sounds tended to be reported closer to the area where the earthquake was centered, whereas more muted sounds were reported at greater distances from the epicentral area. There were some places where no sound was reported even though earthquake shaking was felt.

The area in Maine where the strongest shaking was felt was also the area where the loudest sounds were reported. The March 22, 1904, issue of the *Machias Union* reports that at Columbia Falls, Maine, "A heavy earthquake shock was felt here Monday morning at one o'clock, which shook the buildings and sounded like heavy thunder. This was followed in a few minutes by two other distinct shocks, but the movement was slight although there was a heavy rumbling sound for some time."

The March 23, 1904, issue of the *Bar Harbor Record* states, "A heavy detonation followed by three distinct shocks was felt. . . . Some thought a terrific explosion had occurred, others that it was the 'crack of doom'. Quite a prevalent idea was that the kitchen hot water heater had exploded. . . . A young cornetist who had exercised his talent during the evening, woke with the impression that he was playing a false note. Those on the street at the time of the shock say that a crackling and groaning, as of a huge sheet of ice breaking, was first heard."

The March 22, 1904, issue of the *Rockland Daily Star* from Rockland, Maine, contains the following statements about the earthquake sounds in that town:

*When the first shock came with a thunderous noise it sounded like an explosion. John L. Donahue, clerk at the Thorndike, sprang from bed believing that burglars had blown open the safe of the Rockland Trust Company downstairs. John T. Berry Jr. rushed for a revolver and threw open a window of his room expecting to get a shot at fleeing burglars. . . . Night watchman Magee while patrolling Main Street hastened to the bank district fearing that a bank vault had been blown open and for a time the mystery of the strange noise was unexplained. The general impression at first was that the noise was caused by the explosion of dynamite at the quarries or powder stored somewhere nearby. . . . The descriptions given by various Rockland people of the rumbling noise vary. One man said his better half screamed loudly at the first shock and he tried to quiet her by telling her it was the ice man. He said it sounded just like the ice man awakening the sleeping city about 4 a.m. in the good old summer time. Another man said it sounded like half a dozen trolley cars rushing past his house, and still another described it as a weird noise like the approach of a hurricane. In a South End home the inmates were badly frightened by the rattling of several bricks from the roof chimney.*

The March 25, 1904, issue of the *Rockland Opinion* published at Rockland, Maine, contains the following description: "Most honest people were asleep, of course, but few continued their slumber during the disturbance. First, there was a roaring, grinding noise from the bowels of the earth, growing louder as it approached, apparently from the north, and culminating in a distinct tremor of the earth, sufficient to rattle windows and dishes, but not sufficient to do any harm. The noise then gradually died away in the distance. A few minutes later the roaring noise was resumed and continued for a few seconds, but the earth did not perceptibly tremble then."

Reports came in from many Maine towns. At Southwest Harbor "a loud rumbling noise accompanied the shocks." At Calais "the tremors were preceded by a noise like thunder." Milbridge reported a "rumbling sound." Old Town indicated that the earthquake was "accompanied by rumbling sounds which lasted for a considerable period." At Sullivan Harbor "every one with a boiler in his house or a gas machine thought one or the other had exploded."

In New Brunswick, at towns close to the Maine border, there are reports of earthquake sounds from number of towns. At St. Stephen "there was a heavy rumbling" according to one report, and the earthquake was preceded "by a rumbling noise as of a mighty wind or approaching railway train" in another report. From Grand Manan Island came the report that "the rumbling sound to one just awakened out of his or her slumber was like a heavy squall of wind with distant thunder." At Woodstock "the shock came accompanied by a rumbling noise." A report from Hampton states that the earthquake sound "might be likened to the rattle of a fete of musketry." At St. John a "slight rumbling sound" like "distant thunder" was heard during the first shock and "no sound was noticeable" during the second shock a few seconds later.

At greater distances from the center where the earthquake waves originated, the earthquake sounds were generally lower in tone and intensity than was reported from the localities where the greatest damage took place. In Maine the noise that accompanied the earthquake was described as a "rumbling sound" at Sanford, Gardner, Sacco, Biddeford, and Camden. At Rumford the sound was described as a "heavy, low rumble" and at Winthrop it was called a "dull rumbling sound." Alfred indicated that the sound was like that of a "heavy truck," whereas at Kennebunk it was described as a "noise not unlike the rumble of a passing train." At Embden the earthquake shaking was "accompanied by a rumbling noise like distant thunder." At Richmond there was "a roar that sounded like the oncoming of a train." At Bath "J. M. Clark on Middle Street said the sound resembled a jigger passing on the street."

The *Lewiston Evening Journal* of March 21, 1904, contains a number of descriptions of the earthquake, including impressions of the sounds that people heard:

*One man says it sounded like a gale of wind. . . . Another says that he heard a strange rushing sound which was probably the sound of himself rushing for the bed clothes. Another says that it sounded like snow on the roof. . . . One of the Journal's editors has this testimony to offer. He was awake when the quake came. It seemed at first like a house moving in a heavy wind. It shook with vibrations beginning gently, having a distinct climax and then subsiding. It is impossible to say how long it lasted. Probably not over ten seconds. He noticed no second shock. He spoke to a member of the family and said, "Did you hear that?" "Yes, the wind must be blowing heavily." "No," was the reply, "there is no wind. It is an earthquake. No question about it."*

The *Six Town Times* issue of March 25, 1904, published in Portland, Maine, states that at South Freeport, Maine, "The noise was accounted for in different ways. Some thought it was the electrics, some their safes were being blown open and some thought some one had fallen out of bed or down stairs."

The March 22, 1904, issue of the *Daily Eastern Argus* at Portland, Maine, provides the following account of the earthquake sounds:

*The general opinion was as described in yesterday's paper, namely, a rolling motion preceded by a roar that sounded like a heavy truck team, a horseless engine or something like that passing and a general shaking up of whatever buildings the people happened to be in at the time. . . . One man says . . . that it sounded as though the family living up stairs was having a war dance all over the house. The people up stairs in the same house say that it sounded to them as though the people down stairs were having a terrible time chasing a dog through their rooms and that the dog jumped up and knocked the lamp off the table.*

Southwest beyond Maine, some scattered accounts of the earthquake sound are quite similar. Boston, Massachusetts, reported a "dull rumbling sound," and it was simply called a "rumbling sound" at Worcester and

Lowell, Massachusetts, and at Goffstown, New Hampshire. A report from Providence, Rhode Island, compared the sound of the earthquake to the "noise of a passing street car."

Well to the north and east of the area where the earthquake was centered, the reports of the earthquake sounds were similar to those from southern and western Maine and from the southern New England states. In New Brunswick at Carleton, the sounds were compared to a "number of heavy wagons driven over rough ground," whereas at Chatham it was claimed that a "rushing sound preceded the earthquake." Both Fredericton and Richibucto reported a "rumbling noise" associated with the earthquake, and a report from Miramichi indicated that the earthquake noise was "barely audible." In Nova Scotia the town of Cornwallis reported a "rumbling sound" and at Fairview Mr. John MacAloney "was awakened by feeling the house jar, at the same time hearing a faint sound that [he] took to be distant thunder." Accounts from the towns of Shelburne and Truro suggest that the earthquake shaking was not accompanied by any sound.

## Earthquake Lights

Although the earthquake took place in the middle of the night, there are only a couple of reports that may describe earthquake lights at the time of the event. By 1904 electric lighting had been installed at a number of places, and so it is possible that one or more of the reports of flashes of light may have been electrical arcing across on-off switches or electrical junctions. A report in the March 21, 1904, issue of the *Daily Gleaner* for Fredericton, New Brunswick, states that "some people assert that there were two or three flashes of lightning." Flashes of light were also reported at Alton, New Hampshire, according to the March 21 issue of the *Manchester Union*, published in Manchester, New Hampshire. A report in the March 23, 1904, issue of the *Hants Journal* from Windsor, Nova Scotia, states, "They [the earthquake shocks] were preceded by two or three flashes of lightning, and heavy wind." No rain or thunderstorms were reported anywhere in the region on March 21, although there were some thunderstorms that were reported for the following night. At East Sullivan, Maine, it was reported that lights flashed over the village. Only the last of these reports resembles descriptions of earthquake lights in other earthquakes.

## Animal Behavior

Perhaps because of the occurrence of this earthquake sequence in the middle of the night, there is a paucity of accounts of the reactions of animals to the earthquake. At Searsport, Maine, the earthquake "frightened dumb beasts," and animals were reported disturbed at Bowdinham, Maine. At West Gouldsboro, Maine, "cattle lowed and horses were seized with fear." Unfortunately, no other details about animal reactions are given in the available accounts, so it is impossible to say at what stage or stages in the earthquake occurrence did the animals react.

## Location and Magnitude of the 1904 Mainshock

In his 1911 paper H. F. Reid assigned an epicenter of 45.0°N, 67.5°W to the 1904 mainshock, which would put the epicenter just east of Crawford, Maine. In their 1958 book, *Earthquake History of the United States*, N. H. Heck and R. A. Eppley assigned the epicenter to 45.0°N, 67.2°W, which is a location just north of Dennysville, Maine. Since 1958 all later scientists who have compiled earthquakes catalogs that included New England or who studied the earthquake in eastern Maine have used the Heck and Eppley epicenter.

The problem with both the Reid and the Heck and Eppley epicenters is that they are not near the places that felt the small aftershocks that followed the earthquake. As described above, the greatest amount of damage to structures appears to have extended from St. Stephen, New Brunswick, to Ellsworth, Maine, and so the epicenter of the earthquake was likely somewhere between these localities. The largest number of aftershocks was reported from West Gouldsboro, Maine, where 14 aftershocks were felt the morning after the mainshock, with more aftershocks felt later that day as well as the next day and even the day after. The people at nearby Sullivan Harbor felt aftershocks all during the day following the mainshock, although the number of aftershocks is not given, and across Frenchman Bay at the town of Bar Harbor, Maine, at least seven aftershocks were felt. At West Columbia, Maine, aftershocks were felt for four

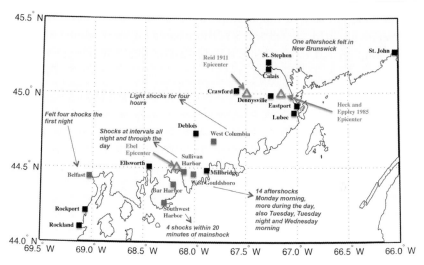

Localities where the 1904 earthquake and its aftershocks were experienced

hours after the mainshock. Towns farther northeast from West Columbia apparently felt at most three or four aftershocks, and the same is true for towns west of Bar Harbor. The area around West Gouldsboro included the communities where the loudest earthquake sounds were apparently heard.

All of this evidence suggests that the epicenter of the 1904 mainshock was in Maine somewhere near West Gouldsboro and Sullivan Harbor and across Frenchman Bay from Bar Harbor. This puts the epicenter somewhere in the vicinity of 44.5°N, 68.1°W. This is south-southwest of the Reid epicenter by about 40 miles (70 kilometers) and southwest of the Heck and Eppley epicenter by about 50 miles (80 kilometers). The new epicenter proposed here is the one that is most consistent with the evidence from the earthquake damage, the earthquake sounds, and the reported aftershocks. The one town that reported a possible foreshock is Belfast, Maine, which is well west of the epicenter favored in this book. It is possible that a small earthquake took place near Belfast minutes before the larger earthquake that was centered farther to the west took place.

The magnitude of the 1904 earthquake has been determined by a number of different investigators based on the highest intensity reported for the event, on the total area of the modified Mercalli IV contour, and on the total felt area of the earthquake. Published magnitudes based on maximum intensity are 4.5 and 5.7. Those based on the modified Mercalli IV contour are 6.0, 6.0, and 5.9. Those based on total felt area are 5.0, 5.3, 5.3, 5.4, and 5.5. The average of these magnitudes is 5.4 ± 0.5. Thus, the magnitude of the 1904 mainshock is probably somewhere between 4.9 and 5.9.

# CHAPTER 10

# 1929: A Strong Earthquake Triggers a Destructive Tsunami

ALTHOUGH THE 1929 EARTHQUAKE WAS CENTERED WELL AWAY FROM the northeastern U.S., it was felt noticeably but with no damage throughout the region. However, the most notable aspect of this seismic event was not the consequences of its earthquake ground shaking. Rather, this earthquake triggered a major tsunami that was destructive in Newfoundland and was experienced along the Atlantic coast from Nova Scotia to New England. Destructive tsunamis are rare in the North Atlantic Ocean basin. Even so, the 1929 event carried an implied warning that a major tsunami could happen elsewhere along the east coast of North America due to a strong offshore earthquake.

With an irony that was not lost on the people at the time, the 1929 earthquake struck at about 3:35 p.m. EST (4:35 p.m. AST for those in the maritime provinces of Canada) on November 18, 1929, the 174th anniversary of the great Cape Ann earthquake of 1755. It was a dark and gloomy day throughout the New England region as a major rainstorm was sweeping up the East Coast, with snow in parts of eastern Maine and Nova Scotia. Even with the cold rain, a number people left buildings and ran into the streets when they experienced the shaking. The headlines of the *Boston Globe* issue of November 19, 1929, summarize the experience:

*QUAKE SHAKES NEW ENGLAND*
*CAUSES BUT TRIVIAL DAMAGE*
*Tremor Originating off Coast Rocks Wide Area from New York*

*North to Maritime Provinces — Mild Panics in Cities When Large Buildings Sway on Their Foundations*

## Felt Area and Shaking Effects on Land

Although the earthquake was widely felt, the effects of its ground shaking were relatively minor across the area where it was felt. The only damage due to the ground shaking appears to have been in Nova Scotia. A report on the earthquake published by the Dominion Observatory of Ottawa states that most of the damage due to the ground shaking was confined to Cape Breton Island, where chimneys were overthrown or cracked, objects were thrown from shelves, and some roads were blocked by landslides. In addition to the damage at Cape Breton Island, the November 19, 1929, issue of the *Globe and Mail* of Toronto, Ontario, contains a report from Halifax, Nova Scotia, that reads, "A dozen chimneys crashed in the Charlotte Street section of Sydney, and several barns were reported to have collapsed in the outlying districts. . . . A couple of chimneys crashed at Kentville."

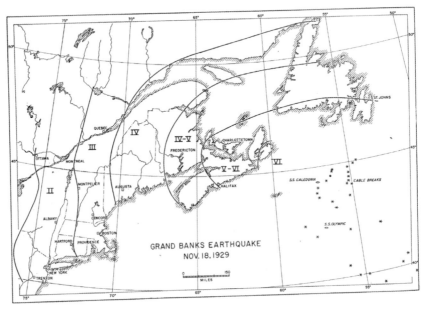

Isoseismal map of the 1929 earthquake FIGURE FROM THE DOMINION OBSERVATORY OF OTTAWA

Elsewhere the earthquake effects were confined to objects being vibrated from shelves at St. John, New Brunswick, to furniture being moved at Worcester and Springfield, Massachusetts. Two landslides into the Bay of Fundy along the coast of New Brunswick were attributed to the earthquake ground motions. At some places the earthquake shaking was sufficiently severe to frighten people. Halifax reported that several people fainted during the shaking, and the people of Truro, Nova Scotia, compared the event to the major munitions explosion of 1917 that rocked Halifax Harbor. In some places in Maine and New Hampshire, people were rattled enough by the earthquake shaking to run from their buildings. The earthquake was felt across all of Prince Edward Island, although there were no reports of the intensity of the shaking there.

There were some initial reports of damage that were never confirmed. The *Boston Globe* issue of November 19, 1929, reported that an iron bridge at Grand Narrow on Cape Breton Island had been damaged due to the earthquake shock, but that report was later discounted as untrue. The November 19, 1929, issue of the *New York Times* stated that the earthquake damaged chimneys in Boston, but the Boston newspapers of the time period reported no such damage.

The area over which the earthquake was felt was quite substantial. Initial reports claimed that the earthquake was felt in the U.S. as far west as Binghamton, New York, and as far south as New York City, where the shaking was described as "light." In Quebec, Canada, the earthquake was said to have been felt in Quebec City but not in Montreal. The Dominion Observatory of Ottawa report from 1948 summarized the results of surveys that it conducted in Canada and that the U.S. Coast and Geodetic Survey conducted in the U.S. With over 300 returns for these two surveys, the earthquake felt area was extended to Ottawa, Ontario, to the west; Claymont, Delaware, to the southwest; and the island of Bermuda to the south. The felt effects pointed to an offshore epicenter, which had also been inferred by seismologists from their seismographic recordings immediately after the earthquake occurred.

## Earthquake Duration, Number of Shocks, and Earthquake Sounds

Reports of the duration of the earthquake shaking varied widely from place to place, as has been typical of all strong earthquakes in the region. However, there does seem to be some pattern to the reports. There are no reports of the duration of the ground shaking from Newfoundland, but estimates from Nova Scotia ranged from three to five minutes. In New Brunswick and Maine, the estimates of the duration of the ground shaking were generally between 15 seconds and one minute, although one report from Fredericton, New Brunswick, indicated that the shaking was felt for several minutes at the provincial parliament building. In southern New England the earthquake reportedly lasted 30 seconds at New London, Connecticut, but two to four minutes at New Haven, Connecticut. A headline in the November 19, 1929, issue of the *Boston Globe* read in part, "Many Folk Unaware of Three-minute Shock."

A clue about the duration of ground shaking is contained in the November 19, 1929, issue of the *New York Times*, which reported that the highest amplitude seismic waves that showed up on the seismograph at Yale University in New Haven were about five minutes after the first wave was detected and lasted for several minutes. The first arriving seismic wave is the P wave, followed later by the S wave, which has higher amplitudes than the P wave. The highest amplitudes are in the surface waves, which arrive after the S waves. The surface waves are generally much lower frequency than the P wave and S wave, and so are most likely to be noticed only in tall buildings at large distances (several hundred miles) from the earthquake epicenter. Thus, it is most likely that those in tall buildings sensed several minutes of ground shaking.

At large distances from the epicenter, the earthquake was sensed by some people as multiple shocks, presumably because the P wave, S wave, and surface waves were each experienced as separate earthquake shakes. According to the *Boston Globe* issue of November 19, 1929, there were reports that the earthquake consisted of as many as three separate tremors, although it is not clear where these reports came from. One report indicated that the earthquake was experienced as two separate tremors in Maine, and it was also felt as two separate shocks at Providence, Rhode Island.

There were only a few reports of the sounds that accompanied the earthquake shaking. In Nova Scotia the earthquake shaking was said to be accompanied by a deafening sound. The earthquake sound was reported as a rumble at Rothesay and Moncton, New Brunswick, and South Paris, Maine. According to the November 19, 1929, issue of the *Boston Globe*, "Kennebunk [Maine] householders reported 'rapping sounds' which sent them flying to the doors to welcome visitors." There are no reports at all of earthquake sounds in southern and western New England, presumably because those areas were so far from the earthquake epicenter that the acoustic frequencies had been attenuated out of the seismic waves.

## FELT EFFECTS AT SEA

One of the most unusual aspects of this earthquake was that it was felt by a number of ships that were at sea hundreds of miles from the nearest land. Ships moored at harbors and at sea not far from shore commonly feel earthquakes because the seismic P wave can travel from the rock through the water and shake the ships. For example, a number of ships felt the 1755 Cape Ann earthquake, but all were in the Boston Harbor area or were sailing less than 100 miles offshore. In the case of the 1929 earthquake, the ships *Olympic* and *France* were each about 312 miles (500 kilometers) southeast of Nova Scotia and both reported feeling the earthquake. The ship *Neriss* was 100 miles (160 kilometers) out when it experienced the earthquake. The ship *Caledonia* was about 150 miles (250 kilometers) southeast of Cape Breton Island, Nova Scotia, and quite close to the epicenter of the earthquake when it felt the shock. The November 25, 1929, issue of the *New York Times* contained the following report from Captain Collie of the *Caledonia*:

> *It was a bewildering two minutes. All of the passengers rushed from one side of the ship to the other, but could see nothing. The Caledonia had passed Sable Island and the water was quite calm. There was little wind. Suddenly the ship was seized with violent trembling. It was as if the ship had run over a sandbar.*
>
> *Thinking the ship had fouled some derelict, I ordered engines stopped. The water had suddenly become very choppy and the ship*

*bumped. It reminded me of my experience during the Tokio earthquake. It was only then that I realized it was a wave that had bumped us.*

*We inspected the ship thoroughly and found no damage had been done.*

## A Major Tsunami and Submarine Slump

The greatest destruction in the 1929 earthquake was not due to the earthquake ground shaking but rather to a large tsunami that was triggered by the earthquake. Tsunamis are rare in the North Atlantic Ocean, and so coastal areas were quite unprepared when the tsunami arrived. In 1929 most people referred to a tsunami as a tidal wave on the mistaken impression that the waves are associated with the ocean tides. In reality tsunamis can occur at any tidal stage, although those that occur at high tides are clearly the most destructive.

Because tsunami waves travel much slower than seismic waves, the tsunami did not reach land until long after the earthquake shaking had passed. The area where the greatest tsunami was experienced and where major damage was experienced was along the south coast of Newfoundland. This coastal area has a number of inlets from the sea with narrow coastal beaches that lead to sharp cliffs that rise to a forested highland. In 1929 the coastal areas were populated by a number of small fishing villages and the highland was uninhabited. The area that experienced the greatest tsunami damage was around Placentia Bay, particularly on the southeast shore of the Burin Peninsula.

The tsunami came ashore in southern Newfoundland about two hours after the earthquake. A rush of water that raised the sea level between 15 feet and an estimated 40 feet moved into Placentia Bay, inundating everything along the coastal areas. In some low-lying areas, the water pushed as much as half a mile inland. The November 21, 1994, issue of the *Globe and Mail* in Toronto, Ontario, ran a story about the 1929 tsunami. That story includes the following account from one of the survivors of this catastrophe:

*About 7:30 p.m. on the moonlit evening of Nov. 18, 1929 seven-year-old Norah Hillier heard a loud roar, looked out of the window of her Newfoundland outport home a few metres from the sea and thought she saw thousands of sheep riding a mountain of water.*

*What the terrified child witnessed was the foam on the deadliest and most destructive tidal wave in Canadian history. "We saw all this white coming and I cried 'Oh, all the sheep!' It seemed the water was mountains high," Mrs. Hillier recalled in a recent interview. "In a matter of seconds we were up to our waists in water. . . . My oldest sister pushed shut the door and we all held onto the doors, waiting for someone to rescue us. We were so frightened. We didn't know what it was."*

*Mrs. Hillier recalls her father returning home shortly after the first wave hit, finding dry socks for the girls and then leading the shivering and terrified children through peat bogs to nearby hills, where bonfires had been lit by those who had already reached safety.*

*They watched as the wave pulsed three times and finally the waters became as smooth as glass.*

The deadly tsunami brought death and destruction to the villages of this coastal region, with significant damage at the towns of Lamaline, Point au Gaul, Taylor's Bay, Lord's Cove, Lawn, St. Lawrence, Corbin, Lance au Lean, Great Burin, Step-a-side, Kelly's Cove, Ship Cove, Burin

Tsunami damage on the Burin Peninsula, Newfoundland, following the 1929 earthquake FROM THE CANADIAN GEOLOGICAL SURVEY

North, Burin East, Port au Bras, Mortur, and Rock Harbour. Initial reports on the number of lives lost in this area due to the tsunami vary from 25 to 40, with at least 50 people injured. A more recent determination of the death toll puts it at 27 lives lost at the time and one death years later due to injuries suffered in the tsunami. Many of the waterfront buildings were heavily damaged or destroyed by the tsunami, with debris piled five feet high in places. Some of the buildings that were destroyed warehoused coal and food provisions for the long winter season, forcing the local inhabitants to salvage what they could from the waterlogged debris. Fishing vessels had been dashed against each other and some were thrown onto the shore. This dealt a major blow to the largest single contributor to the local economy and to a primary mode of transportation for local residents. Coastal roads were washed out in places, making land transportation between the villages difficult.

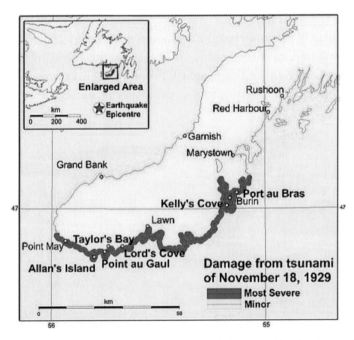

Areas around the Burin Peninsula, Newfoundland, impacted by the tsunami following the 1929 earthquake FIGURE FROM THE CANADIAN GEOLOGICAL SURVEY

Recovery on the Burin Peninsula, Newfoundland, following the 1929 earthquake and tsunami FROM THE CANADIAN GEOLOGICAL SURVEY

The December 3, 1929, issue of the *Boston Globe* summarized the outcome of this terrible tragedy: "Along a stretch of some 50 miles of coast line, where formerly snug settlements of hardy fisherfolk dotted coves and inlets, apparently safe and secure, the terrific onslaught of the tidal wave has resulted in desolation and distress."

The tsunami was experienced not just in Placentia Bay of Newfoundland but in many other places as well, albeit with less devastating effects. Within the hour or so after it struck Placentia Bay, the tsunami had reached other parts of coastal Newfoundland. No significant damage was reported, although a six-foot wall of water was reported at the head of St. Mary's Bay. At Catalina near the border with Labrador, the tsunami started as a water withdrawal, leaving ships stranded until the water returned. About 8:00 p.m. AST the tsunami began to affect the coast of Nova Scotia. At Canso the tsunami was about two feet above high tide and came in with enough force to damage wharves and push one ship onto the land. At Glace Bay in Nova Scotia, the water surged and then withdrew over an interval of about 15 minutes, doing this a total of three times. A water surge eight feet above high tide was observed at Sydney around midnight. Some flooding occurred in the Sydney area due to the tsunami. At Cape Breton a man was reported killed when he was swept off a barge by the tsunami. The tsunami did affect the barge, but the report of the death was erroneous. He was at home having dinner at the time the tsunami washed over the barge. In Halifax Harbor a drydock was inundated by the tsunami.

The tsunami apparently also was experienced along the northeast coast of the U.S. In Massachusetts a surge of water four feet above high tide was noted. The tsunami topped a sea wall in Winthrop to flood Memorial Drive and put Long Wharf underwater in Boston. The tsunami was also observed in New York City. A report in the November 19, 1929, issue of the *New York Times* states, "The Long Island shore was lashed by an extraordinarily high tide, however, which broke over sea walls and inundated the roads, marooning many automobiles hub-deep in water."

It must be noted that at the time of the earthquake there was a strong nor'easter that affected the New England coast. Nor'easters are often accompanied by storm surges that can overtop sea walls and cause coastal flooding. Furthermore, the 1929 earthquake took place at a time when the ocean tidal fluctuations were larger than normal. Thus, for Boston and New York, it is not clear how much of the flooding was due to the tsunami and how much was due to these other influences.

There were also some effects of the tsunami reported in parts of the North Atlantic far from northeastern North America. The tsunami was detected at Charleston in South Carolina. Bermuda experienced a surge of water, likely from the tsunami, about 7:30 p.m. that broke the mooring chains of a dredging ship. The Azores reported an unusual ocean wave about 4:30 a.m. on the morning following the earthquake. Reports of the tsunami were also received from the coast of Portugal and the island of Martinique. This is evidence that the tsunami was strong enough to traverse the entire Atlantic Ocean basin.

Tsunamis are caused by sudden changes in the elevation of the ocean floor. They can be caused by undersea earthquakes where the slip on the earthquake fault causes vertical movements of the ocean floor, or they can be caused by sudden submarine slumps of sediments down slopes on the ocean floor. Some seismologists believe that most or all tsunamis associated with earthquakes have major sediment slumps as a contributing cause. In the case of the 1929 earthquake, there is clear evidence that a major submarine slump accompanied the earthquake. This is known because sitting on the North Atlantic Ocean floor south of Newfoundland in 1929 were about 25 cables that carried telephone and telegraph signals between North America and Europe and between North America and Newfoundland. Of these, 12 of the cables were broken, some in two or even three different places. Because the severing of a cable would immediately interrupt communications, the times of the cable breakages can be precisely determined. Furthermore, after the earthquake ships were sent to sea to fish the cables from the ocean bottom and repair the breaks, which means that the locations of the breaks were also precisely determined.

Most of the cable breaks took place precisely at the time of the earthquake, indicating that there was a major submarine slump that accompanied the earthquake faulting in the rock below the sea bottom. There were several additional cable breaks that took place about 80 minutes after the earthquake. The initial cable breaks took place about 165 miles (265 kilometers) south of Newfoundland in an area where the ocean floor slopes steeply to the south, away from the shallow continental shelf at an area called the Grand Banks. This is the same area that seismologists have determined was the epicenter of the 1929 earthquake. The cable breaks that occurred 80 minutes later were well south of the earthquake epicenter by as much as 300 miles (500 kilometers). The cable breaks were spread about 200 miles (300 kilometers) from east to west. Isolated cable breaks were also reported about 3 hours and about 10–12 hours after the earthquake. Modern sonar images of the ocean bottom in this area indicate a large, fresh submarine slump that could have been triggered in the 1929 earthquake. The slump covers a very large area, approximately one and a half times larger than the province of Newfoundland.

## FORESHOCKS AND AFTERSHOCKS

No foreshocks were felt prior to the occurrence of the mainshock, and only two aftershocks immediately following the mainshock were reported. The first aftershock took place at 7:03 p.m. AST (6:03 EST) and the second aftershock was at 10:03 AST (9:03 EST). Both aftershocks were detected by regional seismographic instruments and both were reported felt by the people around Placentia Bay in Newfoundland.

## LOCATION AND MAGNITUDE

The 1929 earthquake gave good recordings at seismographic stations that were operating at the time in North America and Europe, and from these recordings both the location of the earthquake and its magnitude can be determined. The epicenter of the earthquake was at approximately 44.5°N, 55.0°W, putting it under the edge of the Grand Banks south of Newfoundland. This is about 165 miles (265 kilometers) south of the Burin Peninsula of Newfoundland, where the greatest effects of the tsunami were experienced. It is also the area where the largest concentration of cable breaks was located. The magnitude of the mainshock has been measured as 7.2. The two aftershocks are thought to have occurred in the same general area as the mainshock, but magnitudes have not been reported for either of the aftershocks. The area where the 1929 earthquake was centered continues to be seismically active today, with earthquakes as large as magnitude 4.8 (in 1971) having been recorded from that area in recent decades.

# CHAPTER 11

# 1940: Two Strong Earthquakes Rock New Hampshire

EXCEPT FOR THE 1904 EARTHQUAKE IN MAINE, MOST OF NEW ENG-land had avoided a direct hit by a damaging earthquake since 1755. That changed just before Christmas in 1940, when New England was rocked by a pair of strong earthquakes that were centered in the Ossipee Mountains region of New Hampshire. Although not major shocks, these earthquakes brought some damage and a lot of consternation to the residents of the region.

The first earthquake struck during the early morning hours of Friday, December 20, 1940. The newspaper headlines from December 20 give initial reactions to the sudden shock. The 7:00 a.m. edition of the *Lowell Sun* in Lowell, Massachusetts, had the headline "SLEEPERS JOUNCED AS QUAKE SHAKES LOWELL" along with a front-page article that was headed "Temblor Felt from Jersey to Montreal" with the subheading "No Serious Damage Inflicted; Lasts for Nearly Minute." The "Latest" edition of the *Lowell Sun* for the same day had a banner headline that read, "QUAKE AWAKENED SLEEPING CITY — NO DAM-AGE CAUSED." The front-page article in that edition was the same as for the earlier edition, but it was titled "City Wakened by Early Morning Quake" with the subheading "No Damage Done; Rumble Felt from Jersey to Canada." The *Boston Globe* edition of December 20, 1940, featured a banner headline that read, "QUAKE SHAKES NEW ENGLAND" with a front-page article that was headed "Scantily Clad Folk Rush into Streets as Homes Are Rocked."

The second strong shock took place about 9:43 a.m. on December 24, 1940. Newspaper headlines for this day summarize the local reactions to this second earthquake. The *Fitchburg Sentinel* from Fitchburg, Massachusetts, had the headline "SECOND EARTHQUAKE IN 5 DAYS JARS N.E." The front-page article was headed by the title "Temblor As Severe As Friday's Shock; Has Same Center." The *Lowell Sun* for the same day featured a banner headline that read, "NEW QUAKE ROCKS CITY" with a front-page article that was headed "Second Quake Hits N.E.; No Damage Caused Here." The county edition of the *Lowell Sun* had the banner headline "NEW QUAKE ROCKS N.E.; EXPERTS PREDICT MORE." There were two front-page articles on this second earthquake, one that was titled "Tremor Felt in Lowell Half Minute" and the other titled "Lowell Jarred by Second Quake in Five Days." A small box that contained the weather forecast was on the front page of this edition of the *Lowell Sun*. The forecast for December 24 read, "THE WEATHER: Fair and Warmer (P.S. — No Earthquakes and a Merry Christmas)."

The December 20 shock occurred about 2:27 a.m., and so most people were asleep in bed at the time that the earthquake shaking struck. Many people were suddenly awakened by the earthquake, and most were unsure what was happening. The December 21, 1940, issue of the *Lowell Sun* has a good summary of the first reactions of many:

*Steam boilers in homes got a lot of attention yesterday morning, when the earthquake rumbled through this area. Almost every householder, awakened by the tremor, rushed into the cellar to make sure the boiler hadn't left its moorings. Hardly anyone guessed the rumbling was an earthquake, but instead thought the heating system was about to blow up or that thieves were trying to gain entrance. Some householders even went so far as to go out to their back yards to make sure thieves weren't prowling about. Others stormed the police and fire stations with telephone calls after they found out that their steam boilers were still in place. Among some of the questions asked police were: "Where was the explosion?" "Was there a plane crash?" "Is another hurricane on the way?" "Am I drunk or am I hearing things?" "Whose home blew up?"*

WEATHERMAN SAYS:
Rain and Milder.
Complete report on Page 8

USE NEWSPAPER ADVERTISING FIRST And Reach the LARGEST NUMBER of Buyers

# Biddeford Daily Journal.

PUBLISHED FOR ALL THE PEOPLE OF BIDDEFORD, SACO AND YORK COUNTY

VOL. LVI. NO. 298.   ESTABLISHED 1884   BIDDEFORD, MAINE, FRIDAY EVENING, DECEMBER 20, 1940.   14 PAGES ** PRICE THREE CENTS.

# EARTHQUAKE ROCKS MAINE, NO DAMAGE

## Clique Sabotages Nazi-French Collaboration

### Germans Find Hostile French Groups Are Interfering With Plans

#### Laval To Be Reinstated To Appease Hitler

By LOUIS P. LOCHNER

Berlin, Dec. 20.—(P)—The French cabinet shakeup of last Saturday, known here as "the Putsch of Vichy," has taught the German government one great lesson, men in the know here say.

That lesson, they assert, is that there is an influential group at work within the French government to scuttle, if possible, attempts at a French-German rapprochement such as planned between Reichsfuehrer Hitler and the French former vice premier, Pierre Laval.

German government circles, they reported, long had suspected that not all who were giving lip service to the plan for a "new order in Europe" under German leadership were sincere about it.

Laval's sudden removal unanimously the heads of these countries gave who had forced Laval because they leave him to be acceptable to Germany.

There is no longer even the slightest doubt but that the Wilhelmstrasse was completely surprised by the Vichy upheaval.

The French chief of state, Marshal Philippe Petain, it is arranged in well-informed circles in Berlin, but about him a group of men who just Laval because they leave him to be acceptable to Germany.

As the German-Italian sources had continued, they contended, Laval seemed playing of the way toward a French-German plan.

But, at the story goes, no sooner did he Italians suffer reverses when the Italians called for reverses on Page Two

#### Action Near On Arms Speedup Plan

##### Roosevelt To Meet With National Defense Commission

Washington, Dec. 20.—(P)—President Roosevelt's meeting today with the national defense commission prompted advance forecasts in official circles that definite action to ease on the arms speedup problem.

These quarters looked for a decision on one of several plans calling for a reorganization of defense administration machinery aimed at obtaining the "impossible" by stepping up present production rates to a virtual wartime tempo.

It was understood that the defense industry production of top speed for two reasons.

The first was that approximately $11,000,000,000 worth of additional British orders are being negotiated with President Roosevelt.

(Continued on Page Three)

#### Work To Start Today On South Portland Ship Yard

Portland, Dec. 20.—(P)—Preliminary work was scheduled to start today on a new shipyard in South Portland that will put bigment at least 30 of the freighters on Britain needs so badly.

The first keel would be laid in two and one-half months and the yard completed in four months under plans announced by the Todd interests in New York late last night after conferring with the British to complete the shipyard. Britain is expected to operate on a basis of about $1,000,000 a year. So—other shipyards will be built on the West coast.

Pershing John B. Reilly of the Todd Shipyards Corporation said $5,000 would be employed here by a new affiliate known as the Todd-Bath Iron Corporation of which William S. Newell

### Trapped Italian Army In Africa Battles Fiercely

Would Keep U. S. Out of the War

Mrs. Roosevelt Greets Princess Juliana

#### Attempts To Break Through Blocked Line

By The Associated Press.

Cairo, Dec. 20.—By land, sea and air the British reported their forces kept up a remorseless pounding of Bardia today with Italians trapped in that beleaguered Libyan port battling fiercely to break through their blocked line of retreat to the west.

Supporting the forces encircling Bardia, where the British estimate 20,000 Italians are holding out, the RAF blasted the Libyan coast westward to Derna, 175 miles from the Egyptian frontier. Practically the entire Fascist military at Derna camp was declared in flames.

Heavily raiding Derna simultaneously with a similar assault of Bardia, the RAF continued its set off fires and explosions with direct hits on barracks, police headquarters, motor transport parks and garages at the former base of the Whale House on enemy east.

"When our last aircraft left the scene practically the whole of the camp was ablaze," today's communique said. "Similar raids were carried out on enemy troop concentrations and motor transport to the northwest of Bardia.

(Continued on Page Two)

#### "Three-Power" News To Break Soon

Berlin, Dec. 20.—(P)—Authoritative sources disclosed that today to reinsurance an important news release would be issued pressing any of "intimating prospect of further developments of consequence" between nations involved in the three-power pact.

Officials were silent concerning the contents of the release but one prevailed conjecture was that it might constitute a rejoinder to President Roosevelt's close the other night.

These sources also were expected today or tomorrow to include the French consultations within the French government.

It was intimated that the German comment would become available after the French chief of state, Marshal Philippe Petain, delivered a radio address which he has promised his nation.

No comment was available on the report from abroad, Yugoslavia, that German Foreign Minister Joachim Von Ribbentrop's planes were keeping Balkan relations moving. The diplomatic comments concerning the Adriatic in just fragmentary information.

#### DeWitt MacKenzie

##### Allied Victories Over Italy Are Godsend To British Preparations To Defend Against Invasion

The allied victories over Mussolini in the Mediterranean theatre should prove a Godsend to Britain as intricate preparation for the expected Nazi attempt to invade England.

This threat of invasion is dwarfed by British Premier Churchill as his country's "supreme danger." There can be no doubt of the accuracy of that characterization.

Britain probably is facing her greatest trial by arms[1] since the great war began. It will be inaugurated by a titanic scale of preparation by the German masses during the period of invasion effort. It may be that news intent the British will have to strike to withdraw her forces and the establishment of Hitler's German-ruled "new order."

The Italian defeats in the Egyptian and Greco-Albanian fighting, however, have strength-

### Two Thirty Temblor Shakes Windows And Doors In New England

#### Weather Bureau Reports It Lasted Thirty Seconds

Portland, Dec. 20.—(P)—A strong earthquake roused thousands in Maine to frightened wakefulness at about 2.29 a. m. (E. S. T.) today, but appeared to have caused no damage.

Most of Maine felt the shock—the Weather Bureau fixed its duration as 30 seconds—but its intensity was slight in Aroostook, the state's most northerly county.

Elsewhere the temblor rattled windows and doors, tumbled crockery from cupboard shelves, shook even steel-framed buildings and reportedly knocked several sleepers from their beds.

In Portland, only 45 miles from the epicenter of the general quake, cars in the freight yards at South Portland were thrown to their sidings and the city were moved several feet in some automobiles in a well-town garage lined several feet in New Hampshire—alarmed residents told of hearing a loud Christmas tree atop the Portland fire headquarters swayed as if shaken by a giant hand; the thermostats of a gust shaken in Maine cities; the control of a locomotive shaken by a giant earthquake, sleet or lightening registered in many a telephone exchange; police and fire stations and the early morning patrolmen; the town and many cars tumbled off the telephone operators others and the early morning patrolmen and tremors shook and the telephone calls toll hour; their door furnace boilers had exploded; numerous others aked and the shock's impact made them think after the quake.

(Continued on Page Two)

#### British Pour Bombs Into Valona Port

##### Raid Not Challenged By The Italian Navy, 100 Tons Released

By The Associated Press.

London, Dec. 20.—British air power consisting of battleships, cruisers and destroyers has swept the heavy Adriatic and the battleships poured nearly 100 tons of high explosive shells into the Albanian port of Valona, the admiralty announced today.

The raid, through the 24-mile strait of Otranto, at the first of the Italian fleet, was not challenged by the Italian navy and no fighter clipping was found; the admiralty said. Valona is a vital supply port for Italian forces in southern Albania.

British communiques announced the bombarding Littorio base of the harbor of the Durazzo in Greece, the admiralty assisting the warships, machine operation that British preservation of the Mediterranean, and bombardment made in a tight heavy penetration of the Adriatic for Italian shipping.

The bombardment announced yesterday Italian base of Bardia where, the admiralty said, British Lithium naval preservation, although the British positively and Bardia operations, but the unusual consequences of the British Press Association in their scope.

"It would seem that for movement on Page Six

#### DeTristan Family Again Harassed By Extortionist

Santa Ana, Calif., Dec. 20.—(P)—working recently through a letter sent the Count and Countess De Tristan through the Santa Ana post office, has demanded more money.

Mme. De Tristan, 20.—Another victim of a sustained kidnap plot for ransom—have been harassed saying an extortionist again to extract money and was sought in connection with a cash cabbage patch near Santa Ana.

The suspect, described as an elderly grey-haired man in a thinly-roasted patrol, at the district attorney's office said FBI agents.

#### Italians Retreating in Libya, Says R. A. F.

R. A. F. observers reported the Italian communication lines well outside of Bardia (1), Other land forces retreated across Sirte desert to retire on the great naval base (2). The British are attempting to drive them beyond Tobruk (3). Italian forces have been driven beyond the port of Salum, Port Capuzzo and Sidi Barrani, and the former positions as far east as Mersa-Matruh (2). The British retreat positions as far east as Mersa-Matruh (2). The British retreat positions as far east as Bardia (1). The Italian retreat positions as far east as Sidi Barrani (2). At Bardia (1).

#### Merchant Ship Sunk By Nazis

Berlin, Dec. 20.—(P)—DNB, official German news agency, reported today that a Nazi reconnaissance plane had sunk a 3,200-ton British merchant ship south of the Isle of Wight off Britain's south coast yesterday.

The news agency said the plane made a dive attack and dropped one bomb which struck amidships, tearing the craft apart.

The same source reported that the deck officer.
"I don't hear him."
"Madam," the officer explained, "you have just been visited by an earthquake."

#### Import Control For U. S. Is Possible

Washington, Dec. 20.—The possibility of import control for the United States, hitherto unthinkable but now a serious trade regulation—arrived on inevitable speculation today.

The first question laid that way such an idea was mooted consideration came from Federal Russell L. Maxwell, administrator of export control, during a review of the work done by his department and his agency in directing the American way of export flow.

Ninety students of the situation caught in their faces, that it can be readily "suppress danger." There can be no doubt of the accuracy of the situation.

This basis was pertinent reference to the subject, recurrent at the end of the 2,000 even generous be delivered last night. There was no amplification and, with an example, available government officials produced full assurances to any phase that

#### Woman Reports Man Rattling Porch Window

Saco, Maine, Dec. 20.—An excited woman telephoned early today to report that there was a man rattling the window on her porch.

"Is he there now," asked the desk officer.

#### Sharp Earth Tremors Felt Through County Early This Morning

Most of the residents in this section knew that the occasion today those who sat out this morning in the temblor were made between of organizing an earthquake. Those who did not feel the earth tremors this morning would do well to increase their fire insurance, long queues slacken of some of the apartment houses at that dwellers were disturbed in the walls. Many reported that dishes rattled so that they froze off many iced their beds.

For two minutes about 2.29 buildings shook noticeably. First thing moved that residents seemed to be that the heating apparatus was breaking down, causing a sudden shake and were about to blaze up, several residents reported that they rushed to the basements to see as they feared that the house was being shaken by braces nearby passing.

In some apartments, learn Main street reminders awaked so much in their rooms while an investigation of the heating plant had been made and everything had come to front, in the city building the employer such

#### Italians Pound British Points

Rome, Dec. 20.—(P)—Heavy Italian counter-thrusts in Africa, where Italian guns effectively pounded British warriors and merchant forces, were reported today by the Italian high command.

"Heavy fighting," was reported in the southern flank of the Albanian front while in the northern flank of this Italian elements away a range, blood, and town.

Italy claimed to have the southern flank of the Adriatic to such a force means one of an apparently was weighed and merchant ships in Libyan harbors had been made and everything had come to front. In the (fighting for the corporate report).

(Continued on Page Five)

#### WPA Engineer William Cullinan Resigns Post

Portland, Dec. 20.—The resignation of William E. Cullinan, Jr., district manager and engineer of the Portland WPA office, was announced today by State Administrator John P. Flaherty.

Cullinan, who will join the Civil Aeronautics Authority in Boston, an associate airport engineer, will be succeeded by James W. Damon, district engineer at Halifer.

In Biddeford, Maine, the *Biddeford Daily Journal* of December 21, 1940, contained a summary of people's reaction in their community. An article states,

> *Meanwhile, the citizens who were startled by the rumbling bent one another's ears with stories of their experiences.*
>
> *They included the policeman who thought of letting the inmates out of station cells so they wouldn't get hurt, the man who woke up and thought he was cold and shivering but learned it was the bed that was shaking, the scores who ran to the basements expecting to find the heaters exploded and those who couldn't get back to sleep because aroused dogs wouldn't stop barking.*

A columnist for the *Carroll County Independent–Carroll County Pioneer* of Carroll County, New Hampshire, wrote the following colorful story of one local's reaction to the earthquake during the early morning hours of December 20: "Ransome Goodrich, Wolfeboro's able and capable radio and oil burner man, woke up and thought his burner had gone bad. He dressed and lit his pipe and took his tools and went down cellar and set there smoking and humming to hisself and took his burner all apart and overhauled it and cleaned it and went back to bed about two hours later. In the morning when he heard it was an earthquake he kicked hisself with one swift kick from Wallace's steps to Steve Corkum's store."

Unlike the December 20 event, the December 24 shock was almost immediately recognized as an earthquake by most who felt it. In part this was because of the experience of the strong earthquake just four days earlier. It was also because the second earthquake occurred during the daytime hours when people were awake and about. In many communities immediately following the December 24 shock, the telephone lines were jammed as people called police departments, fire departments, newspaper offices, relatives, or friends to see if they had just experienced another earthquake. The December 24 edition of the *Lowell Sun* noted that the occurrence of this earthquake during daytime hours seemed unusual: "Although New England has felt scores of more minor earthquakes during the past several years, today was the first time a shock was recorded during the daytime."

In fact, earthquakes can occur at any time of the day or night, and some strong earthquakes have taken place during daytime hours, such as the 1884 event that took place near New York City. The impression expressed in the *Lowell Sun* that recent earthquakes tended not to take place during daytime hours represents a local variation rather than a long-term pattern in the way earthquakes take place in the region.

The newspaper reports are mixed about which was the stronger of the two major shocks that took place four days apart. The December 24 issue of the *Kingston Daily Freeman* of Kingston, New York, printed the following comparison of the two earthquakes: "In New England tremors were reported from Maine to Connecticut, and although in many sections they were described as 'slight' and less severe than the shock of last Friday, residents of Lowell, Massachusetts described the 'quake as sharper than last week."

The December 24 edition of the *Biddeford Daily Journal*, contained contradictory reports about the relative strengths of the December 20 and December 24 earthquakes. One article states that the second earthquake was "not as severe as the mild quake felt here last week," but also indicates that at Phillips, Maine, the second shock "was more severe than the earlier one." News reports from Montreal stated that the second earthquake was much heavier than the first. A news item from Syracuse, New York, stated that the second earthquake was more severe than the first. In contrast, the *New York Times* contained an item that the first earthquake was stronger than the second. Other reports from throughout the region indicated that the two earthquakes were of comparable strength. Curiously, a temperature recorder at Badger Farms Creamery in Portsmouth, New Hampshire, acted as a type of seismograph. The pen on the recorder wiggled due to the earthquake shaking and left a brief excursion from the temperature line that it was recording. The December 20 earthquake caused an excursion of five-sixteenths of an inch, whereas the December 24 earthquake caused an excursion of half an inch, suggesting that the second earthquake was stronger than the first at Portsmouth.

## Damage Due to the Earthquakes

With two strong earthquakes at the same remote location having taken place only four days apart, assessing the damage caused by each separate earthquake can be difficult. The Ossipee region where these earthquakes were centered is a mountainous area with scattered small towns, meaning that it was challenging for news reporters and scientists to explore and document the damage that was experienced. There were only a few descriptions of damage that immediately followed the December 20 earthquake. The December 21, 1940, edition of the *Biddeford Daily Journal* contains a report from one local expert who visited the epicentral region. It reads,

> *Roger L. Arringdale, Portland business man who for 20 years has made a hobby of studying earthquakes, rushed to New Hampshire's Lake Ossipee region, center of the shock, and reported he found one basement wall pushed inward about two feet.*
>
> *He said the walls had cracks large enough so he could insert his fist. About 30 chimneys in the area were damaged slightly, he added.*

Arringdale indicated that the greatest effects of the earthquake were at the towns of West Ossipee, Chocorua, and Tamworth in New Hampshire.

There were scattered newspaper reports of minor building damage from several other localities outside the Lake Ossipee region. The reported damage included broken windows in Concord, New Hampshire; a cracked wall in a police station in Keene, New Hampshire; shattered windows in East Boston and Charlestown, Massachusetts; and bricks that were shaken free from some brick walls and chimneys in South Boston. It also reported that plaster was shaking from walls and ceilings in Brookline and Springfield, Massachusetts. The December 20 issue of the *Fitchburg Sentinel* of Fitchburg, Massachusetts, reported that at Medford, Massachusetts, "a wall partly shaken down by a previous quake several years ago, was further demolished." What previous earthquake could have caused the initial damage is not clear. The previous strong earthquake shake to have affected the greater Boston area was the February 28, 1925, magnitude 6.2 earthquake that was centered in the Charlevoix Seismic Zone.

Reports of objects in buildings that were shifted due to the earthquake shaking came from a wide area throughout the northeastern U.S. and nearby Canada. According to newspapers published within a day or so of the earthquake, items fell from shelves or were shifted by the ground shaking throughout the Boston area in Massachusetts; in Augusta, Biddeford, Bingham, Caratunk, Lewiston, and Portland in Maine; in Montreal in Quebec; and in Albany in New York. Sleepers were awakened throughout the region due to the earthquake shaking, and there are several reports of persons being thrown from their beds by the earthquake, including a baby who fell out of its crib. There were also some stories of persons who had trouble standing without holding on to something during the height of the earthquake shaking.

New damage reports followed the occurrence of the second large earthquake on December 24. The December 25 issue of the *Boston Globe* contained the information that "Tamworth in the Ossipee area suffered serious loss, with chimneys of 65 homes leveled." Additionally, 100 chimneys in the Tamworth area were damaged and needed to be repaired or torn down. Furthermore, the same issue of the *Boston Globe* reports that for the Ossipee area, "Many cellar walls caved in. Mr. and Mrs. Harry Sargeant of Chocorua were obliged to vacate their home, because the main chimney had crashed through the roof."

*United States Earthquakes 1940* indicates that it was the December 24 shock that damaged chimneys at Center Ossipee. According to other newspaper reports, at Wonalancet, New Hampshire, in the Ossipee area, in addition to fallen chimneys and broken windows, furniture was overturned by the earthquake and a number of buildings settled on their foundations. Ossipee High School suffered some damage to ceiling rafters that had to be repaired before the school could reopen after the Christmas break. The state reformatory in Concord suffered cracked and buckled walls due to this earthquake, and in addition to some fallen plaster, the front wall of St. Paul's School in Concord was cracked by the shaking. In North Conway, New Hampshire, a crack in a chimney due to the earthquake caused a fire in a house that resulted in significant damage.

Tombstone in Ossipee, New Hampshire, shifted by the 1940 earthquake

Other communities in central New Hampshire also reported damaged chimneys and fallen or cracked plaster.

Other newspaper accounts indicated that many communities at significant distances reported chimney damage, something that was not seen following the December 20 event. After the December 24 shock, several chimneys were reported damaged in Portland, Jefferson Centre, Brownfield, and Augusta, Maine, and a water main was said to have broken in Portsmouth, New Hampshire. Whereas for the December 20 earthquake scattered damage extended south from the Ossipee region into Massachusetts, for the December 24 earthquake, the chimney damage extended primarily east toward Maine. In addition, newspapers indicated that a water main broke in Chicopee Falls, Massachusetts, and windows were broken in Dorchester, Massachusetts.

As in the December 20 earthquake, shaking due to the December 24 earthquake moved objects and vibrated items from shelves across much of the New England region and beyond. Many items including Christmas trees were moved by the earthquake throughout Massachusetts and to southern Rhode Island. One widely reported story was about a rare ancient Japanese gargoyle at the Peabody Museum in Salem, Massachusetts, that fell from a shelf and shattered during the earthquake shaking. Items were knocked from shelves at Kennebunk and Augusta, Maine, to the east, and ornaments fell from Christmas trees at Kingston and Syracuse, New York, to the west.

Sometime after the December 24 earthquake, seismologists from Weston Observatory in Weston, Massachusetts, canvassed the region by sending out postcard questionnaires that had been prepared by the U.S. Coast and Geodetic Survey. They also received many letters from private residents from many parts of the region. These data along with the newspaper reports and personal reconnaissance totaled over 600 separate observations about the effects of the earthquakes. The strongest shaking was apparently experienced at Tamworth, New Hampshire, with strong shaking also taking place at West Ossipee and Chocorua, New Hampshire. Many chimneys were damaged in these towns, although the surveys suggested that the damaged chimneys were those that were in poor condition and needed repointing. In general, only those parts of chimneys that were above the roofline took damage in the earthquake shaking. Also, it was unclear whether those chimneys that collapsed in the second earthquake were weakened due to damage in the first earthquake. At Whittier, New Hampshire, heavy tombstones were rotated, another indication of the strength of the ground shaking. At Portland, Maine, no chimneys suffered damage in the December 20 shock but about a dozen chimneys suffered damage in the December 24 earthquake. This may indicate that the December 24 event was somewhat stronger than the December 20 earthquake.

## TOTAL FELT AREAS OF THE EARTHQUAKES

From newspaper reports it appears that the December 20 and December 24 earthquakes were felt over roughly comparable areas. From newspapers published on December 20 and 21, it is known that the first

Isoseismal map of the December 20, 1940, earthquake

strong earthquake was felt as far west as Buffalo, New York, and Toronto, Ontario; as far north as Montreal; as far east as Aroostook County, Maine; and as far south as central New Jersey. On December 21 several newspapers printed a map showing the area over which the earthquake was felt, with the felt area approximately delimited by Bangor, Maine; Montreal, Quebec; Rochester, New York; and Philadelphia, Pennsylvania. One newspaper report indicated that the earthquake was felt in Ottawa, Ontario. As this earthquake took place in the middle of the night when most persons were in bed asleep, the farthest reaches to which the earthquake was felt are likely not well determined because at those distances the ground shaking would have been too mild to wake most sleepers. Of course, the eastern extent of the felt shaking could not be ascertained because it clearly reached beyond the Maine coast.

The same cities and towns that reported feeling the December 20 earthquake also provided reports about experiencing the December 24 shock. In addition, newspaper accounts indicate that the December 24 earthquake also was felt at Fort Kent in Maine, at Quebec City and Sherbrooke in Quebec, at Owen Sound in Ontario, and at Saint Johns and Fredericton in New Brunswick. At Fredericton a Canadian press report contained the following story:

> *A clock which had not run for years stood on a mantel in the office of J.B. Dickson, Deputy Attorney-General of New Brunswick.*
>
> *Today, as earth tremors rumbled through eastern Canada, the old clock began to tick. Hours later it was still going, although five hours fast.*

Canvassing in Ohio, Maryland, and parts of Pennsylvania indicated that the earthquakes were not felt in those areas. Although the felt area of the December 24 earthquake appears to have been a little larger than that of the December 20 shock, the occurrence of the December 24 earthquake during daytime hours increased the chances that persons at large distances from the earthquake epicenter would have felt and reported that particular shock.

Finally, although strictly speaking this was not a direct felt report, there was one displaced item that earned special attention because it probably indicates how far from the epicenter the earthquake of December 20 might have been felt. This item, as it appeared in the December 21 issue of the *New York Times*, reads, "In Washington, D.C., M. W. Lewis of suburban Hyattsville related how a 10-cent piece acted as his seismograph. He told Dr. Frederick Sohon of Georgetown University's seismology department, according to The Associated Press, that he wagered with a friend last June 24 that a dime would stand indefinitely on edge. When he awoke yesterday the dime lay flat."

## DEATHS AND INJURIES REPORTED DUE TO THE EARTHQUAKES

The newspaper accounts of the December 20 earthquake contain only one account of an injury that could be attributed to the earthquake. The December 21 issue of the *Biddeford Daily Journal* of Biddeford, Maine, reported that a woman slipped on ice and injured her leg as she was hurrying to her sister's house following the earthquake. Fortunately, most people were in bed at the time of the earthquake, meaning that they likely were not in situations where they could be harmed.

On the other hand, one death and at least one injury were attributed to the occurrence of the earthquake on December 24. The description of the death was printed in the December 29 issue of the *New York Times*, based on an account that the newspaper had received from Carroll County, New Hampshire, the area where the earthquake was centered.

*For the first time in 340 years since the Pilgrims landed with unshaken faith and footing on Plymouth Rock an earthquake had directly caused a death in New England.*

*While her husband was fighting a chimney fire at the near-by home of their daughter on Tuesday morning, Mrs. Fred B. Brown, terrorized by the rumble and shake of the tremor, collapsed in her kitchen and died. Dr. Francis J. C. Dube, County Medical Referee, attributed death to overstraining of the heart of the 72-year-old grandmother.*

The December 25 edition of the *Boston Globe* reported that one man in Rockland, Maine, was hit in the head by a paint can that was thrown off a shelf by the seismic waves. At East Weymouth, Massachusetts, a man working under a car that was up on jacks became pinned under the car when it was knocked off the jacks by the earthquake shock. He extricated himself a few minutes later without any noticeable injury. A report from Portland, Maine, indicated that a woman was dazed when she fell and struck her head during the earthquake shaking.

## DURATIONS OF THE EARTHQUAKES

The reported durations of the two mainshocks vary widely from locality to locality and even at the same locality, as is typical for other strong earthquakes in the region. Only a few estimates of the duration of the ground shaking in the December 20 earthquake were included in the newspaper accounts. This likely was because most persons were asleep at the time of the earthquake and therefore could not make a good estimate of how long it lasted. One account that appeared in multiple newspapers was that the earthquake lasted 27 to 30 seconds based on a seismograph reading from Weston Observatory as reported by Fr. James J. Devlin, S.J., of the observatory. Fr. Joseph Lynch, S.J., at Fordham University in New York City, reported that the duration of the earthquake on his seismograph was only two to three seconds. The few estimates of the duration of the ground shaking for the December 20 earthquake range from 30 seconds to five minutes. The December 20 and 21 issues of the *Biddeford Daily Journal* of Biddeford, Maine, had different reports of the duration of the earthquake. One report indicated 30 seconds, one indicated two minutes, and one indicated three to four minutes. That newspaper further stated that three shocks were felt in that city as the earthquake waves passed. At Kingston, New York, the earthquake was experienced as two separate shocks. It is common that localities at far distances from earthquake epicenters report two and sometimes three separate earthquake pulses as the P waves, S waves, and surface waves separate due to their different travel velocities.

In contrast to the earthquake of December 20, there are many estimates of the duration of shaking of the December 24 earthquake that were published in newspapers following the event. At many localities the estimates of the duration of the ground shaking ranged from 10 to 30 seconds, although some localities such as Portsmouth, New Hampshire, and Utica, Watertown, and McGraw, New York, reported durations of one to two minutes. One report from Newport, Rhode Island, thought that the earthquake lasted three minutes, and a report from New York City suggested that the earthquake lasted seven minutes. It is likely that for both the December 20 and December 24 earthquakes, the duration of the ground shaking was in the range of 10 to 30 seconds at most localities. Just as for the December 20 earthquake, the December 24 earthquake was felt as multiple shocks at localities far from the epicentral area. At Owen Sound, Ontario, the earthquake was felt as three separate shocks, whereas it was felt as two separate shocks at Montreal, Quebec, and Kingston, New York.

## FORESHOCKS AND AFTERSHOCKS

The December 1940 earthquakes were the first strong seismic events in New England that were recorded by nearby seismographic stations, which provided data that augmented the reports of locals who felt the earthquake shocks. State-of-the-art Benioff seismographs were being operated by Jesuit priests at Weston Observatory in Weston, Massachusetts, and by Harvard University seismologists at their seismic observatory at Harvard, Massachusetts. In addition, Mr. Joseph Arringdale operated a somewhat older and less sensitive seismographic instrument at Portland, Maine. These instruments gave good recordings of the two strong mainshocks, and they registered traces of the stronger aftershocks that took place in the epicentral region.

Apparently, the first strong earthquake, on December 20, occurred without any warning. Neither the seismograph records at the nearby seismic stations nor the local newspapers provide evidence that any foreshocks preceded that earthquake. Somewhat surprisingly, no aftershocks were reported during the few days that followed that mainshock. The seismographic instruments in Massachusetts did not record any aftershocks from December 20 to 24, and the newspapers contain no reports that anyone felt further seismic activity during this time period.

In contrast, the December 24 earthquake had one foreshock and was followed by a number of aftershocks. At 8:00 a.m. on December 24, the seismographs detected the signals of a small earthquake from the Ossipee region. Local residents also felt this earthquake. The second strong earthquake struck at 8:44 a.m. on December 24, and some newspaper accounts indicate that an aftershock was experienced in the epicentral area about 10 minutes after that. Another aftershock was detected by the seismographs in Massachusetts at 9:33 a.m. and was felt by local residents, and it was followed by still another aftershock at 1:12 p.m. This last earthquake was reported felt in western Maine. Weston Observatory, the center for earthquake monitoring in New England at the time, also reported aftershocks as detected by seismic instrumentation on December 25 at 12:04 a.m., on January 1, 1941, at 10:43 p.m., and on January 4, January 18, January 20, January 22, and February 12.

It is clear that there were some small aftershocks that were felt in the Ossipee region following the December 24 earthquake that were not detected or reported by Weston Observatory, and there likely were some foreshocks as well to the second strong earthquake. An item in the *Carroll County Independent–Carroll County Pioneer* of Carroll County, New Hampshire, of December 27 reads,

*Upheaval Forecast by Weird Sounds*
  *Premonitory rumblings, ghostly and hollow, like the ominous grumbling of distant thunder, were heard on Sunday afternoon and again on Monday evening at mountainside homesteads in the Town of Ossipee. They presaged the temblor of Tuesday morning. And more of them followed.*
  *Human beings were not the only ones to be struck with awe at the vagaries of nature. Cats leaped out of cosy chairs, lashed their tails and yowled. Dogs cowered and whimpered or barked loudly like a boy whistling his way past a cemetery. All had sufficient cause.*

This item reads like a description of foreshocks and aftershocks that were so small they were heard and felt only in the town of Ossipee. The December 25 issue of the *Manchester Union Leader* of Manchester, New

Hampshire, reported that Harry Damon of Tamworth, New Hampshire, felt a total of 11 earthquakes on December 24 between the time of the foreshock at 8:01 a.m. and an aftershock that he felt about 3:00 p.m. In the days following December 24, the people of central New Hampshire apparently felt a number of aftershocks. For example, the *Portsmouth Herald*, published in Portsmouth, contained an item that reads, "So it was another earthquake in the series yesterday!" This may have been an earthquake that was reported from the Ossipee area at 2:55 p.m. on December 27. The book *United States Earthquakes 1940*, published by the U.S. Coast and Geodetic Survey, states that at Tamworth, "One observer reported 129 aftershocks through January 31, 1941." These likely were small aftershocks that were only felt in the immediate epicentral region around Tamworth.

## Earthquake Sounds

No firsthand accounts of the sounds that accompanied the shaking in these two strong earthquakes have been found in contemporary newspapers. In part this reflects the style of news reporting in 1940, since newspapers were more likely to produce summaries of what had happened rather than to print verbatim quotations from individuals describing what they experienced. Also in part this probably is due to the fact that central heating with cellar boilers had become widespread throughout the region, and the first impression of many persons was that the boiler had exploded or otherwise malfunctioned in the cellar. Of course, the sensation of an explosion could be due to a noise or a vibration (or both), and so the impression that there had been an explosion may or may not be an indication that a noise emanating from the ground was heard.

For the December 20 shock, the earthquake shaking was most commonly reported to have been accompanied by a "roaring sound." This was true for Barre, Vermont; Fitchburg, Massachusetts; and Portland, Maine. In Fitchburg one person who was awake at the time of the earthquake claimed that "the quake began with a rumble that increased in volume almost to a roar. He said he thought it sounded like a truck at first and then like an explosion."

The initial "rumble" likely was the P wave and the later "explosion" most probably accompanied the arrival of the S wave. The December 24 shock was also accompanied by a "roaring sound" in Portland, Maine, and a "rumbling sound" in Syracuse, New York. Alfred, Maine, said that the earthquake shaking was accompanied by a "loud rumble." At Tamworth, New Hampshire, and the nearby towns near the earthquake epicenter, the earthquake sounds that accompanied all of the events were described as a "rumbling sound." Curiously, the December 24 edition of the *Syracuse Herald* from Syracuse, New York, reported that Rochester, New Hampshire, had heard a roaring sound during the December 20 shock but not during the December 24 event. The reason for this difference is unclear, especially since many thought that the December 24 was the stronger of the earthquakes.

## EARTHQUAKE LIGHTS

No mentions of earthquake lights are contained in the reports of either of these earthquakes.

## ANIMAL BEHAVIOR

There were only a few reports of unusual animal behavior due to the earthquakes. In their report on the earthquake in the *Bulletin of the Seismological Society of America*, authors Fr. James J. Devlin, S.J., Fr. Lawrence C. Langguth, S.J., and R. L. Arringdale reported that the dogs at the Chinook Kennels in the Tamworth area barked and ran about during the earthquake shaking. They also stated that there were rumors in Tamworth that the dogs in town started barking before the earthquakes. At Alfred and Portland, Maine, and Portsmouth, New Hampshire, news reports stated that dogs and cats in those towns were disturbed by the earthquake. Curiously, one dog seemed undisturbed by the early morning earthquake of December 20. The December 21 issue of the *Biddeford Daily Journal* of Biddeford, Maine, contained a report that reads, "Leslie Tebbetts who lives at Wells Beach woke up startled, looked at his dog who was not disturbed and went back to sleep again declaring to himself he had a nightmare."

The earthquakes caused some poultry losses to farmers in New Hampshire and Massachusetts. The December 27 issue of the *Portsmouth (New Hampshire) Herald* has the following news item:

*Quake Hit Poultrymen*
*Center Ossipee—Poultrymen in this area are just now begin-*
*ning to discover their true losses due to the recent earthquake. On*
*some farms egg production has been cut one-third and hatchings are*
*reduced, many birds being found dead in their shells.*

The December 29 issue of the *New York Times* had a similar new item. It reads,

*Mrs. Irene C. Goodson, proprietor of the Ridgehaven Turkey Farm at*
*Chocorua Village, largest of its kind in New England, reported that*
*250 turkeys had been found dead in their shells when hatches were*
*removed today.*
*At Wilbur S. Goodson's Pinetop Poultry Farm in Tamworth*
*15,000 hen's eggs in the process of hatching were destroyed by the*
*earthquake.*

A news item in the *Boston Globe* of December 28 notes that "among the casualties of the recent earthquake was the death by fright or shock of five hens belonging to Harry F. Hastings of Athol. They simply could not take it."

## Ground Cracks and Water-Level Changes

Because the earthquakes happened in late December, the ground was frozen and snow covered, and there was ice on the lakes and ponds throughout the region. There were several reports of cracks in the frozen ground following the earthquakes. The December 27 edition of the *Carroll County Independent–Carroll County Pioneer* of Carroll County, New Hampshire, contained the following discussion of ground cracks:

*Although no yawning chasms opened up, the earth was cracked in several places radiating north from the epicenter. A fissure eleven and a half inches wide and deep as a scooping hand followed the railroad bed for miles between Ossipee and Madison. Section men made it safe before the noon train steamed along.*

*A crevice two and a half inches wide slashed across the farm of Elwin Drew in Madison and ribbons the diameter of a carpenter's pencil slit Turkey Street in Tamworth and High Street in Madison. Similar tracings of the earth's inner fury left their marks elsewhere.*

The paper by Devlin, Langguth, and Arringdale noted that cracks about a half inch in width and running in all directions were seen in the frozen snow in the fields around Tamworth, New Hampshire, following the earthquakes. They attributed these cracks to the effects of the ground shaking on the frozen soil. According to the December 25 edition of the *New York Times*, a fissure opened in the ground near the Farnum Ski Club, and there was settlement of some sections of land in the Tamworth area. Some ground cracks also were reported at George's Mills, New Hampshire.

One report that showed up in several newspapers was that Lake Ossipee had dropped about a foot or even more due to the earthquakes. Devlin, Langguth, and Arringdale stated in their paper that the lake had dropped a foot in level, but they attributed the drop to the removal by a utility employee of a board from a dam at one end of the lake. A change in the lake level was disputed in a different way in the December 25 edition of the *Manchester Union Leader* in Manchester, New Hampshire. An item in that newspaper reads, "The shocks brought out a new batch of rumors, including one that the level of water in Lake Ossipee had fallen two feet, but all proved false. Sheriff James Welch of Tamworth and lakeside dwellers said ice in the lake was broken up and sand from the bottom was pushed up into windrows three feet high on the north shore, but that was all."

The January 3, 1941, edition of the *Carroll County Independent–Carroll County Pioneer* printed several readings of the relative level of

Lake Ossipee from throughout December 1940, and these readings indicated that the level of the lake had been quite steady, with a small rise of a few inches at the end of the month due to a storm at that time.

There were a few reports of the effects of the shaking on rivers due to the December 24 earthquake. There were multiple reports that the ice on the Cocheco River settled due to the earthquake and that there were ripples seen on the Salmon Falls River at East Rochester, New Hampshire. A report in *United States Earthquakes 1940* stated that small waves were observed on the Presumpscot River. In addition to these observations, a number of persons reported that the water in their wells was muddied by the earthquakes. On the other hand, hundreds of wells in the Tamworth area were reported to have run dry due to the December 24 earthquake.

## Magnitudes and Locations of the
## 1940 Ossipee Earthquakes

In 1940 there were several scientists in New England who were actively studying the earthquakes in the region, trying to figure out where they occurred, why they were taking place, and what might happen in the future. Since 1935 Weston Observatory in Weston, Massachusetts, a seismic observatory run by the Jesuits priests of New England, had been accumulating earthquake readings from seismographs and publishing bulletins of earthquake locations in the region. Following the first strong earthquake, on December 20, seismologists at the time determined its epicenter to be somewhere at the southern end of Lake Ossipee with a depth of focus between 25 and 50 miles below the surface of earth. For the second strong earthquake, on December 24, the seismologists put that epicenter at the northern end of Lake Ossipee in the Tamworth area. These epicenters and focal depths were determined using the best methods at the time. The epicenters were found from arcs drawn on a map of the region, with the center of each arc at the location of a seismic station and the radius of the arc related to the times of the P-wave and S-wave arrivals at that station. The center of the area where the arcs intersected was reported as the earthquake epicenter, and the focal depth was estimated based on the size of the area where the arcs converged.

By the 1980s seismologists had much better methods for locating earthquakes. Instead of arcs drawn in pencil on a map, an earthquake epicenter was found from the P-wave and S-wave times using a computer program based on a mathematical analysis of the data. The focal depth of an earthquake was estimated based on the seismic waveforms recorded at distant stations in places like Europe and South America. Based on results using these modern methods, seismologists today can show that the epicenter of the December 20 earthquake was a few miles west of Tamworth, New Hampshire, and that of the December 24 earthquake was a couple miles north of Tamworth. The December 20 earthquake originated from about 6 miles (10 kilometers) below the surface of the earth, whereas the December 24 earthquake originated at a depth of about 4 miles (6 kilometers). Both earthquakes had magnitudes of about 5.5.

## CONTEMPORARY EXPERT OPINION ABOUT THE 1940 OSSIPEE EARTHQUAKES

Like today, in 1940 the news media turned to local experts to explain what had happened, why it had happened, and what might happen in the future. Following the December 20 earthquake, many newspapers contained statements from scientists opining on the strength of the shock, its rarity, and what the shock might portend about future earthquake activity in the region. Most of the scientists called it a minor earthquake capable of little or no damage, and it was noted that the shock was much smaller than many that had been experienced in California. The experts did note that the earthquake was larger than usual for the region. One seismic expert termed it a "severe earthquake."

Regarding the prospects of strong earthquake activity in the future, the opinions of the experts were decidedly mixed. Prof. Kirtley F. Mather, a geologist on the faculty at Harvard University, stated that "there will be another earthquake in six or eight months which will be felt by many people in southern New England and might do a little damage." He used as the basis of his appraisal the past earthquake history of the region, and he stated that the most likely location of the next earthquake would be "in the St. Lawrence Valley." In contrast, Dr. L. Don Leet, who was the director of the Harvard Seismological Observatory, felt that there was not any danger of a "great seismic catastrophe in the near future," although he cautioned that seismologists cannot predict "the time and nature of coming earthquakes." Fr. Michael J. Ahern, S.J., and Fr. James J. Devlin, S.J., of the Weston Observatory concurred with Dr. Leet's opinion.

The occurrence of a second strong earthquake on December 24 just four days after the first shock and with an epicenter near that of the first shock clearly surprised the local experts. Several indicated that the occurrence of two strong earthquakes just days apart was unprecedented in New England earthquake history. Furthermore, the second earthquake shifted not just the earth but the opinions of the local seismic experts as well. Professor Mather declared that this second earthquake was the one he had predicted days earlier and that he expected no further significant earthquakes, although small ones might continue during the next months. Dr. Leet, on the other hand, declared to the press that he expected further earthquake activity, including "probably a major one" in the Ossipee area of New Hampshire. Fr. J. Joseph Lynch, S.J., of the seismic observatory at Fordham University, felt that there was no cause for alarm of another serious earthquake. In any case the newspapers indicated that the sales of earthquake insurance soared in New Hampshire and surrounding areas follow the earthquakes.

Although the experts could not agree on what future earthquake activity might occur, they did concur that the cause of the earthquakes was the continuing uplift of the crust of the earth following the melting of the last continental glaciation in the region 10,000 to 20,000 years ago. This idea was metaphorically expressed in a headline in the December 20 issue of the *Biddeford Daily Journal* of Biddeford, Maine, that read, "N. E. Merely Straightening Its Back." By 1940 geoscientists knew that the weight of the ice during the continental glaciation had depressed the crust of the earth. Once the ice melted, the crust slowly rebounded, uplifting the area that had been previously glaciated. The glacier had covered all of New England and had extended as far south as Long Island, New York, and there is abundant geologic evidence throughout New England of the glacial rebound. The scientists also knew that earthquakes occur on faults, and geologic mapping had found evidence of many old faults all through the northeastern U.S. and southeastern Canada. Seismologists had already detected many earthquakes throughout this region (an average of 10 per year in New England, according to Dr. Leet), and so the connection between postglacial rebound, faults, and earthquakes seemed to be the logical explanation at the time.

Today the seismological evidence strongly supports the idea that the occurrences of earthquakes in northeastern North America are due to pressures in the crust that arise from the movement of the tectonic plates over the surface of the earth. Postglacial rebound probably plays only a minor role in causing the earthquakes throughout the region. However, the evidence and theories of plate tectonics were unknown in 1940, and so postglacial rebound was the only force known to the scientists of the time that could deform the crust. Because the seismologists had estimated a very deep focus for the earthquakes, they knew that they could not tie the earthquakes to any individual surface fault, and they did not do so in the newspaper reports of the time. Even today the fault or faults upon which the 1940 earthquakes took place are unknown.

## CHAPTER 12

# 1944: An Earthquake During a World War

IN THE MONTH OF SEPTEMBER 1944, THE UNITED STATES WAS embroiled in the most catastrophic global war ever seen on earth up to that point in time. Day after day the news was filled with descriptions of battles, military tactics, victories, and losses from both the European and Pacific theaters of war. At home everyone was pitching in to help the war effort wherever possible. Whether it was working in factories to produce weapons, coping with the daily challenges caused by rationed goods, or joining the military to work directly on the effort, the lives of all Americans were dramatically affected by the Second World War. It was against this backdrop that a strong earthquake suddenly shocked the northeastern U.S. and adjacent areas of Canada at 12:40 a.m. on September 5, 1944. Many people in the region immediately recognized that an earthquake had occurred based on their experiences of a pair of strong earthquakes in New Hampshire in 1940 and of a large earthquake centered in western Quebec in 1935. However, with the war on everyone's mind, some people wondered whether they had felt an earthquake or if the Germans had come to their town.

Although the earthquake was centered in northern New York State near the border with Ontario, telephone switchboards in cities like Boston, New York, and Toronto were flooded with calls almost immediately after the shaking was felt. In those days telephone calls were connected by a human switchboard operator from the caller's phone to the phone being called, and the sudden deluge of calls overwrought the night staffs at the switchboards. In Toronto one exhausted switchboard operator finally just gave up answering calls altogether.

## *Quake Jars Thousands in N.E.*

# BRITISH PLUNGE INTO HOLLAND

### SHOCKS FELT FROM CANADA TO DELAWARE

12:40 A. M. Tremors Also Jolt Ohioans, But Damage Is Light

ALLIED DRIVES INTO LOW COUNTRIES AND GERMANY are proceeding with lightning speed. Covering 225 miles in four and a half days, British Second Army forces have taken Lille, Brussels, Antwerp and reached Breda, seven miles inside Holland, thereby cutting off 100,000 Germans between Abbeville and mouth of Scheldt river. Canadians from Abbeville are moving up against these newly isolated Nazis. U. S. First and Third army columns are reported attacking outer Siegfried Line defenses around Aachen and Prel.

## *Antwerp Captured; Yanks Press Rhine*

### ALLIES POINT TO FLANK ALL GOTHIC LINE

**8th Army Canadians Pound Rimini Anchor; 5th Army Keeps Pace**

ROME, Sept. 4 (AP)—Powerful Canadian forces of the Eighth Army had the vital Adriatic coastal city of Rimini almost within their grasp tonight after a slashing attack carried them across the Conca river and gave them a solid bridgehead two miles deep within less than seven miles of the important terminus of the Po valley highway.

By DREW MIDDLETON
(Boston Herald-N. Y. Times Cable)

LONDON, Sept. 5 (Tuesday)—The flood tide of Allied military might has swept northward across Belgium into The Netherlands and eastward to the German frontier where it is rushing on the outer defenses of the Siegfried-line.

British tanks smashed through Brussels and Antwerp, then raced across the Dutch frontier to capture Breda, seven miles to the north, and to begin the liberation of The Netherlands.

**100,000 Nazis Isolated on Channel**

The whole of Pas de Calais, the channel ports and about 100,000 Germans have been isolated by the thrust which has carried the British Second Army 225 miles in four and a half days.

The First and Third American armies have pushed far beyond the last positions at which they were officially reported. Armored formations of First Army have reached the German frontier on a wide front through Belgium, according to the Algiers radio. Aachen, a German rail-road center three and a half miles over the border, is being shelled, although there are some unconfirmed reports and some unofficial information from which indications that it is already being assaulted by tank forces.

Although there is a blackout of news from the Twelfth Army Group, there is no reason to disbelieve reports concerning its progress, only scattered groups of Germans are serving as rearguards between the two American armies and German defensive positions in the Reich.

### PATCH'S MEN RACE 47 MI. ABOVE LYON

**Reach Montrevel on East Bank of Saone, French Gain on West**

ROME, Sept. 4 (AP)—Lush southward on both banks of the Saone river tonight in pursuit of German forces fleeing from the heart of France. Firsth communications show victory at Lyon, to which the last enemy resistance had been stilled.

*(Continued on Page First)*

### U. S. Sea and Air Blows Smash 107 Jap Aircraft, 44 Vessels

Three-Day Assault Rakes Bonins; Enemy Pounded South to Celebes

*(By the Associated Press)*

A thundering series of American air and naval actions over the vast Pacific war front was officially reported today to have resulted in the destruction or damaging of 107 Japanese planes and 44 ships and barges.

### SOVIET-FINN FIGHTING ENDS

Nazi Withdrawal Issue Still Clouded

STOCKHOLM, Sept. 5 (AP)—Finland's three years of war with Soviet Russia ended with a dramatic "cease firing" order today, and guns of both sides along the 300-mile front from Viipuri to Salla subsided into silence.

### Reds Nearing Border of Yugoslavia

LONDON, Tuesday, Sept. 5 (AP)—Spinning troops racing down the Danube valley toward a junction with the forces of Tito have reached Turnu Severin, the Danube river town Bucharest.

### 10,000 Dazed Nazis Quit Around Mons

By HAROLD DENNY
(Boston Herald-N. Y. Times Wireless)

WITH THE FIRST UNITED STATES ARMY IN BELGIUM, Sept. 4—The rout of the German troops which have been cut off in the west by lightning American and British drives in Belgium seems now to be complete. Since yesterday afternoon they have been surrendering in huge groups observing little fight. The German forces appear to have no general plan. Divisional commanders simply are given a point to which they are to conduct their forces and receive new instructions.

### U. S. Seizes 4 Pennsylvania Coal Mines

By LEWIS WOOD
(Boston Herald-N. Y. Times Special)

WASHINGTON, Sept. 4—The seizure of four more Pennsylvania coal mines.

### Use of Force Wins Parley's Full Backing

By JAMES B. RESTON
(Boston Herald-N. Y. Times Special)

WASHINGTON, Sept. 4—The Dumbarton Oaks conference has reached general agreement on the basic principle.

### VACATIONISTS BACK AFTER LABOR DAY BOOM

### 11-FOOT SHARK CAUGHT AT NAHANT

### Engineers Relish Folies 'Eye-Beam'

By CATHERINE COYNE
(Wireless to the Herald)

### Germans Resume Robot Barrage

LONDON, Tuesday, Sept. 5 (AP)—Another robot bomb attack on the London area.

Newspaper front page from Boston, Massachusetts, for September 5, 1944

Although the newspapers carried articles about the earthquake, the seismic event clearly took second billing to the latest news from the war fronts. The *Ogdensburg Journal* published in Ogdensburg, New York, featured the earthquake on page 3 of its September 5, 1944, issue, even though the town was strongly shaken by the earthquake. The front page of that issue was devoted to war news. The *Boston Herald* published in Boston, Massachusetts, put out an extra edition on September 5, 1944, with a banner headline about the earthquake that was just above a larger banner headline about the war. The headlines read, "Quake Jars Thousands in N.E." "BRITISH PLUNGE INTO HOLLAND."

Only one of the twelve columns of news on the front page of that edition of the *Boston Herald* was about the earthquake, with the rest of the front-page articles containing war news.

## DAMAGE IN THE EPICENTRAL AREA

Although it was not a major seismic event, the September 5, 1944, earthquake did a great deal of damage to the cities of Cornwall, Ontario, and Massena, New York. These cities, which lie on either side of the international border, apparently were in the area of the strongest seismic shaking radiated by the earthquake. Furthermore, sections of both of these cities are situated on soft sandy or clay soils that amplified the ground shaking compared to that experienced on nearby firm soils and rock.

Most of what is known about the earthquake damage in Cornwall and Massena came from three scientific investigations that were carried out immediately after the earthquake. Dr. Ernest A. Hodgson of the Dominion Observatory of Ottawa, Canada, conducted a detailed damage survey in the epicentral region. Dr. Charles P. Berkey, a geologist in the United States Engineer Office in New York, also came to the epicentral region to inspect the effects of the earthquake. Scientists from the United States Coast and Geodetic Survey carried out their own field investigations of the epicentral region. The last group also canvassed a wide area of the eastern U.S. to ascertain the total felt area and felt effects of the earthquake, and the Dominion Observatory carried out a similar investigation for Canada. Because they were focused on war coverage, newspapers of the time contain relatively few reports of the damage effects.

Most of the buildings at Cornwall, Ontario, sustained some damage due to the earthquake. The city contained just over 3,000 buildings at the time of the earthquake, and about 2,000 chimneys were damaged to the point that repairs were required. The upper wall of the house of Mrs. Alex Clark collapsed into the street due to the seismic waves. The front wall of the Bank of Commerce caved inward, and some blocks atop the post office were shaken down to the sidewalk. Fortunately, because of the late hour of the shock, the streets were empty and businesses were closed, and for this reason no one was hurt by these collapses. A number of masonry walls were cracked by the earthquake shaking, and reports of cracks in plaster walls and broken windows were common across the city. Because of earthquake damage, two schools in Cornwall were judged unsafe following the earthquake and were closed. Besides the structural damage to buildings, objects were knocked from shelves throughout the city, with many homes and businesses sustaining broken glass and china. Some pipes were broken by the earthquake shaking. From data provided to Dr. Hodgson by the Cornwall city engineer, it appears that the bulk of the damage took place in the parts of the city built on deep or sandy soils. Areas built on harder surficial materials sustained much less damage. An estimate of the total damage in Cornwall at the time was placed at about $1 million.

At the nearby city of Massena, New York, about 10 miles (16 kilometers) from Cornwall, the story was very similar. Reports suggest that every building in Massena sustained some damage due to the earthquake. About 90 percent of the chimneys in the city, roughly 2,500 to 3,000 in number, were damaged, and the town hall suffered badly from the shaking. One school reported 60 broken window lights and severely cracked cement floors. Plaster walls were found to have cracks in many buildings. The town water pipes were broken in some places, although the city was able to locate and repair those in short order. Objects were knocked from shelves and walls throughout the city, and many houses reported plumbing fixtures that needed repairs. The damage at Massena was valued at about $1 million. Dr. Hodgson, who had visited both Cornwall and Massena immediately following the earthquake, had the impression that the earthquake effects were slightly worse at Cornwall than at Massena. As at

Tombstones near Massena, New York, damaged by the 1944 earthquake

Cornwall, the damage at Massena appears to have been greater in those areas of the city that were built where the surficial materials were composed of deep, soft soils.

One interesting set of observations of damage due to the earthquake was taken at cemeteries at Cornwall and Massena. As documented by Dr. Hodgson, a number of cemetery monuments in both cities were rotated or knocked over due to the earthquake shaking. The cemeteries in the Cornwall area where the greatest damage was observed were on sandy soil, indicating that the local soft soils amplified the ground shaking. At Cornwall a large majority of the cemetery monuments were rotated in a counterclockwise manner, whereas at Massena the cemetery monuments were predominantly rotated in a clockwise direction. This observation was used by the seismologists to infer that the epicenter of the earthquake may have been between these two cities. At a cemetery about 4 miles east of Massena, there was an urn on a grave marker that was damaged by the earthquake. The earthquake shaking was sufficiently strong at this cemetery to break the urn at its neck and to hurl the body of the urn about three feet from its base. The ground surface showed no marks of urn, indicating that the urn did not roll to its final resting spot but rather flew through the air to where it landed.

The field investigations revealed that the severe earthquake damage was limited to a small area that included the cities of Cornwall and Massena. Damage was markedly less just 5 miles (8 kilometers) east of Cornwall, and a similar observation was made about 5 miles (8 kilometers) south of Cornwall. However, significant damage was found as far as 15 miles (24 kilometers) west of Massena. Thus, the strongest shaking seems to have extended farther to the west of the epicenter than to the east.

Because this earthquake occurred during the time of a major war, construction materials were in short supply, as were workers to do the reconstruction work. A shortage of bricks and of masons hindered the ability of many people to get immediate repairs to their chimneys, although local officials moved quickly to find resources to make up for this shortage. Fortunately, the earthquake took place at a time of warm weather when many chimneys were not in use, and some good weather following the earthquake provided the opportunity to arrange necessary repairs before the chimneys were needed for cold-weather heating.

## Injuries Due to the Earthquake

There were no deaths attributed to the earthquake, and only a couple of injuries were reported. In Cornwall one person was said to have been injured during the shaking, and in Massena one woman was cut by a picture frame that fell on her head. The lack of deaths and paucity of injuries in this earthquake are unquestionably due to the late hour of the event, as most people were at home and in bed. Had the earthquake occurred during the middle of the day, the injury and casualty count probably would have been higher.

## Damage Outside the Epicentral Area

There were scattered reports of some minor damage well outside the epicentral area. In New York State reports of chimney damage came from several places in St. Lawrence County as well as from Malone, Fort Covington, and Keeseville, the last about 65 miles (105 kilometers) from Massena. The earthquake shaking broke some water mains in Plattsburgh, and a window was broken in Rochester. Vermont likewise reported minor effects. In Shelburne some windows were broken, and at the offices of the *Burlington Free Press* in Burlington, water sloshed onto the floor from some fire buckets that were stored in the building. Also at Burlington some guns were knocked to the floor from their rack in a police station, and at St. Johnsbury furniture was moved across the floor by the earthquake shaking.

The earthquake affected the city of Toronto, Ontario, in a number of ways. The electrical service throughout the city went down at the time of the earthquake, but it was restored about nine minutes later. One hospital lost power for about 20 minutes. A few chimneys were damaged in East Toronto, items were knocked from shelves at many places throughout the city, and the shaking triggered some burglar alarms to sound. Burglar alarms were also set off in Hamilton, Ontario, where a church steeple sustained some damage from the seismic waves. Items fell from some shelves in London, Ontario, and Tonawanda, Pennsylvania, and the ground shaking moved some furniture in Buffalo, New York. The earthquake ground motions rang church bells in Oneonta, New York, and some plate-glass windows were broken in Greenfield, Massachusetts, due to the earthquake shock. One report claimed that some chairs in Connecticut were knocked over by the earthquake shaking. In Boston there were a few reports of broken dishes and cracked windows due to the seismic shock. A water main break in New York City was blamed on the earthquake shaking.

One very minor effect was reported at Washington, DC, due to the earthquake. The September 6, 1944, issue of the *Boston Globe* has a report that reads,

> *Earthquake Stops Senate Clock*
> *Washington, Sept. 5 (AP) — The Senate's clock stopped today and J. Mark Trice, deputy sergeant at arms, hazarded a guess that maybe its innards had been jolted by last night's earthquake.*

## LONG-DISTANCE FELT EFFECTS AND TOTAL FELT AREA OF THE EARTHQUAKE

For places at far distances from the epicenter of the earthquake, the felt effects showed local variations that reflect the amount of amplification

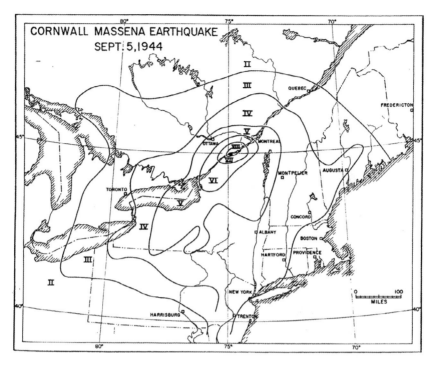

Isoseismal map of the 1944 earthquake

of the seismic waves by local soil conditions. This was especially evident in the large coastal cities, where local soil conditions can vary considerably over short distances and where sections of the cities are built on man-made land. According to the September 5, 1944, issue of the *New York Times*, the earthquake was generally felt on the east side of Manhattan, whereas it was felt only in the tall buildings at Times Square. The earthquake shaking along Park Avenue in Manhattan was strong enough to awaken many people. Queens police reports indicated that most of the calls about the earthquake were received from Jackson Heights, Forest Hills, and nearby sections of Jamaica, whereas it was not felt at the police headquarters in Jamaica. The administration building and hangars at La Guardia Airport felt noticeable shaking, but persons on the eastern side of the field and at the adjacent seaplane base reported feeling nothing at all. At Toronto, Ontario, the September

5, 1944, edition of the *Globe and Mail* reported that the area of East Toronto along Lake Ontario felt the earthquake more strongly and for a longer period of time than those areas away from the water. For Boston the *Boston Herald* extra edition of September 5, 1944, reported that the earthquake was felt particularly severely in the Back Bay, a section of the city that is built on man-made land that had been put atop the soft soils of the Charles River estuary.

The total felt area of the earthquake was well-established by the canvassing carried out by American and Canadian scientists. To the west the earthquake was felt noticeably in Detroit, Michigan, and some reports of felt shaking came from as far west as Milwaukee, Wisconsin. To the south the earthquake was felt in Norfolk, Virginia. To the east the earthquake was felt throughout Maine and into New Brunswick. In Canada the earthquake was felt noticeably in Quebec City and Chicoutimi, Quebec, to the northeast and as far as James Bay to the northwest. The total estimated felt area of the earthquake was about 800,000 square miles (about 2 million square kilometers).

## Duration of the Earthquake

There are only a few reports of how long the earthquake shaking was felt. In part this was because many people were asleep at the time of the earthquake, and in part this was because of the limited coverage the newspapers gave to the earthquake. The September 5, 1944, edition of the *Globe and Mail* reported that the earthquake duration in Toronto was a long three minutes, although some in Toronto indicated that the earthquake shaking lasted only about 40 seconds. The same edition of the *Globe and Mail* reported durations of two to three minutes at Manchester, New Hampshire; Portland, Maine; and Worcester, Massachusetts. Parts of upstate New York indicated that the ground shaking lasted 30 seconds to one minute, and a report from Ottawa, Ontario, stated that the earthquake was felt for 15 to 20 seconds.

The September 5, 1944, edition of the *Globe and Mail* contained some detailed reports of the ground shaking. At Montreal, Quebec, a telegraph operator on duty at the time of the earthquakes reported that "there was a five-second tremor at 12:39 followed 10 seconds later by a severe shock which lasted some time. Soon afterwards a less severe third shaking occurred. The whole series of shocks was over in less than a minute."

Three separate tremors, each lasting about 8 to 12 seconds, were also said to have been experienced at Toronto.

The September 5, 1944, issue of the *New York Times* contains a detailed observation of the earthquake shaking as made by A. V. Madge, a Montreal astronomer. This observation reads, "He said he timed the first tremors at ten seconds after 12:30 A.M. and then continued for seventeen seconds with increasing intensity and then dwindled after a total rumbling of 1 minute and three seconds."

## FORESHOCKS AND AFTERSHOCKS

No reports have been found of any foreshocks being felt in the Cornwall-Massena area during the weeks or months prior to the September 5 mainshock. However, the seismograph at Ottawa, Ontario, detected small earthquakes on August 9 and August 10, 1944, with waveforms that are consistent with a location in the Cornwall-Massena area. There was a small earthquake detected at Ottawa on February 18, 1944, that might also have come from the Cornwall-Massena area. Unfortunately, determining the precise locations of these three earthquakes is not possible using the available data from the single seismic station, and thus these three events must be regarded only as possible foreshocks.

Following the mainshock there were many aftershocks that were detected by the seismographs in Canada and were felt by the local residents. Seismographic stations detected six aftershocks on September 5 and another six aftershocks during the next week. Several additional aftershocks were detected during the rest of September and in October of 1944. Occasional aftershocks were observed throughout 1945, 1946, and 1947 from the location of the mainshock.

Dr. Ernest Hodgson of the Dominion Observatory at Ottawa, Ontario, provided a graphic description of one of the aftershocks that he felt during post-earthquake investigations in the epicentral area. In an article in the January 1945 issue of the *Journal of the Royal Astronomical Society of Canada*, he described an aftershock that he and his colleagues experienced on Saturday, September 9, 1944:

*The group was at dinner in the Cornwallis Hotel at 7:25 that evening, when a severe aftershock was experienced, which brought all diners to their feet in a hurry. Fortunately, the tremors lasted only a few seconds; there was no time for panic. The disturbance began as a faint rumble, quickly becoming stronger and followed by an explosive bang, which felt as though the boiler had exploded in the basement, after which it terminated with a few rumbling sounds. It was decidedly the most severe shock which the writer has ever felt in his limited personal experience. It was registered at Ottawa, where the seismographs showed it to be of about the same intensity as the one at 5 a.m. on September 5. These two have been, so far, the most severe of the many aftershocks, which were at first experienced every few hours and then at increasingly longer intervals, continuing up to the date of writing this account.*

Dr. Hodgson's description of the faint rumbling sound coming first and then the earthquake building up to an explosive "bang" makes perfect sense. Even at a close distance to the epicenter, as undoubtedly Dr. Hodgson was, the P wave is the first arriving wave. The P wave in the rock converts to a sound wave at the earth's surface, and what Dr. Hodgson heard was the sound wave in the air generated by the seismic wave in the earth below. A few seconds later the much stronger S wave arrived. Near the epicenter this is the strongest wave that is felt. Because the S wave can convert to a P wave and therefore a sound wave at the earth's surface, in addition to stronger shaking, the S wave is accompanied by a much louder sound, and hence the explosive bang that Dr. Hodgson experienced. Dr. Hodgson's report makes clear that a large number of small aftershocks that were not detected by the Ottawa seismograph were felt by the Cornwall and Massena residents during the first few days after that mainshock, something that other reports suggest as well.

## EARTHQUAKE SOUNDS
The scientists who went to the epicentral area immediately following the mainshock collected many reports of the sounds that were heard at the time of the earthquake. Dr. Charles Berkey compiled a very detailed report of

the earthquake sounds. People reported that the earthquake sounded "like thunder" or "like a truck or train rumbling past." Perhaps most interesting is that the observers indicated that the sound invariably preceded the actual earthquake, similar to what Dr. Hodgson described for the aftershock that he experienced. The September 5, 1944, edition of the *Globe and Mail* in Toronto, Ontario, reported that a rumbling noise "as of a big truck passing" was heard in Hamilton, Ontario. A rumbling noise was also reported from Montreal, Quebec, with the following elaboration: "One worried Montrealer asked if the shock might be caused by a new weapon the Germans were using, while another wondered if explosions in Europe might have caused the shock."

At Chicoutimi, Quebec, the police reported that they heard a noise "like a bomber passing overhead." Clearly, the war in Europe was not far from the minds of those who experienced the earthquake.

## ANIMAL BEHAVIOR

There are only a few descriptions of animal reactions to the earthquake, and all of those descriptions apparently concern how animals behaved at the time of the mainshock. The *New York Times* edition of September 5, 1944, states, "Farmers along the coast reported that the quake had disturbed livestock, particularly along the Hudson Valley."

The *Globe and Mail* edition of September 5, 1944, reported that chickens were frightened and ran outdoors at the time of the shock in Niagara Falls, Ontario. Dogs and cats were said to have been scared by the earthquake shaking in Springfield, Massachusetts. One dog was so frightened by the earthquake that town officials were called to dispose of the animal.

## GROUND CRACKS, GROUND LIQUEFACTION, AND WATER-LEVEL CHANGES

There were some notable changes in groundwater levels and apparent liquefaction effects associated with the September 5 earthquake. Dr. Ernest Hodgson, in his 1945 report in the *Journal of the Royal Astronomical Society of Canada*, stated that in the vicinity of Massena, New York, some wells dried up whereas other wells started to flow. This also happened along the north shore of the St. Lawrence River in nearby Ontario. He indicated that there was a crack in deep alluvium north of Massena Centre that oozed water and sand. The September 6, 1944, issue of the *New York Times* reported that one crack in the epicentral region was 30 feet (10 meters) long.

A retrospective article on the earthquake dated October 22, 2012, in the *Adirondack Almanack* contains a paragraph about groundwater-level changes and soil liquefaction effects. It reads,

> *The earth itself performed some peculiar acrobatics, sending three geysers streaming into the air from fissures that opened on a farm north of Massena. After nearly 8 hours, the flow subsided, and sand came to the surface. Where drought conditions were ongoing, wells that had been dry were filled, and some overflowed, requiring piping to channel the water elsewhere. Others went dry and remained that way. One farmer dumped 99 barrels of water in his well, hoping to draw from it as needed, but found it had all drained away. Town water supplies were opened to distressed farmers, who hauled more than 3 million gallons to feed animals and fill other needs. Three months after the earthquake, it was noted that one-fourth of the 4500 farms in the area were hurting for water. A call went out to well drillers to open 1000 new wells.*

One report, published in the 1949 *Publications of the Dominion Observatory, Ottawa* by W. G. Milne, contains an unusual observation that may or may not have been related to the impending earthquake. This report reads,

> *A day before the Cornwall earthquake, at a few minutes past seven in the evening, three groups of independent observers reported that the waters of Lake Placid in New York State suddenly were disturbed by some unknown force. The disturbance was reported as waves of a long-period on an otherwise very calm lake. One person reported a sudden upheaval followed by the swell but all three confirm the swell. This may or may not have been a forerunner to the earthquake, and there*

*can be a great deal of doubt as to whether the two are at all related. However, such reports are noted here for future reference should they occur again.*

Whether this unusual wave on Lake Placid was related to the earthquake is unknown. However, emissions of gas from the earth have been reported before some earthquakes, and this might explain the Lake Placid observation. On the other hand, Lake Placid is located about 60 miles (100 kilometers) away from the epicentral region of the earthquake, a distance that makes it unlikely that there is a direct connection between the wave seen on the lake and the earthquake that took place just over five hours later.

## Earthquake Lights
Neither the newspaper accounts nor the scientific reports about this earthquake contain reports of earthquake lights being observed by the local residents. If any earthquake lights had taken place, it is probable that they would have been seen since the earthquake took place not too long after midnight on a late-summer evening near two small cities. The simplest conclusion is that there were no earthquake lights associated with this earthquake.

## Location and Magnitude of the
## 1944 Cornwall/Massena Earthquake
Because the 1944 earthquake occurred at the time of a great global war, the number of available seismographic observations was limited. Seismic stations in North America were fully operational, but seismic stations in Europe and Asia, both of which might otherwise have recorded the event, were down because of the war. Fortunately, the seismic data from North America were sufficient to allow a computation of the epicenter of the earthquake. Dr. Ernest Hodgson, in his 1945 report in the *Journal of the Royal Astronomical Society of Canada*, speculated that the epicenter must have been very near Massena Centre based primarily on the observed effects of the earthquake. He put the depth of the earthquake at 20 miles (32 kilometers). Dr. W. G. Milne, in his 1949 *Publications of the Dominion*

*Observatory, Ottawa* report, used seismographic readings from eastern North America to compute an epicenter in the St. Lawrence River about 3 miles (5 kilometers) northwest of Massena Centre. A relocation of the earthquake published in 1984 by Dr. James W. Dewey and Dr. David W. Gordon of the U.S. Geological Survey put the epicenter about 5 miles (8 kilometers) south of Cornwall, Ontario, and about the same distance east of Massena, New York. This last determination is the best estimate of the epicenter of this earthquake. The best estimate of the focal depth of the earthquake is 12 miles (20 kilometers) from work published in 1996 by Dr. Allison Bent of the Geological Survey of Canada.

There is some uncertainty about the magnitude of this earthquake due to the available recordings. Earthquake magnitudes are computed from the strength of the seismic waves as measured on seismograms. For a strong earthquake like this, local and regional seismograms registered poor recordings because the needles on the instruments moved so fast that they only left a faint image of the ground motion on the seismogram or because the instruments malfunctioned in some other way due to the strong earthquake waves. One typical malfunction was that the needle writing the seismic trace separated from the paper due to the earthquake motions. Because the seismic shaking was much weaker at far distances, seismographic stations farther away did not have this problem and thus gave faithful recordings of the earthquake waves. Unfortunately, in 1944 the number of operating seismic stations at far distances was greatly reduced due to the war. Dr. Milne, in his 1949 *Publications* report, states that Dr. Beno Gutenberg of the Seismological Laboratory at the California Institute of Technology in Pasadena, California, computed a magnitude of 6.5 for the earthquake. Later studies put the magnitude anywhere from 5.1 to 5.6. The most recent and most reliable study of the size of this earthquake, by Dr. Allison Bent, determined that the moment magnitude of the event was 5.8.

## Contemporary Expert Opinion about the 1944 Cornwall/ Massena Earthquake

As they did for other earthquakes in the mid-20th century, contemporary experts claimed that the 1944 earthquake was caused by postglacial rebound. The *Boston Globe* on September 10, 1944, ran an article with an interview of Dr. L. Don Leet, seismologist at Harvard University. Dr. Leet opined that the time between strong earthquakes in the region was decreasing, and based on that he suggested that more earthquake activity might be possible. Furthermore, he noted that strong earthquakes might be centered anywhere in the region. He stated that scientists cannot predict earthquakes but that cities in the region should be prepared for another strong earthquake. In the article he was quoted as saying, "I don't want to be alarmist, but it is my duty to warn that Boston and other large New England cities should be prepared to cope with the emergencies caused by an earthquake. If one should come in Winter, especially, the destruction which could be caused by the fires resulting and the probable disruption of the water supply might be very great. We should organize to meet the situation."

In the September 6, 1944, edition of the *New York Times*, Dr. Leet warned that another earthquake could hit the region "within a matter of days, certainly within the next five years." In fact, no strong earthquake took place in the five years after the 1944 earthquake, and the next strong earthquake in northeastern North America was not until 1982.

# CHAPTER 13

# 1982 and 1988: Two Recent Strong Earthquakes in Canada

TWO STRONG EARTHQUAKES TOOK PLACE ALMOST SEVEN YEARS APART IN the 1980s at different locations in eastern Canada; there are many similarities between them, and for that reason they are discussed together in this chapter. Both mainshocks had similar magnitudes and had similar felt effects throughout the northeastern U.S. Both earthquakes were well-recorded by regional seismographs that were operating throughout the region, and those seismographs were able to capture in detail the foreshocks and aftershocks that accompanied each earthquake. Both earthquakes took place at locations that were unexpected to seismologists at the time, and because of this they expanded the scientists' thinking about the seismic hazard of the region. And even though these two seismic events took place more than 30 years ago, they are considered recent earthquakes because they occurred during the modern time period of seismic data acquisition, analysis, and interpretation. New instrumentation not available to earlier seismologist gave many recordings of the earthquakes, and computer analyses of the observed data using modern mathematical data-processing methods provided understandings of the earthquake sources that were not possible before the 1970s. The development of the ideas of plate tectonics in the 1960s provided a context for the earthquakes that had not been available to earlier seismologists.

The 1982 earthquake occurred at 7:54 a.m. EST (8:54 AST in the Maritime Provinces of Canada) on January 9, with an epicenter in New Brunswick. It was felt across all of the New England states. The mainshock was followed by a vigorous aftershock sequence that produced several aftershocks that approached the magnitude of the mainshock. The aftershocks of this earthquake are described in more detail later in this chapter.

The 1988 earthquake took place on November 25 at 6:46 p.m. EST, with an epicenter in Quebec. Like the 1982 earthquake, it was felt across all of the New England states. Curiously, the mainshock on November 25 had been preceded by a strong foreshock two days earlier, and so the people of the epicentral region were still thinking about earthquakes when the mainshock took place. Unlike the 1982 earthquake, the 1988 mainshock was followed by very few aftershocks.

## LOCATIONS, MAGNITUDES, AND FELT AREAS OF THE 1982 AND 1988 EARTHQUAKES

By the 1980s earthquake seismology in northeastern North America had become a sophisticated scientific discipline. There were dozens of seismic stations installed all throughout the region, with the data being continuously telemetered to seismic monitoring centers in New England, New York, Pennsylvania, and Canada. Computers were used to pinpoint earthquake locations that were much more precise than those of earlier decades. Because of this technology, within a couple hours of any earthquake, seismologists were able to report the magnitude and location of the mainshock, and they were already seeing the signals from the first aftershocks arriving at their centers.

The epicenter of the 1982 mainshock was determined to be in north-central New Brunswick in the Miramichi uplands, and hence it is called the Miramichi earthquake by seismologists. The earthquake epicenter was in a rugged area of forested granitic bedrock with a sparse local population. The magnitude of the mainshock was 5.7. The mainshock was felt in Canada throughout all of New Brunswick, Prince Edward Island, and Nova Scotia, at Ile d'Anticosti in the Gulf of St. Lawrence, and along both shores of the St. Lawrence River from the Gulf of St. Lawrence to just northeast of Quebec City. In the U.S. the earthquake was felt throughout all of the New England states and as far southwest as Albany, New York. A magnitude 5.5 aftershock on January 11 was felt throughout

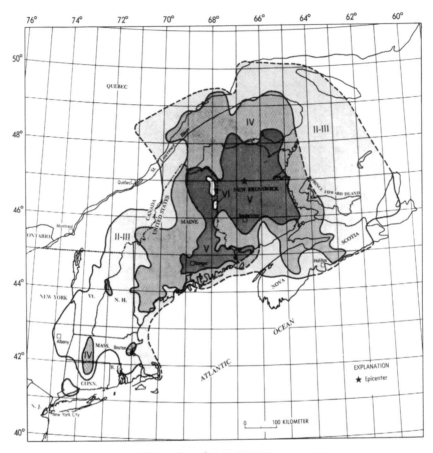

Isoseismal map of the 1982 earthquake FIGURE FROM THE USGS

New Brunswick, on the western side of Prince Edward Island, in central Nova Scotia, and throughout northern and central New England. There were also scattered reports of this earthquake being felt in the Boston, Massachusetts, area.

The 1988 earthquake in Quebec province was centered near the town of Saguenay, about 120 miles (200 kilometers) north of Quebec City and about 80 miles (130 kilometers) northwest of the Charlevoix Seismic Zone, which was discussed in chapter 4. Seismologists computed a magnitude of 5.9 for the 1988 mainshock. Two days before this mainshock, there was a magnitude 4.7 earthquake centered in the same

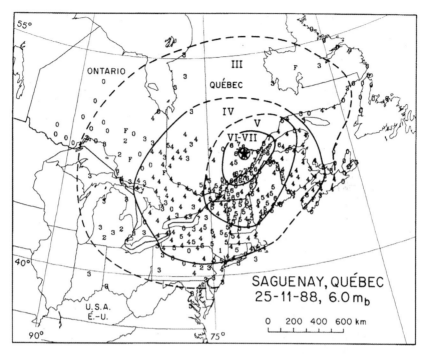

Isoseismal map of the 1988 earthquake FIGURE FROM THE GEOLOGICAL SURVEY OF CANADA

place, a seismic event that itself caused no damage but gave the local population a considerable fright. This shock was a foreshock of the magnitude 5.9 event two days later. The foreshock was not followed by any other detected earthquake activity before the occurrence of the mainshock, which was a damaging earthquake. Both the foreshock and the mainshock took place at a depth of about 17 miles (28 kilometers), putting them among the deepest known earthquakes in northeastern North America. The mainshock was followed by a low level of aftershock activity that lasted only a few weeks after the mainshock. The mainshock was felt on Cape Breton Island to the east, in Labrador to the northeast, along the southern shore of Hudson Bay to the northwest, along the northern shore of Lake Superior to the west, and in Indiana and Virginia to the southwest. All of New England and the Middle Atlantic U.S. states reported feeling this earthquake.

The 1988 earthquake appears to have taken place at the southern boundary of the Saguenay graben, a valley that down-dropped about 575 million years ago when ancestral North America started to rift away from a continent to the east. The Saguenay graben is called a failed rift valley by geologists because although the earth's crust started to stretch and the valley formed during the initiation of this stretching, the rift stopped before an ocean basin opened between the two sides of the rift valley. There is a fault on each side of the rift valley, and these faults probably formed during the time of active rifting 575 million years ago. Although the existence of the rift faults is confirmed from evidence in the surface geology, it is unknown how far those faults extend to depth in the earth's crust. The location of the focus of the 1988 earthquake suggests that the earthquake might have taken place on one of these rift faults if the southern rift fault projects vertically from the surface down to 28 kilometers. However, rift faults often bend away from a vertical orientation on their deeper sections below the earth's surface, and thus the association of the 1988 earthquake with the Saguenay rift fault that is seen in the surface geology is at best ambiguous.

## DAMAGE AND FELT EFFECTS DUE TO THE EARTHQUAKES

There was no severe damage in either the 1982 earthquake or the 1988 mainshock. The epicentral region of the 1982 earthquake was almost totally uninhabited, with the closest town lying about 30 miles (50 kilometers) away from the epicenter. The remote location of this earthquake probably greatly reduced the amount of damage caused by the shock. In New Brunswick cracks in walls were reported in New Denmark and Bathurst. In Fredericton no building damage was reported, but the shaking was strong enough to move heavy objects and to shake pictures from walls and dishes from shelves. In Maine after the earthquake some minor cracks were found in the masonry walls of some buildings in Presque Isle, and one homeowner reported that some cupboards were shaken loose from the wall in his basement. Residents in Aroostook County also reported road cracks up to an inch wide following the earthquake. In all of these cases, although the cracks were attributed to the earthquake shaking, it is not known if any of the cracks were in existence prior to the earthquake.

There was some notable damage to unreinforced masonry structures due to the shaking of the 1988 Saguenay earthquake. The epicenter of this earthquake was about 22 miles (35 kilometers) south of the Quebec towns of Jonquiere and Chicoutimi, and Saguenay was about 25 miles (40 kilometers) from the epicenter. Almost all of the damage in this area was confined to walls made of unreinforced brick, cinderblock, or stone. Several schools suffered cracks in masonry walls, and at one secondary school in Chicoutimi, the tops of some cinderblock divider walls fell, destroying the suspended ceilings and littering the floor of the school with debris. Fortunately, no one was hurt by the failures of these walls because the school was unoccupied at the time of the earthquake. In Chicoutimi, the earthquake shaking caused significant cracking in some walls in the provincial government building, and at La Baie the police and fire stations sustained cracks to a nonstructural masonry wall. In addition to this masonry damage in the area near the epicenter, for a bridge across the Saguenay River, the earthquake shaking caused the plate of one of the bridge's girders to separate from the abutment on which it was installed. Also, in Jonquiere two pipes carrying natural gas were damaged, which led to fires from the leaking gas. It is estimated that about 300,000 persons lost power as a result of the earthquake affecting the power distribution system, although most of the power was restored within two hours of the occurrence of the seismic event.

In addition to the damage at the towns closest to the epicenter of the earthquake, there also was some isolated damage to structures at much greater distances from the epicenter. At Quebec City, about 95 miles (160 kilometers) away, the Saint-François-d'Assise hospital suffered collapses to two chimneys, one each on different wings of the building. Also, the counterweight for an elevator in one of the buildings dislocated and damaged a support beam. In addition to these more significant failures, the hospital suffered a number of minor cracks in exterior brick walls and interior plaster walls. The nearby Notre-Dame Pavilion of this same hospital complex also suffered cracks in its masonry walls. These hospital buildings were located in the Lower Town of Quebec City on the soft sediments along the St. Charles River. Apparently, the river sediments

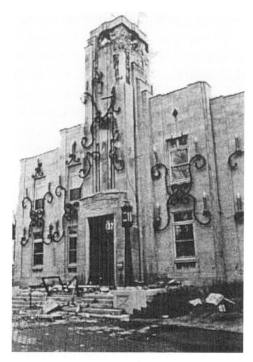

significantly amplified the earthquake ground shaking compared to that experienced at other parts of the city that are built on rock.

A similar story of isolated damage to unreinforced masonry construction built on soft soil also came from Montreal, at a distance of about 210 miles (340 kilometers) from the epicenter. The Montreal East City Hall lost many exterior masonry panels due to the earthquake shaking. This building was built on the thick, soft sediments that lie along the St. Lawrence River, and the structure had suffered prior damage due to settlement into the riverbank muds. No

Damage to the Montreal East City Hall in the 1988 earthquake

other nearby buildings were damaged by the earthquake shaking, suggesting that an inadequate foundation on the soft river sediments was a contributing factor to the new damage that the building experienced in the earthquake shaking. There was also a disruption to train travel in the Montreal area due to damage to tracks and to a bridge west of Montreal as a result of the slumping of a soil embankment.

## Deaths and Injuries Reported Due to the Earthquakes

No deaths or injuries were reported due to the occurrence of any of the 1982 earthquakes in New Brunswick. The paucity of population in the epicentral region likely contributed to this fortunate result. There were some deaths and a number of injuries reported following the 1988 Saguenay mainshock. The November 26, 1988, issue of the *Globe and Mail* in Toronto, Ontario, reported that one man died of a heart attack at a restaurant in Quebec City during the earthquake shaking. The November 26, 1988, issue of the *Boston Globe* of Boston, Massachusetts, contained a report that there was a traffic fatality in Quebec City that occurred at an intersection where the traffic lights were not working due to the loss of electricity in the region. The November 27, 1988, issue of the *Boston Globe* indicated that following the earthquake about 50 persons were treated for minor cuts and bruises at Chicoutimi, Quebec.

## DURATIONS AND SOUNDS OF THE EARTHQUAKES

In prior decades, namely, the 1940s and earlier, newspapers contained many detailed reports about topics such as how long earthquake shaking lasted or what sounds were heard as seismic waves were felt. Newspaper reports described how an earthquake was experienced at different localities, and there were many firsthand accounts of how the earthquake was felt or heard, often including addresses of the persons who supplied the accounts. By the 1980s newspaper articles about earthquakes were written quite differently. Details about an earthquake such as how long it lasted or how it sounded were given usually in summary statements that covered a large area such as a state or region, with few or no firsthand reports about those topics from any specific locality. During the 1980s much of the newspaper coverage was devoted to descriptions by local experts of what happened and why it happened. For the 1982 and 1988 earthquakes, the newspaper accounts contain very little information about how long the earthquake shaking lasted or how the earthquake was heard in different parts of the region. This lack of specific information is a function of the style of modern newspaper reporting rather than a lack of reports of how long an earthquake was felt or how it was heard.

For the 1982 earthquake centered in New Brunswick, the descriptions of the earthquake duration and earthquake sound were often contained in the same report. For example, the January 10, 1982, issue of the *Boston Globe* contains the following report from a Houlton, Maine, woman: "Our whole building shook.... It was a big vibration, a strong vibration that lasted 20 or 30 seconds. They thought our building was blowing up. It sounded like the boiler was going to explode. You could hear a loud rumbling. We're in a soundproof building, so it must have been very loud outside."

The January 11, 1982, issue of the *Globe and Mail* in Toronto, Ontario, reported that the earthquake was felt for up to one minute in the province of New Brunswick. It also contained a description of the earthquake sound from one Marion Prey of New Denmark, New Brunswick: "It sounded something like an airplane but the vibration was greater—it was really shaking the house.... It sounded something like thunder when it really roars."

At Boston, Massachusetts, the January 10, 1982, issue of the *Boston Globe* states that the mainshock was accompanied by a low rumble. Another person in Boston reported that she felt the shaking of the mainshock but heard no sound. Curiously, the duration of the mainshock as experienced at Boston is not given in the *Boston Globe* article, but the same article includes a report that the magnitude 5.0 aftershock about three hours after the mainshock was felt for about 15 seconds.

There are only a few reports of the duration of the felt ground shaking in the 1988 earthquake and no reports at all of the earthquake sounds that accompanied the shaking. The November 26, 1988, edition of the *Globe and Mail* reported that the earthquake shaking lasted as much as two minutes in Quebec but only a few seconds in Toronto. The November 26, 1988, issue of the *Boston Globe* put the duration of the felt ground shaking at Boston in the range of 10 to 30 seconds. The *New York Times* edition of November 26, 1988, indicated that earthquake waves were felt for about 30 seconds in New York City and its suburbs.

## FORESHOCKS AND AFTERSHOCKS

Both the 1982 and 1988 earthquakes were preceded by foreshocks and were followed by aftershocks, but the foreshocks and aftershock activity were quite different for each of the two mainshocks. The 1982 mainshock was preceded by a magnitude 3.7 earthquake that occurred in the epicentral area about 42 days before the mainshock and a magnitude 1.8 foreshock in the same place just three days before the mainshock. The 1982 mainshock triggered a long-lasting and energetic aftershock sequence. One aftershock of magnitude 5.3 occurred less than three hours after the mainshock, and a magnitude 5.5 aftershock struck two days later. A magnitude 5.0 aftershock occurred on March 31, 1982, and a magnitude 4.7 aftershock took place on June 16, 1982. Hundreds of smaller aftershocks were detected by regional seismographs during the weeks that followed the mainshock. The earthquake activity in the Miramichi epicentral area has remained elevated up to the present time relative to the earthquake activity that was detected prior to the 1982 mainshock. Thus, it appears that the aftershocks of this earthquake have lasted several decades and continue even today.

The 1988 earthquake was preceded two days earlier by a magnitude 4.7 foreshock, with that foreshock being one of the largest events in Quebec in several years. The 1988 Saguenay mainshock was followed by a very sparse aftershock sequence. Due to the installation of portable seismic instruments in the epicentral region following the occurrence of the magnitude 4.7 foreshock, there is an unusually complete record of even the very small aftershocks that took place in the epicentral area following the occurrence of the mainshock. The aftershock activity was of a very short duration, with most of the aftershocks occurring before December 10, 1988. Only 86 aftershocks had been detected by June 1989, and this epicentral area has been seismically quiet since then. Thus, whereas the 1982 earthquake at Miramichi, New Brunswick, was followed by a highly active aftershock sequence, including several strong aftershocks, the 1988 earthquake at Saguenay, Quebec, was followed by a very sparse aftershock sequence, and only one of the aftershocks, a magnitude 4.1 event just four hours after the mainshock, had a magnitude above 2.7.

## LIQUEFACTION, SOIL FAILURES, AND LANDSLIDES

There were no reports of soil liquefaction, soil failures, or landslides reported due to the 1982 Miramichi earthquakes. The mainshock and strongest aftershocks took place during a cold midwinter, when the ground throughout New Brunswick, Quebec, and northern New England was deeply frozen and less susceptible to liquefaction or slumping of soils. Furthermore, the rugged surface geology of the Miramichi region is generally not prone to liquefaction or soil slumping except in a few areas in the sediments along streams and rivers. If there were any landslides in the steeper local topography, they probably would not have been observed due to the sparse population of the Miramichi region in winter.

The 1988 earthquake at Saguenay, Quebec, had several reports of sandblows and other types of soil liquefaction from several of the towns in the Saguenay River valley. Just like for the Miramichi region, in the area of the Saguenay earthquake, liquefaction effects and soil failures would likely occur only in sediments along the rivers and streams, and in the case of the 1988 earthquake, all of the soil liquefaction reports came from populated areas where local residents observed sandblows, ground cracks, or soil slumps immediately following the earthquake. A snowfall covered the ground in the Saguenay area the day after the mainshock, making it impossible to use aerial reconnaissance to look for fresh soil liquefaction effects immediately following the earthquake. Soil liquefaction effects and failures were reported from the towns of Hèbertville, St-Amboise, Grande Baie, Ferland, and Boileau.

At one house in Ferland, about 15 miles (25 kilometers) northeast of the epicenter, a sandblow and soil ground fissures cracked the foundation of a house and deformed the basement walls. The sandblow next to the house forced water backward into the house from the septic system through the sewage drain pipe, causing a basement toilet to erupt water and sand. A bathtub in the basement of the same house was found to contain a layer of fine sand about 8 inches (22 centimeters) thick that had been pushed out of the drain by the sandblow. Other sandblows were found at farther distances from this house. Another house in Ferland sustained damage to basement walls due to a sandblow that erupted beneath the structure. In this case the sandblow flooded the basement with about 18 inches (30 centimeters) of water and sand. The water drained from the basement shortly after the earthquake, leaving the homeowner with a thick layer of sand on the basement floor and a damaged house foundation.

There were a number of rockslides and landslides that took place as a result of the strong ground shaking generated by the Saguenay earthquake. The rockslides and landslides generally took place in the Laurentide Mountains south of the Saguenay River valley. One landslide at Sainte-Thècle, Quebec, about 110 miles (180 kilometers) south of the epicenter, was large enough to dam a creek with 30 feet (10 meters) of rock and soil. A section of a hillside that was about 270 feet (82 meters) wide gave way in this landslide.

One result of the scientific investigations into both the soil liquefaction features and the landslides induced by the 1988 earthquake is that evidence for similar features probably caused by earlier earthquakes were found at a number of places in Quebec. Although the ages of the earlier features were not ascertained in the published scientific studies, they provide strong evidence of prior strong earthquakes within the past few thousand years in this area.

## EARTHQUAKE LIGHTS

One of the most intriguing aspects of the 1988 Saguenay event is the large number of reports of earthquake lights that emerged following the mainshock. Scientists were first alerted about these reports the day after the mainshock when a number of people in the epicentral region called a local radio station to report seeing unusual lights in the sky around the time of the earthquake. The mainshock had taken place at 6:46 p.m. local time, about two hours after sunset, when many people were out and about following the end of the workday. Prof. Marcel Ouellet of the National Institute of Scientific Research (INRS) of Quebec University at St. Foy near Quebec City learned of these reports and decided to carry out a widespread search for descriptions of the earthquake lights from the Quebec region. Professor Ouellet compiled a comprehensive database of reports of earthquake lights by publishing requests for information on sightings of earthquake lights in local newspapers. He sent each respondent a questionnaire asking detailed questions about what was observed, and in some cases he telephoned respondents for further clarification. In total he obtained 46 accounts that he considered reliable observations of earthquake lights. The reports came from many of the towns along the Saguenay River and around Lake St. John north of the epicenter, as well as from Quebec City and other towns south of the epicenter.

Professor Ouellet's survey found that the first reliable observation of an earthquake light was made at about 6:30 p.m. on the evening of October 31, 1988, almost a month before the Saguenay mainshock. There were another eight reports of earthquake lights during November 1988

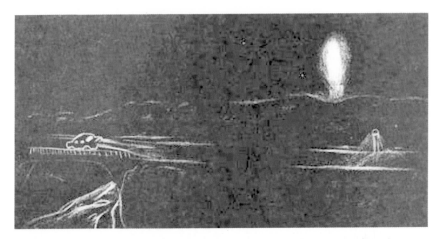

Drawing of a report of an earthquake light that occurred five days before the foreshock of the 1988 Saguenay earthquake FIGURE FROM SEISMOLOGICAL RESEARCH LETTERS

prior to the occurrence of the magnitude 4.7 foreshock, with two of these occurring within about five hours of the foreshock. The November 23 foreshock, which took place at 4:10 a.m., had eight confirmed sightings of earthquake lights that were approximately coincident with the earthquake shaking. Two reports described earthquake lights observed during the evening of November 23, and another three reports were made for the evening of November 24. There were two observations of earthquake lights at Chicoutimi about 25 minutes before the mainshock. The mainshock itself on November 25 had another nine confirmed reports of earthquake lights either coincident with or just minutes after the shaking of the mainshock. Four observations of earthquakes lights were made on November 26, with two observations in the month of December 1988 and six in the month of January 1989. The last confirmed report of an earthquake light was dated January 21, 1989. The January 1989 sightings of earthquake lights took place during a time of resurgent aftershock activity in the earth around the location of the mainshock hypocenter.

Several varieties of earthquake lights were described by the observers. The most common type of earthquake light that was reported was a globular incandescent mass often described as a fireball. These were generally glowing balls that were typically no more than a few yards (a few meters)

Drawing of a report of an earthquake light from near the epicenter of the 1988 Saguenay earthquake FIGURE FROM SEISMOLOGICAL RESEARCH LETTERS

in diameter and lasted as long 15 seconds. The reported color of the glowing balls varied from observation to observation. Most of the time the incandescent balls were said to be yellow or orange in color, although some reports described balls that were green, reddish purple, or white. Some of the globular masses were described as stationary, but in many cases the masses were observed to emerge from the ground and to hover a few to several feet (1 to 3 meters) or more in the air. The masses were often reported to move laterally or vertically, and some reports indicate that glowing streamers appeared to extend away from the main glowing masses as they moved.

One observer noted that a glowing mass seemed to emerge from the ground, rise to a height of about 100 yards (91 meters), and move several yards (several meters) toward the southwest before extinguishing itself. The same phenomenon repeated itself a few more times. What looked like sparks or glowing droplets that quickly disappeared seemed to fall from the main incandescent mass, which was about 3 feet (1 meter) in diameter, as it rose. One observer was a trapper who was in the woods only about 15 miles (25 kilometers) from the epicenter at the time of the November 25 mainshock. He said that the sky was clear and the wind was calm. At the same time that he felt the strong earthquake ground shaking, he became suddenly surrounded by a bright, fast-moving glowing light that was between blue and white in color. The trees seemed to crackle as the light passed through them. He thought that this glowing mass was about 600 yards (550 meters) wide and about 16 yards (15 meters) high. The light lasted only a few seconds before it disappeared.

There were several reports with descriptions of flashes of light that were reminiscent of lightning. The sky was clear at the times of both the foreshock and the mainshock in November 1988, and in any case lightning storms are very rare in Quebec in the fall and winter months. The lightning-like earthquake light was described as a flash that lasted a few seconds, sometimes repeating itself one or more times much the way that multiple lightning flashes take place. No sound was associated with any of the flashes. During the magnitude 4.7 foreshock, several persons reported seeing what looked like sheet lightning. In one case an observer in a dark room with PVC blinds covering the windows suddenly saw the room light up as though there had been a sudden lightning flash just outside the window. In some reports a significant part of the night sky was suddenly and briefly illuminated by a strong flash of light. One such event on January 19 was said to have been preceded by a hissing sound.

A third type of earthquake light that was reported in the Saguenay epicentral region is luminous bands of light. Luminous bands that are earthquake lights remind observers of the lights of an aurora borealis, although the lights of an aurora borealis occur high in the sky whereas luminous bands associated with earthquakes tend to occur near the ground. Two different observers reported luminous bands at the time of the mainshock on November 25. One person reported about six bands that glowed with different pastel colors, whereas the other person indicated about seven bands that were all white in color. According to both observers, the bands lasted for about five minutes and hung in the atmosphere over the Saguenay River. One observer was north of the river and one was south of the river, but they both agree on the location of the luminous bands. There was also a report of luminous bands observed about three weeks before the November 23 foreshock. A check of auroral activity for the dates of these observations showed that it was unlikely that an aurora borealis would have been observed in this part of Quebec on either of these dates.

One other report of an earthquake light described a flamelike luminosity that was observed during a magnitude 2.5 aftershock on November 26 at 3:10 a.m. According to observers, there was a flamelike glow that flared up on a paved road a few yards (a few meters) away from their car. They saw the flamelike light flare several times in a repetitive manner.

All of the kinds of earthquake lights from the Saguenay region from October 1988 to January 1989 in the Ouellet database are similar to earthquake light observations that have been reported in other past earthquakes from around the world. The causes of the various types of earthquake lights are only poorly understood, and instrumental studies of them are very rare because of their ephemeral nature and unpredictable occurrences. Nevertheless, the agreement of the times and types of observations that were gathered by Professor Ouellet support the veracity of these observations.

In contrast to the experience in 1988 in the Saguenay area, there are no known reports of earthquake lights associated with the 1982 Miramichi earthquakes. This is perhaps not surprising because the large Miramichi earthquakes all occurred during daylight hours and there were almost no people living within 30 miles (50 kilometers) of the 1982 mainshock epicenter. For the 1988 Saguenay earthquake, 34 of the 46 observations of earthquake lights were made at less than 30 miles (50 kilometers) from the mainshock epicenter.

## ANIMAL BEHAVIOR

There were no reports at all about animal behavior due to the 1988 earthquake, and there was only one newspaper account that mentioned animal behavior associated with the 1982 earthquake. This article was in the January 11, 1982, edition of the *Globe and Mail* of Toronto, Ontario, and it bore the headline "Dog in N.B. begins shaking six hours early." The article describes the behavior of a dog owned by Tom Donovan of Red Bank about 16 miles (25 kilometers) southeast of the earthquake epicenter. The article gives the following report from Mr. Donovan:

*He said the dog, normally thrown out of sorts only by an impending thunderstorm or rifle shots, became terrified at about 3 a.m. and began scratching and whining ceaselessly at the door leading to the bedrooms upstairs.*

*"If it was the summer I'd notice the dog is afraid and there must be a thunderstorm coming," he said. "But when it's 25 below on a clear night, and no rifle shots, I thought she must be getting kind of weird or something."*

*People from as far away as Dartmouth, N.S., and the Gaspe region of Quebec gave reports of their dogs and cats going crazy when the tremors started, but Fluffy seemed to have advance notice.*

This is the only report of an earthquake in New England and nearby areas where an animal is reported to have reacted prior to the occurrence of the earthquake.

## CONTEMPORARY EXPERT OPINION ABOUT THE 1982 AND 1988 EARTHQUAKES

A significant fraction of the newspaper reports about both the 1982 and 1988 earthquakes are devoted to interviews of earthquake experts in Canada and the U.S. concerning the causes and effects of shocks. For both earthquakes the experts indicated surprise at the unexpected locations of the earthquakes, and their interpretation was that the seismic hazard was more widespread than previously believed. The experts further indicated that most earthquakes in the region have small magnitudes and that the sizes of these earthquakes were relatively infrequent in the region. Thus, strong earthquakes like these were rare, although not unexpected.

The theory of plate tectonics says that the earth's surface is divided into a number of tectonic plates that move over the surface of the planet. The plates rub together at their edges, and these plate-edge areas are where most of the world's earthquakes take place. Dr. Robert Wetmiller of the Department of Energy, Mines and Resources in Canada provided an explanation of the 1982 Miramichi earthquakes in the April 3, 1982, edition of the *Globe and Mail*. Talking about the Miramichi earthquakes, Dr. Wetmiller was quoted as saying,

*They are indicative of the kinds of event that can occur in the region. This is normally a relatively stable area and the daily series of events is quite unprecedented, especially in terms of the aftershocks we've recorded daily.*

*It's certainly a rare opportunity to study this kind of phenomenon.*

*Unlike the West Coast, where the plates are coincidental with the coastline, the plates off the East Coast are in the middle of the Atlantic Ocean. But we do know there can be considerable activity within the body of a plate and this seems to be an instance of that.*

The quote is not quite correct, because it is the boundary between the North American plate and the European and African plates that is in the middle of the Atlantic Ocean. In any case the earthquake rate of northeastern North America in the middle of the North American plate is not negligible, but it is much lower than the rates of seismic events seen at plate boundaries.

It was known since the 1906 San Francisco earthquake that earthquakes are caused by excess pressures on local rocks that cause those rocks to crack and slip to relieve some of the excess pressure. The buildup of excess pressure to cause earthquakes is easy to explain at the boundary between two tectonic plates, since the movements of the plates relative to each other naturally create large, local pressure changes. Whereas in the 1940s the only known source of pressure buildup in northeastern North America was the rebound of Canadian crust following the melting of the ice sheets of the last major continental glaciation, things were quite different in the 1980s. Seismologists knew that the movements of the tectonic plates could cause pressure to build up within the plate interiors. Furthermore, they had strong seismological evidence that the excess pressure that was triggering earthquakes in northeastern North America was oriented parallel to the direction of movement of the North American plate and was not oriented in the direction of the postglacial rebound. These explanations were provided to reporters following the strong earthquakes at Miramichi and Saguenay.

The faults in the rocks between the two plates are the places where the earthquakes take place at plate boundaries. One thing that baffled seismologists of the Northeast at the time of the 1982 and 1988 earth-quakes, and still is not well understood by seismologists today, is knowing where to expect earthquakes within the middles of tectonic plates, since there are no obvious faults on which those earthquakes might take place. In northeastern North America there are many faults, and these faults are distributed all throughout the region. Furthermore, almost of these faults are hundreds of millions of years old, and there is no reason to expect such old faults to be active today. One theory to explain where strong earth-quakes might be expected was provided by Prof. Gene Simmons, who at that time was a faculty member in the Department of Earth, Atmo-spheric, and Planetary Sciences of the Massachusetts Institute of Tech-nology. Prior to the 1982 earthquake, Professor Simmons had argued that most strong earthquakes in the region took place at the edges of volcanic rock formations called plutons, which pushed up into the crust and then cooled and solidified more than 100 million years ago. The idea is that the rocks of a pluton are somewhat stiffer than the surrounding rocks, and hence plate tectonic rock pressures can concentrate at the edges of the pluton. The 1982 Miramichi earthquakes took place within the center of a pluton, and the 1988 Saguenay earthquake had no pluton anywhere in its vicinity at all. These earthquakes were judged to be negative evidence that strong earthquakes in northeastern North American tend to concentrate at the edges of plutons.

# CHAPTER 14

# Future Earthquakes in Northeastern North America: What Might Happen Next?

THE PREVIOUS CHAPTERS HAVE DESCRIBED THE MOST IMPORTANT AND most damaging earthquakes that have affected the northeastern U.S. and nearby provinces in Canada in the past. However, they represent only a few of the many thousands of earthquakes that are known to have occurred in the region since the coming of Europeans to settle northeastern North America in the 1500s and early 1600s. Like in all other parts of the world, most of the earthquakes in this region of North America have been of small magnitude and caused no damage. They were a sudden and brief distraction in the lives of the people at the time. It was the rare large magnitude earthquakes that damaged man-made structures and caused injuries and deaths.

One feature of the past earthquake activity in the region is that it gives scientist important data that can be used to estimate what future earthquakes might take place. From more than a decade of GPS measurements, it is now well-established that the tectonic plates are moving steadily and smoothly year in and year out over the surface of the earth. This is why the rates of earthquake occurrences are rather constant with time. Whether one looks at California, Japan, New England, or China, there is relatively little variation in the numbers of earthquakes that take place from one year to the next, although each area has its own unique average earthquake rate. It is the inexorable movement of the tectonic plates and the resulting steady rate of earthquake activity that gives seismologists the confidence to say that the past rates of earthquakes will continue into the future. Thus, if we can get a good estimate of the average rate at which damaging earthquakes have taken place in the past in the northeastern U.S. and nearby southeastern Canada, then we will have a good guess of what that future average earthquake rate is likely to be. Furthermore, the Gutenberg-Richter distribution of earthquakes described in chapter 1 allows seismologists to break down how the average earthquake rate will distribute at different magnitude levels. Larger earthquakes are rarer events, and so they are less likely to occur in any given time period.

Although average earthquake rates are useful for estimating the probability of an earthquake, they are not good predictors of exactly when the next earthquake will occur. Earthquake occurrences seem to be a highly random process, with no set pattern seen in the occurrences of earthquakes with time. There is no regular periodicity between earthquakes (and especially between strong earthquakes). In a random process there is no pattern between the events. Sometimes the events occur closely spaced in time, and sometimes they are widely spaced in time. The pattern shifts without warning. For example, if a strong earthquake occurs, another strong earthquake occurs one year later, and a third strong earthquake occurs 99 years after that, the average time interval between the earthquakes is 100/2, or 50 years. However, the average time interval between the earthquakes does not give any useful information for predicting when the next strong earthquake might occur. Seismologists must look for more subtle patterns in the occurrences of past earthquakes, and we cannot do this work until we have a complete and reliable record of the occurrences of the past earthquakes going back many centuries and perhaps even millennia.

Another problem that has not been solved by seismologists is predicting where the next strong earthquake might take place. Earthquakes have been located throughout all of the northeastern U.S. and southeastern Canada, with some parts of the area experiencing more earthquakes and some parts of the area experiencing fewer earthquakes. This spatial spread of the earthquakes happens at short as well as long time scales, and there do not seem to be any noticeable patterns of where earthquakes tend to occur in different time periods. Many people believe that if seismologists can find one or a few faults in the region, then they will know where future earthquakes will occur. This is a simplistic view of what is really a very complicated question. Because of past plate tectonic interactions going back over one billion years, northeastern North America is riddled with countless old faults that formed during past geologic epochs. For example, there are probably hundreds of faults that have been mapped by geologists just in the Boston metropolitan area, and probably all of these faults formed several hundred million years ago. The major problem today is that the modern earthquakes are not aligning on these old faults, and for this reason seismologists have insufficient evidence to determine which of these faults might currently be seismically active and therefore capable of hosting a future major earthquake. To make matters worse, some of the earthquakes in the region, such as the 1755 Cape Ann earthquake, have had offshore epicenters where geologic mapping is extremely difficult and very costly.

It is possible to estimate the potential locations where some future large earthquakes might take place even if there is no direct evidence of which faults are active. It is known from all parts of the world that large earthquakes generally take place at localities where small earthquakes have been previously recorded. Furthermore, localities that have more small earthquakes tend to have more frequent strong earthquakes. For this reason it is thought by many seismologists that any locality in northeastern North America that has experienced small earthquakes has the potential for being the epicenter of a strong earthquake at some point in the future. Of course, a strong earthquake at any single locality might not happen for many, many years (perhaps thousands of years or even longer from now), and the probability of a strong earthquake centered at any given locality in the region is small. On the other hand, if in the future active faults in the region are identified and the past earthquake history on those faults can be worked out, then it should be possible to estimate the probabilities of future strong earthquakes on those faults.

In the following sections, what is known about the past earthquake activity in different parts of the northeastern U.S. and adjacent southeastern Canada is summarized, and the potential of future damaging earthquakes is estimated. Thousands of earthquakes are known from historical records in the region, with by far most of them being small shocks that

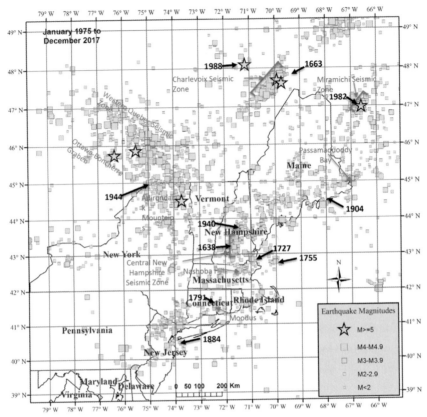

Earthquakes from 1975 to 2017, along with the locations of past strong earthquakes and major seismotectonic features

caused no damage and were felt at only one or just a few communities. Only some of the earthquakes were more widely felt, and just a small number of the earthquakes were damaging, the most important of which for New England are described in the preceding chapters. Since the 1970s modern seismic instrumentation has greatly improved the detection and location of earthquakes in the region. Today well over a hundred earthquakes are located annually in northeastern North America. Most of these earthquakes are too small to be felt, but they are helping to refine our understanding of the seismically active parts of the region. About 15–20 local earthquakes are felt each year somewhere in the northeastern

U.S. or southeastern Canada. Every few years there is a widely felt earthquake, and on average about once a decade, there is an earthquake that causes some damage. The rates of earthquake activity have been fairly steady since the 1970s, and those rates are expected to remain comparable into the foreseeable future.

## EARTHQUAKES IN MAINE

Maine comprises half the spatial area of New England, and each year it has approximately half of the earthquakes that take place in New England. Most of the earthquakes in Maine, and all of the more widely felt earthquakes in the state, have taken place from the coastal areas to inland about 60 miles, in the western part of the state, or in the center of the state. Only scattered epicenters of small earthquakes are found in the northern part of the state, particularly in Aroostook County. Because of the strong earthquakes in 1904 and 1869 that likely were centered west of Passamaquoddy Bay, the Downeast area has some of the highest seismic hazard in the state. Other areas most likely to experience potentially damaging shaking in future earthquakes are the northern tip of the state due to strong events in the Charlevoix Seismic Zone, the west edge of the state, and the southern tip of the state due to its proximity to the Cape Ann Seismic Zone. Offshore earthquakes in the Gulf of Maine have taken place near Passamaquoddy Bay and near the southern tip of the state, and they indicate that a strong offshore earthquake that could affect Maine is possible.

Aside from the strong earthquakes in 1904 and 1869, several seismic events of some note in Maine are known from historical records, although none probably reached 5.0 in magnitude. A strong shake was felt in eastern Maine on May 22, 1817. It was widely felt in the state and in New Brunswick. Larger earthquakes were reported in Maine on December 23, 1857, near Lewiston; on July 5, 1905, near Sabbatus; on August 18, 1921, in the Bridgeton-Norway area; and on April 25, 1957, near Portland. A magnitude 4.8 earthquake took place on June 15, 1973, in Maine near the junction of its borders with New Hampshire and Quebec. A magnitude 4.2 earthquake was centered just east of Bar Harbor on October 2, 2006, and caused a number of rockfalls in Acadia National Park. In the center of the state, notable earthquakes occurred on February 8, 1928, and on January 14, 1943, in the Dover-Foxcroft/Milo area. A special, targeted study in 1989 and again in 1990 showed that several microearthquakes, usually too small to be felt, take place each week in a small seismic zone between Dover-Foxcroft and Milo. The earthquakes in this zone are thought to be late aftershocks of a strong earthquake that took place before this locality was settled by Europeans. It is not known how early this earthquake might have taken place, but it might have occurred as recently as the 17th century.

Future strong earthquakes in Maine will likely be centered somewhere in the coastal region of the state, in the western part of the state near the border with New Hampshire, and in the central part of the state near Dover-Foxcroft and Milo. Based on the past earthquake history of the state, an estimate of the average repeat time of earthquakes of magnitude 5.0 or greater in Maine, large enough to cause damage in the epicentral area, is probably between 100 and 200 years. On the other hand, the National Seismic Hazard Maps issued by the U.S. Geological Survey every six or so years indicate that in any 50-year period, the northernmost tip of Maine is likely to feel the strongest ground shaking of any part of the state due to its proximity to the highly active Charlevoix Seismic Zone in nearby Quebec province.

## EARTHQUAKES IN NEW HAMPSHIRE AND VERMONT

Even though they neighbor each other, there is quite a contrast in the earthquake histories of New Hampshire and Vermont. New Hampshire has experienced earthquakes in all parts of the state throughout its history, and the strong earthquake in 1638 is thought to have been centered between what are today Concord and Sanbornton, as described in chapter 2. In contrast, few earthquake epicenters are known in Vermont, and the ones that are known from both historical records and recent instrumental earthquake monitoring were primarily along its eastern or western borders.

In addition to the 1638 and 1940 earthquakes chronicled in earlier chapters, New Hampshire has had some other notable earthquakes centered in the state. On October 9, 1925, a shock of about magnitude 4.0

at Ossipee was an early harbinger of the 1940 events. The magnitude 4.8 earthquake at the Maine–New Hampshire–Quebec border area gave the northern part of the state a strong shake. On January 18, 1982, a magnitude 4.4 earthquake was centered just west of Laconia. A magnitude 4.1 earthquake struck near Berlin on April 6, 1989. On July 23, 1843, an earthquake with an estimated magnitude 4.1 occurred with an epicenter probably offshore southeast of Portsmouth. Another probable offshore earthquake that shook strongly in Portsmouth occurred on November 9, 1810. The strongest earthquake with an epicenter in Vermont was a magnitude 4.0 earthquake on March 31, 1953, with an epicenter somewhere near Brandon and Rutland. On April 10, 1962, a magnitude 3.9 earthquake occurred in the north-central part of Vermont.

No estimates of the average repeat times of local earthquakes in New Hampshire or Vermont have been made by seismologists. However, it is much more likely that a future strong earthquake will be centered in New Hampshire than in Vermont.

## EARTHQUAKES IN MASSACHUSETTS, RHODE ISLAND, AND CONNECTICUT

In southern New England most of the earthquakes since early historical times have taken place in eastern Massachusetts, south coastal Massachusetts, the Narragansett Bay area of Rhode Island, and along coastal Connecticut. A number of earthquakes have also occurred in central Connecticut in the Moodus area and in central Massachusetts along the Connecticut River valley. In addition to the damaging earthquakes described in earlier chapters, several earthquakes in the region approached the magnitude threshold of damage. On February 2, 1766, a strong shock probably centered east of Cape Ann, Massachusetts, rocked southern New England, with another, probably from somewhere near the same epicenter, occurring on June 2, 1785. Offshore Cape Ann also was the epicenter of a moderate earthquake on January 27, 1925. On June 10, 1951, an earthquake of magnitude 4.6 that was centered near Westerly, Rhode Island, strongly shook southern New England. An earthquake with a similar felt area and effects had taken place in Rhode Island on February 27, 1883.

As described in chapter 7, Moodus, Connecticut, is famous for its Native American legends about earthquakes, but that is not the only area in New England for which such legends exist. Roger Williams, who founded Rhode Island, wrote that the local Native Americans in Rhode Island had the word *Naunaumemoauke* for "earthquake" in their language. The Native Americans had legends of four strong earthquakes during the 70 years prior to the landing of the Pilgrims at Plymouth, Massachusetts, in 1620. A number of small earthquakes have been detected around Littleton, Massachusetts, since modern instrumental seismic monitoring began in the 1970s. These earthquakes have occurred in the general vicinity of a hill called Nashoba, which is a Native American word that means "hill that shakes." Native Americans as well as early European settlers in the area claimed that rumbling noises emanated frequently from the ground around the hill. The first known earthquake from the Nashoba area was reported in 1668.

As described in earlier chapters, damaging earthquakes took place in southern New England in 1727, 1755, and 1791, and several other earthquakes approached the threshold at which damage might be expected. It is estimated that earthquakes of magnitude 5.0 or greater take place within 200 miles (300 kilometers) of Boston with an average repeat time of 60 to 120 years. Earthquakes the size of the 1755 Cape Ann earthquake probably have average repeat times of 500 to 1,000 years.

## Earthquakes in the New York City Area and New Jersey

The southern part of New York State that includes New York City as well as the northern part of New Jersey have experienced many small earthquakes throughout recorded history. There also have been some earthquakes on Long Island east of New York City and in southern New Jersey near the border with Delaware. The strong earthquakes of 1737 and 1884 in the New York City area are described in chapter 8. An earthquake of about magnitude 4.8 had an epicenter near Trenton, New Jersey, on August 23, 1938, and a notable earthquake was reported on November 30, 1783, with an epicenter probably in Morris County, New Jersey. The greater New York City area felt a sharp rumble on October 19, 1985, when a magnitude 4.0 earthquake struck at Ardsley, New York.

On March 10, 1992, an earthquake of magnitude 4.2 was centered at East Hampton, New York, on the east end of Long Island. Several small magnitude earthquakes have been detected from beneath New York City itself, including a magnitude 2.6 earthquake on October 27, 2001.

Based on the past earthquake activity of the area, the average repeat time of earthquakes of magnitude 5.0 or greater is estimated to be about 100 years for the greater New York City area. For magnitude 6.0 or greater, the average earthquake repeat time is probably about 600 to 1,000 years. The most likely locations for earthquakes in the greater New York City metropolitan area include the highland areas of northwestern New Jersey, the Hudson Highlands north of New York City, Manhattan Island, and the area around the south of Queens stretching across the bay to Sandy Hook, New Jersey. The Newark Rift Basin, a geologic basin that includes the low-lying areas in New Jersey west of New York City, seems to be less seismically active than the surrounding highlands. In the past some seismologists had speculated that the Ramapo Fault, which is the old boundary fault between the Newark Rift Basin and the highland areas of northwestern New Jersey, was seismically active. Although earthquakes occur near the Ramapo Fault, most seismologists today think that it is not the Ramapo Fault that is currently active but rather smaller faults that cross the Ramapo Fault and extend into the northern New Jersey highlands.

## EARTHQUAKES IN NORTHERN AND WESTERN NEW YORK STATE

In addition to the earthquake activity around New York City, frequent earthquakes have occurred in the Adirondack and Catskill Mountains of northern New York State, and a number of past earthquakes have taken place in western New York State. Curiously, almost no earthquakes are known to have occurred in central New York State in historical times, and this pattern has been confirmed by instrumental seismic monitoring over the past few decades. The Adirondack and Catskill Mountains and surrounding areas have been the most seismically active part of New York State, and they are also the areas in the state where the largest number of strong earthquakes has taken place. The largest earthquake in New York State, the magnitude 5.8 1944 earthquake at Massena, New York, is described in detail in chapter 12. Other damaging earthquakes centered in northern New York State took place on November 4, 1877, somewhere in the Adirondack Mountains; on April 20, 1931, near the southern end of Lake George; on October 7, 1983, at Goodnow (magnitude 5.1); and on April 20, 2002, at Au Sable Forks (magnitude 5.0). All of these earthquakes had magnitudes around 5.0 and caused minor damage in their epicentral areas. A number of earthquakes that did not cause damage but were widely felt in northeastern New York State and nearby Vermont (between magnitude 4.0 and 5.0) are also known from the historical and instrument records. About 6 to 10 earthquakes per year have been detected in recent years in the Adirondack and Catskill Mountains area, although most of them have not been felt.

In western New York State, a damaging earthquake of about magnitude 5.2 was centered at Attica on August 12, 1928. Other earthquakes that were strongly felt but not damaging took place in the Attica area on January 1, 1966, and on June 13, 1967. The Clarendon-Linden Fault in western New York State has been suspected as the structure on which these earthquakes may have been centered, but so far no seismological or geological evidence has emerged to indicate that this is an active fault. In modern times small earthquakes have been detected beneath Lake Ontario and in a band south of Lake Ontario stretching from the Finger Lakes region of New York State west into the Niagara Peninsula of Ontario. The rate of earthquake activity in this region is only about a quarter of that of the Adirondack and Catskill Mountains area in the eastern part of the state. The average repeat time of damaging earthquakes of magnitude 5.0 or greater in northern and western New York State is probably comparable to that of the greater New York City area.

## EARTHQUAKES IN EASTERN ONTARIO AND WESTERN QUEBEC

There are two broad belts of frequent earthquake activity in eastern Ontario and western Quebec, with small earthquakes that are regularly recorded by seismographic monitoring and with occasional stronger and even damaging earthquakes in the historical and recent past. One earthquake belt follows the Ottawa River from around Ottawa, Ontario, to Témiscaming, Quebec, in a valley known by geologists as the Ottawa-Bonnechere graben. The other seismic belt runs from around Montreal, Quebec, to the Quebec-Ontario border north of Temiscaming, and is known as the Western Quebec Seismic Zone. Both are broad trends of earthquake activity. The Ottawa River seismic belt is about 35 miles (50 kilometers) wide, while the western Quebec seismic belt is about 95 miles (150 kilometers) wide.

Damaging earthquakes have taken place in both seismic belts of western Quebec and eastern Ontario. The strongest earthquake known from the eastern end of these belts was on September 16, 1732, about noon, with an epicenter somewhere near Montreal. The earthquake caused major damage at Montreal, with all of the homes in the city suffering damage, more than 500 chimneys having fallen, and parts of the city wall collapsing due to the earthquake shaking. The hospital in the city was destroyed. Some reports from distant localities indicate that between two and seven persons were killed at Montreal in the earthquake, although no deaths are reported in any of the reports that were written at Montreal itself immediately following the earthquake. Some reports also suggest that an unknown number of persons may have been injured in the earthquake. The shaking reportedly lasted about two to three minutes in Montreal. In the Boston, Massachusetts, area, the earthquake last about 30 seconds to one minute and was accompanied by a minor rumble. The earthquake shaking was reported as far south as Annapolis, Maryland, where a clock was said to have stopped due to the shaking. Unfortunately, much of northeastern North America was still unpopulated at this time, and because of this it is not possible to determine the extent to which this earthquake was felt to the east, north, or west. At Montreal about 50 aftershocks were felt during the first day after the mainshock, and aftershocks were said to have occurred for months afterward. Most people were so afraid of their houses collapsing that they refused to reenter their dwellings and slept outdoors for some days after the earthquake. The epicenter of this earthquake was clearly somewhere near Montreal, and the magnitude of the mainshock has been estimated at 5.6 to 6.0.

At the western end of the seismic zone, along the Ottawa River, there was a magnitude 6.2 earthquake at Témiscaming on November 1, 1935, just after 1:00 a.m. This earthquake damaged an estimated 80 percent of the chimneys within about 40 miles (70 kilometers) of the epicenter, cracked brick walls, and caused liquefaction effects along the shores of some of the lakes in the epicentral area. The normally clear water of T Lake was muddied by the earthquake. The earthquake shaking was felt from the epicentral area east to New Brunswick, south to Virginia, west to Wisconsin, and north to Hudson Bay. About 200 miles (300 kilometers) from the epicenter, the ground shaking was still sufficiently strong to cause a landslide along a railroad embankment. People in Témiscaming and other nearby towns described a loud, terrifying roar that preceded the earthquake shaking by a few seconds, and earthquake rumbles and roars accompanied the many aftershocks that the locals felt for several weeks following the mainshock.

More recently, a magnitude 5.0 earthquake that caused some minor damage was centered in the Western Quebec Seismic Zone near Shawville on June 23, 2010. This shock did some minor damage in towns around the epicenter, including causing some cracks in the Canadian Parliament building in Ottawa. In addition to this earthquake, several seismic events that were strongly felt but did not cause damage have taken place in these seismic zones, including 12 earthquakes of magnitude 4.0 or greater since 1975. This rate of seismicity suggests that in these seismic zones the average time between earthquakes of magnitude 5.0 or greater is about 20 years and the average time between magnitude 6.0 or greater earthquakes is about 160 years.

## EARTHQUAKES IN THE CHARLEVOIX SEISMIC ZONE AND SURROUNDING AREAS OF QUEBEC

The Charlevoix Seismic Zone was the site of a very large earthquake that is fully described in chapter 4, and this zone remains today the most seismically active area in northeastern North America. Modern seismic stations in Quebec detect an average of two or three earthquakes each week in the Charlevoix Seismic Zone, most of which are too small to be felt. From 1975 to 2017 there were eight earthquakes of magnitude 4.0 or greater that took place in this seismic zone, close to the rate of events in the much larger seismic zones in western Quebec and along the Ottawa River. Furthermore, there has been earthquake activity in parts of Quebec outside of the Charlevoix Seismic Zone. The 1988 Saguenay earthquake (chapter 13) took place to the north of the Charlevoix Seismic Zone along an old crustal rift zone called the Saguenay rift. Also, earthquakes have been detected outside the Charlevoix Seismic Zone farther upstream along the St. Lawrence River near Quebec City, where an earthquake of magnitude 4.7 was centered on November 16, 1997.

Historical records indicate that a number of damaging earthquakes with magnitudes of about 6.0 or greater have struck in the Charlevoix Seismic Zone since the major earthquake in 1663. These events took place on December 17, 1791; October 17, 1860; October 20, 1870; and February 28, 1925. All were quite damaging to chimneys and other brittle building components in the epicentral region and caused scattered chimney damage in northern New England and in some parts of Quebec away from the epicentral area. All of these earthquakes were widely felt throughout New England, in the Middle Atlantic states, in the states around the Great Lakes, in the maritime provinces of Canada, and throughout Quebec and Ontario. For example, the 1925 earthquake was felt so strongly in Boston, Massachusetts, that some buildings were abandoned by residents who were frightened by the strength of the ground shaking, although no damage was reported in the city due to the earthquake. Similar reports came from the earthquakes of 1860 and 1870.

Given its history, the Charlevoix Seismic Zone has the highest potential for future damaging earthquakes in all of northeastern North America. Since 1791 the average time between magnitude 5.0 or greater earthquakes has been about 30 years. In addition, as noted above, several damaging earthquakes have taken place outside of the Charlevoix Seismic Zone. Thus, the potential for damaging earthquakes in this part of Quebec is roughly comparable to that of the much larger seismic zones in western Quebec.

## EARTHQUAKES IN THE LOWER ST. LAWRENCE RIVER REGION, NEW BRUNSWICK, AND NOVA SCOTIA

Modern earthquake monitoring has detected a zone of diffuse, persistent seismicity in the lowest part of the St. Lawrence River valley of eastern Quebec where the river empties into the Gulf of St. Lawrence. This zone is called the Lower St. Lawrence Seismic Zone, and several earthquakes are detected from that zone each year. Although no earthquake of magnitude 5.0 or greater is known from this zone either historically or from modern instrumental seismic monitoring, the persistent activity in this area along with several past earthquakes above magnitude 4.0 suggest to many seismologists that a damaging earthquake could be centered there at some point in the future. The average repeat time in this seismic zone is estimated to be about 60 to 100 years based on the rates at which smaller earthquakes are taking place there.

Earthquakes have been documented from a number of different places in New Brunswick and Nova Scotia. Several aftershocks each year continue to be detected from the epicentral area of the 1982 Miramichi shocks, and modern earthquake activity has been scattered across the southern half of New Brunswick and in the southern half of Nova Scotia, with no one area having a concentration of seismicity. The strongest historical earthquake in these provinces was an event on February 8, 1855, that caused some minor damage at Moncton, New Brunswick. The potential for future damaging earthquakes in New Brunswick and southern Nova Scotia is approximately comparable to that of Maine, with an estimated average repeat time of magnitude 5.0 or greater earthquakes between 100 and 200 years.

## Offshore Earthquakes and the Potential for a Future Tsunami

Up to this point in this chapter, all of the earthquakes discussed have taken place onshore or just offshore. There also has been persistent earthquake activity detected from farther offshore areas near the edge of the continental shelf. It is difficult to know whether many earthquakes took place in these areas during historical times because the earthquake shaking may not be well-documented in historical records, and an accurate location of smaller events well offshore is pretty much impossible to determine with historical data. On the other hand, modern instrumental seismic monitoring is able to detect and locate many offshore earthquakes, and this monitoring has detected a surprising number of offshore earthquakes. Along the edge of the continental shelf, which ranges from 75 miles (120 kilometers) east of New Jersey and south of Long Island to 125 miles (200 kilometers) east of Cape Cod to 75 miles (120 kilometers) southeast of the southern tip of Nova Scotia, dozens of small and moderate earthquakes have been detected since the 1970s, and a few earthquakes also have been detected even farther offshore from the nearby deep oceanic crust to the east. The largest earthquake in this area was a magnitude 4.5 earthquake south of eastern Long Island on August 20, 1992. In April 2012 a swarm of a dozen earthquakes, the largest a magnitude 3.9, occurred along the edge of the continental shelf due east of Boston, Massachusetts. The geologic setting of these far offshore earthquakes on the edge of the continental shelf is very similar to that of the 1929 earthquake on the Grand Banks south of Newfoundland (described in chapter 10).

The presence of persistent earthquake activity along the edge of the continental shelf east of the northeastern U.S. raises the question of whether a strong earthquake that triggers a damaging tsunami could take place east of New England or south of New York/east of New Jersey. The answer to this question is unclear, but there are some hints that such an event could happen. First of all, the striking similarity of the geologic setting of these offshore areas east of New England and south and east of New York and New Jersey, respectively, with that of the source region of the 1929 earthquake suggests that a strong tsunami-generating earthquake near the coast of the northeastern U.S. might be possible. A second piece of evidence is that there are submarine landslide scars on the U.S. continental slope, where the edge of the continental shelf slopes off into the deep Atlantic Ocean basin to the east. The 1929 tsunami was associated with a large submarine landslide that broke many transatlantic telephone cables on the ocean floor, and the coincidence of damaging tsunamis and submarine landslides has been documented in other parts of the world as well. Finally, some geologic deposits that are about 2,300 years old along the coast of New Hampshire and northeastern Massachusetts are possible tsunami deposits. If these deposits were indeed left by a tsunami that swept ashore along this part of the New England coast, the cause of the tsunami might have been an earthquake along the edge of the continental shelf east of Boston.

The likelihood of a strong offshore earthquake that generates a damaging tsunami along the coast of the northeastern U.S. is difficult to estimate with the currently available data. Studies of the earthquake activity along the edge of the continental shelf from North America to Greenland yield estimates of a 2,120-year average repeat time of an earthquake the size of the 1929 earthquake along a 220-mile (350-kilometer) stretch of the edge of the continental shelf around New England and New York. Another study that looked at the submarine landslide scars along the continental slope near Newfoundland estimated that a 220-mile (350-kilometer) stretch of the edge of the continental shelf would experience an earthquake the size of the 1929 earthquake on average once every 22,800 years. These widely divergent values of estimated average earthquake repeat times show the large uncertainties in these analyses. Even so, they indicate the possible range of average repeat times of potentially damaging tsunamis along the northeastern U.S. coast from Maine to New Jersey.

## EARTHQUAKE SCENARIOS AND DAMAGE

Up to now all of the discussions in this chapter have been concerned with estimating the locations and average repeat times of potentially damaging earthquakes in the northeastern U.S. and nearby provinces of Canada. However, it is also important to know how devastating a large earthquake might be if it occurs in the near future. Fortunately, in 2012 a study was published that made just such estimates of possible earthquake losses for a number of different large earthquake scenarios for New England and surrounding areas. Four of those scenarios spell out the expected damage and losses in southern New England should the proposed earthquakes actually take place.

One scenario is the occurrence of a magnitude 5.0 earthquake with an epicenter at Littleton, Massachusetts, in the vicinity of Nashoba Hill. The 2012 report indicates that there would be no deaths and only a handful of injuries from an earthquake of this location and size. However, about 20,000 people would lose electrical power due to such an earthquake, and building damage would amount to about $560 million. In addition, the damage would lead to losses of economic activity amounting to about $850 million.

A larger earthquake scenario that was explored was the occurrence of a magnitude 5.8 earthquake at Newburyport, Massachusetts. Because of the event magnitude in a well-populated suburban area, 5–10 persons might be killed and almost 500 would probably be injured due to such an earthquake. About 3,000 buildings and other facilities would sustain extensive damage, amounting to about $3.7 billion in losses. An estimated 84,000 people would lose electrical service due to the shock, and about 1,400 persons would be forced to leave their houses because of earthquake damage. Economic activity losses would probably amount to about $4.8 billion.

In yet another scenario a repetition of the 1755 Cape Ann earthquake with a magnitude of 6.5 would have widespread major effects along the Massachusetts, New Hampshire, and Maine coastal areas. This scenario earthquake might not cause any deaths, but it would probably injure about 500 persons. The number of buildings suffering extensive damage would be about 500, with about 30,000 persons losing electrical service. The estimated damage to buildings and other built structures would amount to about $2.6 billion, and the loss of economic activity would be about $3.4 billion. Probably about 150 houses would be damaged to the point where the residents would need to find other places to live.

The largest of the scenario earthquakes in the 2012 report that would affect southern New England is a magnitude 6.5 earthquake centered near Concord, New Hampshire, a similar event to what might have happened in 1638. This earthquake would have widespread consequences across central and southern New England. In this earthquake scenario the estimated number of deaths would be about 50–100, and the number of injuries would probably be about 2,000. About 9,000 buildings would suffer extensive damage, and an estimated 72,000 customers would lose electrical service following the earthquake. The losses to buildings and structures would cost about $5.8 billion, and the loss of economic activity would set businesses back about $8.3 billion. The number of persons who would be displaced from their houses is estimated at 4,500. Damage due to the occurrence of this earthquake would be spread across all of the states in the northeastern U.S., from Maine to New York.

The earthquake scenarios in the 2012 report are being used by emergency management officials, public safety officials, building code officials, mayors, and other public officials for planning purposes to prepare for the occurrences of future damaging earthquakes in the region. States and localities regularly review the seismic provisions in their building codes and are upgrading those codes as required. Emergency management agencies, public works agencies, building inspection officials, police departments, and fire departments are regularly developing, exercising, and refining plans to deal with earthquake emergencies so that they are ready when the next damaging earthquake takes place. The good news is that the region is becoming ever more prepared for the occurrence of future strong earthquakes, but the bad news is that the region still has a long way to go before it is fully prepared. History gives every reason to believe that another damaging earthquake will take place somewhere in the region at some point in the future. When it does, the consequences could be significant.

# Appendix: The Modified Mercalli Intensity Scale of 1931

The following is an abbreviated description of the 12 levels of the Modified Mercalli intensity scale of 1931. Each intensity value is assigned a Roman numeral to indicate that it is a rating of the local ground shaking based on the described felt and damage effects. The value in parentheses following each description of the higher intensities is approximately the lowest earthquake magnitude value at which this intensity level is observed.

I. Not felt except by a very few under especially favorable conditions.

II. Felt only by a few persons at rest, especially on upper floors of buildings. Delicately suspended objects may swing.

III. Felt quite noticeably by persons indoors, especially on upper floors of buildings. Many people do not recognize it as an earthquake. Standing motor cars may rock slightly. Vibration similar to the passing of a truck. Duration estimated. (3.0)

IV. During the day felt indoors by many, outdoors by few. At night some awakened. Dishes, windows, doors disturbed; walls make cracking sound. Sensation like heavy truck striking building. Standing motor cars rocked noticeably. (3.5)

V. Felt by nearly everyone; many awakened. Some dishes, windows, etc., broken. A few instances of cracked plaster. Unstable objects overturned. Disturbance of trees, poles, and other tall objects sometimes noticed. Pendulum clocks may stop. (4.0)

VI. Felt by all; many frightened and run outdoors. Some heavy furniture moved; a few instances of fallen plaster or damaged chimneys. Damage slight. (5.0)

VII. Everybody runs outdoors. Damage negligible in buildings of good design and construction; slight to moderate damage in well-built ordinary structures; considerable damage in poorly built or badly designed structures; some chimneys broken. Noticed by persons driving motor cars. (5.5)

VIII. Damage slight in specially designed structures; considerable damage in ordinary substantial buildings with partial collapse. Damage great in poorly built structures. Fall of chimneys, factory stacks, columns, monuments, walls. Heavy furniture overturned. Sand and mud ejected in small amounts. Changes in well water. Persons disturbed while driving motor cars. (6.0)

IX. Damage considerable in specially designed structures; well-designed frame structures thrown out of plumb. Damage great in substantial buildings, with partial collapse. Buildings shifted off foundations. Ground cracked conspicuously. Underground pipes broken. (6.5)

X. Some well-built wooden structures destroyed; most masonry and frame structures destroyed with foundations. Ground badly cracked. Rails bent. Landslides considerable from river banks and steep slopes. Shifted sand and mud. Water splashed (slopped) over banks. (7.0)

XI. Few if any (masonry) structures remain standing. Bridges destroyed. Broad fissures in ground. Underground pipelines completely out of service. Earth slumps and land slips in soft ground. Rails bent greatly. (7.5)

XII. Damage total. Waves seen on ground surfaces. Lines of sight and level distorted. Objects thrown upward into the air. (8.0)

# Index

*Lewiston Evening Journal,* 1904
  earthquake, 179, 182, 185
lights, earthquake
  1663 earthquake, 68–69
  1727 earthquake, 98–100
  1755 earthquake, 127–28
  1904 earthquake, 187–88
  1944 earthquake, 239
  1988 earthquake, 253–57
*L'Impartial,* on earthquake, 177
l'Incarnation, Sr. Marie de, 54, 55, 61,
  64, 71, 73
liquefaction. *See* soil liquefaction
Long Island, earthquakes on, 153, 268
  *See also* New York City
*Lowell Sun,* on 1940 earthquakes, 203,
  204, 206–7
Lynch, Fr. Joseph, S.J., 215, 224

**M**
*Machias Republican,* on
  earthquake, 181
*Machias Union,* on earthquake,
  182, 183
Madge, A. V., 235
Maine, earthquakes in, 265–66
  1755, 115–16
  1904, 171–90
  1929, 193, 194, 195
  1944, 234
  1982, 246
  1940 New Hampshire earthquakes,
    209, 211, 212
  1884 NYC earthquake, 156–57
Mallet, Robert, 47, 48, 49, 50
*Manchester Union*
  1904 earthquake, 187
*Manchester Union Leader*
  1940 earthquakes, 217–18, 221

maps, intensity, 21–22
Maryland, 1884 NYC earthquake,
  156, 157
*Maryland Gazette,* on 1755
  earthquake, 117
Massachusetts, earthquakes in
  1727, 76–103, 134
  1744, 104–7
  1944, 232, 234
  1755 Cape Ann, 107–31, 267, 268
  1929 earthquake/tsunami, 193, 200
  1904 Maine earthquake in, 186–87
  1940 New Hampshire earthquakes,
    208–9, 211, 218
  1884 NYC earthquake, 160,
    161, 165
  1638 Plymouth earthquake, 36–45
Massena (NY), 1944 earthquake, 228,
  229–31
Mather, Increase, 49, 65
Mather, Prof. Kirtley F., 223, 224
Mayhew, Jonathan, 121, 123
McCaffrey, James, S.J., 53
McIntyrn, Patrick, 166
McKay, Hugh, 173
*Memoirs of the Boston Society of Natural
  History,* 47
Mercalli Intensity Scale, 21, 22,
  279–80
Metcalf, Seth, 116
Middle Atlantic states, earthquakes
  in, xi, xii
  *See also specific states*
*Middlesex Gazette,* on earthquake, 144
Milne, Dr. W. G., 238–39, 239–40
Milwaukee (WI), 1944
  earthquake, 234
Mix, Stephen, 96

1988 earthquake, 252
　*See also* soil liquefaction
San Francisco (CA), 1906 earthquake,
　176–77, 259
Sargeant, Harry, 209
Sargeant, Rev. Christopher, 90, 95
Scheler, Mrs. Charles, 157
Seeber, Dr. Leonardo, 103
seiches, and earthquakes, 168–69
seismic waves, 11–16, 96
　amplitudes of, 14–17
　1755 earthquake, 109
　1884 earthquake, 168
　1929 earthquake, 194
　forms of, 11–12
　magnitude scales of, 18
　and soft soil, 22–23
　and sound waves, 68
Seismological Society of America, 177
Sewall, Henry, 76, 85, 86, 87, 90
Sewall, Samuel, 96
ShakeMaps, 19–20, 21, 22
Shurtleff, William, 80
Silliman, Benjamin, 140, 142
Simmons, Prof. Gene, 260
Simon, Fr. Charles, S.J., 53, 60, 69, 72
*Six Town Times,* on 1904
　earthquake, 186
Skinner, Charles, 136
slickensides, 8–9
　*See also* faults
Smith, Rev. T., 116
Sohon, Dr. Frederick, 214
soil liquefaction, 25–26, 27, 35
　1727 earthquake, 85
　1755 earthquake, 120–23
　1944 earthquake, 237, 238
　1988 earthquake, 252, 253

1904 Maine earthquake, 183
1663 Quebec earthquake, 61–62
sounds, earthquake
　1982, 1988 earthquakes, 249–50
　1727 earthquake, 94–98
　1944 earthquake, 236–37
　1904 Maine earthquake, 183–87
　1940 New Hampshire earthquakes,
　　218–19
　1884 NYC earthquake, 163–65
St. John *Gazette,* on earthquake, 173
St. Lawrence River
　and 1663 earthquake, 63
　Lower St. Lawrence Seismic Zone,
　　273–74
*Statistical Account of Middlesex County,
　A* (Field), 142
Steele, Dr., 135–36
Stiles, Ezra, 144
Stilles, E., 126
Strum, Captain, 153–54
Stuyvesant, Peter, 66
*Summerside Journal,* on 1904
　earthquake, 177
*Sydney Daily Post,* on 1904
　earthquake, 177
*Syracuse Herald,* on 1940
　earthquakes, 219

**T**
Tadoussac (Quebec), and 1663
　earthquake, 62, 63
Tebbetts, Leslie, 219
tectonic plates, movements of, 258,
　261–62, 263
　and thrust faults, 5
　*See also* earthquakes

# About the Author

**John E. Ebel** has been a professor of Earth and Environmental Sciences at Boston College for over 30 years and is the former director of Boston College's Weston Observatory, a seismic research facility dedicated to detect, locate, catalog, and study all earthquakes that occur in New England and vicinity. He holds a BA in physics from Harvard University and a PhD in geophysics from the California Institute of Technology. He has published more than 80 papers and reports on earthquakes in New England and around the world. Additionally, he has been a consultant on seismic hazard for over 20 major engineering projects such as highway bridges, LNG tanks, dams, and other critical structures in the United States, the Bahamas, Colombia, the Dominican Republic, Honduras, Jordan, Puerto Rico, Chile, and Tunisia. He lives in Natick, Massachusetts.